THE LAW OF LOVE

FROM AUTONOMY TO COMMUNION

THE LAW OF LOVE

FROM AUTONOMY TO COMMUNION

Stephen F. Brett, SSJ

University of Scranton Press

Scranton and London

Library of Congress Cataloging-in-Publication Data

Brett, Stephen F. (Stephen Francis), 1949-
  The law of love : from autonomy to communion / Stephen F. Brett.
    p. cm.
  Includes bibliographical references (p.   ) and index.
  ISBN 978-1-58966-207-0 (pbk.)
  1. Sex--Religious aspects--Catholic Church. 2. Christian ethics--Catholic
authors. 3. Autonomy (Philosophy) 4. Sexual ethics. I. Title.
  BX1795.S48B74 2010
  241'.66088282--dc22

                                                            2010017122

Distribution:

University of Scranton Press
Chicago Distribution Center
11030 S. Langley
Chicago, IL 60628

PRINTED IN THE UNITED STATES OF AMERICA

To Father Matthew J. O'Rourke, SSJ,

a faithful mentor and irreplaceable friend.

CONTENTS

ACKNOWLEDGMENTS

Above all, I am thankful to God for His mercy and grace in allowing me to complete this project aimed at restoring openness to the divine in human relations of family life and love in contemporary culture.

Several individuals have been very generous with their time, experience, and talent in reviewing different versions of this effort. In particular, I want to thank Dr. Pamela Haftel Sheff, Gordon Giampietro, Dr. Ed Macierowski, and Dr. Margaret M. Reher.

The patience and professionalism of Jeffrey L. Gainey and John P. Hunckler of the University of Scranton Press have provided a clear light of editing direction for which I am truly grateful.

I am indebted to the Sisters, Servants of the Immaculate Heart of Mary, for their support and encouragement during my very happy assignment at Camilla Hall and Immaculata University. Particularly, I want to thank Sr. Ann Bernadette MacNamara, IHM, for her unfailing encouragement during the writing process. Sr. Elaine Marie Glanz, PhD, the Dean of the College of Undergraduate Studies of Immaculata University, was especially gracious in reviewing the manuscript. It goes without saying that I alone am responsible for any errors of language, fact or judgment that may appear in this work.

I want to express my gratitude to my former students at St. Charles Borromeo Seminary in Philadelphia for their faith, camaraderie, and insights. Many ideas were shaped, sharpened, and refined in classroom discussions there.

The staff members at the Marion Burk Knott Library of St. Mary's Seminary & University in Baltimore have all been especially helpful in my research endeavors.

Finally, I am grateful to the members of the Josephite community for their fraternal support.

INTRODUCTION

Love is always a mystery, a reality that surpasses reason, without
contradicting it, and more than that, exalts its possibilities. Jesus
revealed to us the mystery of God. He, the Son, made us know
the Father who is in Heaven, and gave us the Holy Spirit, the
Love of the Father and of the Son. Christian theology synthe-
sizes the truth of God with this expression: only one substance
in three persons. God is not solitude but perfect communion. For
this reason the human person, the image of God, realizes himself
or herself in love, which is a sincere gift of self.

— Pope Benedict XVI

A work on the mystery of love can rightly start with what is for Christians
the ultimate mystery, the triune God, whose three persons are inseparably
a communion of love. Working alongside many other distinguished theologians in the 1960s, Joseph Ratzinger contributed to the historical documents of Vatican II which held, boldly and famously, that the mystery of
human existence cannot be fully appreciated apart from the reality of
Christ.[1]

What follows is an essay (using that term in its original French
sense of an attempt to understand) about personal desires and philosophical
notions. It begins with the bias that human love is in no way threatened or
constrained by the God of Jesus Christ. Rather, any authentic expression
of love stretches in an infinite arc toward transcendent good, the realm of
trinitarian communion. Just as every human being is created in the image
of the divine, so every experience of human love participates in the undy-
ing, underlying reality of divine love. To the extent that human love means
a sincere gift of self, it images divine love. To the extent that it negates or
violates self-gift, an attempt at love will image human brokenness.

In an ongoing work, *Jesus of Nazareth,* which he began before his
elevation to the papacy, Pope Benedict XVI stresses how rooted is the identity of Jesus in his communion with his Father. That rootedness in the divine

is essential in our understanding the historical reality of Jesus, truly and fully the Christ. It explains the scope and nature of human participation in the work and ways of God. Ultimately our participation in divine love expands and fulfills the unbounded desires of the human heart.

This work argues that the model of autonomy which emerged from the Enlightenment has not provided a sufficient basis for human dignity. The Kantian focus on freedom has led to alienation, isolation, and atomism in the lives of people who may enjoy more freedom but who are uncertain about what to do with it. Kant was the Henry Ford of autonomy, mass-producing it for ordinary people, but we now have clogging congestion and deadly collisions. We are unsure what to do or where to go with our new acquisition. In short, we need to look at the "owner's manual" for humans found in theology and philosophy. Having done that, we need a map to chart where we are and where we want to go with our freedom.

Human sexuality is rooted in divine love. Any understanding of sexual ethics which neglects or denies that rootedness is misleading. Our conversations today about love, sex, family, and children frequently show a direct connection with an "exclusive humanism"[2] that began in the eighteenth century, that is, a humanism exclusive of any sense of the divine. The path and popularization of an atheism or anti-theism by the Enlightenment generated a notion of autonomy concerned with power, independence, and function. This sense of self-identity with unbounded self-expression has not always been helpful in showing how various independent selves are expected to relate to each other in harmony or communion. We shall look closely at this phenomenon.

When set against a larger horizon, autonomy can be an authentic and invaluable dimension of human desire, but when separated from "the sovereignty of good,"[3] ultimately a matter of divine identity and relationship with humankind, autonomy can become worse than a runaway locomotive as it picks up social speed and moves in a direction away from human dignity. Autonomy which is exclusive of the divine easily becomes exclusive from any other, divine or human, in the quest for total freedom of self. When this happens, autonomy becomes power without purpose, desire disconnected from any teleology or roadmap of worthy goals. An exclusively secularized preoccupation with autonomy has too often blinded individuals desirous of life-changing love from the prospects of love that require vulnerability, risk, sacrifice, and communion.

A distinguished moralist whom we shall look at in depth has pointed out that just as there are different understandings of autonomy, so there are correspondingly different meanings of freedom. Servais Pinckaers has contributed to moral discourse the distinction between freedom of indifference and freedom of excellence.[4] Freedom of indifference flows from a content-free notion of autonomy which is devoid of any transcendent or teleological compass; freedom of excellence flows from an autonomy that is ordered and open to the transcendent.

If the autonomy or power to define oneself is linked with worthy and transcendent goals, then the choice made is truly an example of freedom of excellence. Catholic social teaching has often referred to this model of autonomy as subsidiarity, whereby different levels of freedom and authority are recognized and respected. Each level is expected to help (*subsidium* means "help") and support another level in its respective role and mission. A simple example is the relationship between a nurse and a hospital administrator. Each is autonomous in her own domain but in a way that links the two different ranks and roles whereby the work of the nurse supports the mission of the administrator and vice versa.

If, on the other hand, a choice is made in a vacuum, devoid of purpose, teleology, or transcendent finality, it is merely a case of freedom of indifference. Freedom of indifference is not merely indifferent to human love and well-being but is ultimately destructive of human needs because human beings require communion with one another. Indifference to the needs of a neighbor is as deadly as overt hatred.

An illustration from everyday experience quickly demonstrates the consequences of the two kinds of freedom. Technology provides us with countless examples of Pinckaers's distinction between freedom of excellence and freedom of indifference. Traffic lights of red, yellow, and green can be programmed so that the yellow phase can be increased or decreased by as many seconds as the programmer wants. Cameras can be installed to catch drivers who run a red light by attempting to make it through on the yellow light. As a consequence, shortening the yellow phase will increase the number of speeders caught and the fines that they must pay.

But studies have shown that shortening the period of yellow not only increases the number of drivers who go through an intersection on red, but also increases the number of accidents resulting from the fact that the driver with a quick-changing light must make a sudden, often hasty choice. Shortening the yellow for a stoplight increases revenue for the government—arguably a good. But since the hesitation about whether to go or stop also increases accidents as drivers plow into those who have stopped suddenly or a vehicle races to beat the red light, camera, and ticket, one can ask whether this exercise of freedom is morally acceptable in trading safety for revenue.

A longer yellow phase reduces accidents as drivers make a last-minute decision more calmly, but it reduces revenue generated by speeding motorists. The proponent of freedom of indifference would argue that a jurisdiction is free to program its yellow lights for whatever time it wants and can aim toward increasing revenue. A freedom of indifference is willing to sacrifice human safety for increased revenue. It is by definition "indifferent" to the transcendent good of human well-being.

By contrast, a proponent of freedom of excellence would underscore the importance of human safety and forego the increased revenue that would accompany a higher incidence of accidents. If society is metaphorically at a crossroads concerning what kind of freedom it wants, even decisions regarding the technology regulating our actual crossroads is an object of the decision-making involved. Freedom is not an abstraction but a series of practical choices that can spell life or death, safety or hazard. The exercise of freedom aimed at nonnegotiable moral goods such as health and safety is radically different from a free choice indifferent to goals. In short, we have two kinds of freedom springing from different versions of autonomy.

It is almost impossible to exaggerate the importance of autonomy in looking at moral issues today. The distilled essence of the Enlightenment view of autonomy came from Immanuel Kant: "Kant argues that for an action to be moral it must stem solely from an autonomous will. A will is autonomous when it is a law to itself as independent from all foreign causes. . . . In other words, the will is self-ruling as determining its own laws independent of any natural necessity, external command, external reward, or punishment. If the action stems from natural necessity, external commands, or incentives, it is not autonomous but heteronomous, and therefore not moral. . . . Consequently, Kant makes autonomy the foundation of his moral system."[5]

The Enlightenment sense of autonomy as freedom from revelation and religion made its way from eighteenth-century European salons into twentieth-century Western households through a culture that looked to courts to enact and define the modern sense of freedom. Impatient with any standards deemed quaint or outmoded by the intellectual elite, the United States Supreme Court eagerly accepted the standard of autonomy and expanded its scope. Pushing the envelope on sexual ethics was the direct correlation of expanding the boundaries of autonomy. The worlds of philosophy and law combined to make unfettered expression of sexual desire a constitutional right described and protected as privacy.

The mantra of privacy masked the most public reality of all—the triumph of sexual expression at the expense of love, faith, family, children, and the common good. An early acceptance of eugenics by the Supreme Court in 1927 foreshadowed the widespread acceptance of contraception, anticipating and facilitating tens of millions of legal abortions, the separation of male sexual responsibility from the marital covenant, and the inevitable rise of fatherless families in an environment of sexual polarization. These are the legacy of the sexual revolution of the 1960s. While drug companies today work feverishly to find cures for an unprecedented scale of sexually transmitted diseases, the insidious notion of absolute autonomy in the culture is a daily toxin that transmits diseases of hopelessness, confusion, and nihilism to ordinary folks swept along in the currents of sexual autonomy.

As bleak as this picture is, there are many signs of a genuine recovery of a transcendent view of human desire, including friendship and agape, oriented toward a self-sacrificing love that aims at the true well-being of the beloved. Young people who have seen firsthand the erosion of marital love culminating in divorce by their parents want a new path. They are more concerned with true love than free love, and more are coming to conclude that true love waits for marriage. New generations—X, Y, and the millennial babies—will be forced to confront the consequences of the 1960s, fashioning their own lives and reframing the perspectives of mid-twentieth-century America. These young people will need and benefit from the scholarship of philosophers and theologians whose studies shed light on the context of sexual and marital love today.

This essay will summarize critical reflections of philosophers and theologians such as Alasdair MacIntyre, Charles Taylor, Cornelio Fabro, and the late Servais Pinckaers. The goal is to provide a path toward recovery of human sexuality understood not as a boundary-free exercise of freedom but as a desire for authentic goodness, inherently inclined toward a foundational divine goodness and countless instances of related goodness such as truth, beauty, human fellowship, and sexual integrity, connecting desire with the adventure of virtue.

The sexual revolution of the 1960s had its roots in the Enlightenment of the eighteenth century. Like all revolutions, it has produced countless casualties, individuals whose mistaken choices have cost them dearly. At times, as with the AIDS epidemic, it has cost their lives. But not all the blame for intellectual confusion can be laid at the doorstep of Immanuel Kant and European rationalism. The moral theology of the Catholic Church after the Council of Trent in the sixteenth century grew too comfortable with a view of morality as obligation. Law replaced virtue and morality became easily caricatured as moralism.

This work aims to move beyond libertinism and moralism, relativism and legalism. We will assess the remarkable contribution of Pinckaers in his *The Sources of Christian Ethics*, in which a profound theological anthropology shows the inclination of human subjects toward an array of transcendent goods. Then we shall conclude our assessment of Pinckaers's *ressourcement*, his call to return to both classical and Christian sources in reframing moral priorities, by looking at the current landscape for such a recovery in which secularization plays a decisive role.

The synthesis of classical and contemporary themes advanced by Pinckaers is compelling, but a provocative and practical question remains. Will a view of human action so intimately linked with a divine worldview of fundamental goods that are part of creation have any traction in a post-Christian, postmodern, thoroughly secularized world? Put differently, is the Pinckaers perspective simply an interesting but archaic view? Is it incapable of capturing the popular imagination as a counterweight to the headlong secularism of the 1960s?

To answer this question, we look in our last chapter to the work of a brilliant Canadian philosopher, past winner of the prestigious Templeton Award, Charles Taylor. Taylor has examined definitively the roots and consequences of secularization in the West and concludes that religious belief with its attendant moral codes is more vital than ever. The classic is not archaic; the need for recovery of an anthropology that elevates human desires toward the infinite has never been greater.

The vision of Pinckaers, like that of Pope Benedict XVI, is rooted in the orientation of human subjects toward God. At issue here, contrary to what atheist skeptics may think, is not a reliance on a God of the gaps to explain what is otherwise a puzzle. No, the priority for Pinckaers is to do justice to the full meaning of humanity. Unless the door is left open to the infinite, the transcendent, and the unconditional, we will not have the full measure of human life and love.

Pinckaers is critical at once of the Enlightenment that absolutizes autonomy and the post-Tridentine version of Catholic moral theology that succumbs to a view of obligation as uppermost in the Christian life. Neither narrative can tell the story of human love. Pinckaers provides new answers to old questions and forces us to re-examine timeless answers to newly considered questions. Pinckaers looks at obsolete approaches to human striving that emphasize obligation at the expense of virtue. The manuals of moral theology allowed a focus on law to obscure the desire for beatitude found in the Gospels. By reducing morality to moralism, this legalistic approach made inevitable a reaction of emotivism and relativism.

Similarly, Pinckaers critiques the secularized freedom of Enlightenment autonomy arising from a separation of human experience and its divine origins. He finds it sadly lacking in its capacity to describe human subjects in communion with one another. The detachment of the subject from articulations of the moral good found in the virtues leaves people adrift to utter a meaningless "Whatever . . ." as questions of human identity and sexual integrity that require virtues of patience, modesty, humility, and reverence for worthy answers are brushed aside as purely subjective issues without any shared horizon of a common good.

But is a recovery of a virtue-based ethics possible today in a climate of articulate and militant secularization? The work of the Canadian philosopher Charles Taylor strongly suggests that the contemporary search for meaning cannot ignore transcendence and transformation. Secularity and secularization have different meanings, he argues, with the result that the eclipse of God evident in the West since 1500 has not destroyed the foundation for religious belief but has changed the circumstances and conditions of such belief. While the instrumental reason of science has produced unprecedented technological advances, it has not been able to answer the deepest human needs of friendship and communion.

The atomistic perspective and the directionless autonomy of the "buffered self" (Taylor's term to describe how one can be invulnerable to beliefs or values outside of the self) exalts "values" without really attempting to define what a value is. What makes such a definition impossible is the absence of any shared or common understanding of the good. Values become the fig leaves that cover our inability to work out the meaning of sex and love in a way that is arduous but ultimately authentic.

It is my belief and hope that the work of Pinckaers, emblematic of a Catholic return to vital roots of faith and reason, is enormously helpful in moving beyond secularism, on the one hand, and legalism, on the other.

In his prophetic 1968 encyclical *Humanae Vitae*, Pope Paul VI identified an inseparable bond of life and love. Our culture has progressively separated life from love in the detachment of love from sex, the separation of marriage from family, the divorce of faith and reason, and the disengagement of sexual desire from virtue. I believe the road to recovery from these wrong choices runs through a divinely provided inclination to happiness and communion. It is an inherent, ontological orientation to transcendent good. Efforts to achieve sexual fulfillment or human communion in the absence of transcendent good necessarily entail a short-circuiting and shortchanging of human love. I hope this work provides a path toward a recovery and renewal of the human spirit buoyed by friendship, love, and communion.

ONE

AN IDEAL AND A REVOLUTION

The sexual revolution has not yielded peace of mind but confusion, contradiction, and conflict. There is certainty about nothing except the rightness, inevitability, and irrevocability of the path we have gone down.

— Theodore Dalrymple

REDOING THE MAP

If you were asked to name a prominent philosopher who launched a revolution through the power of ideas, you might very well answer, "Karl Marx and the Russian Revolution"—a thoroughly respectable response. Our inquiry looks, however, at a different philosopher. Specifically, it examines a powerful idea historically associated with a philosophical giant and the impact of that idea in contributing to revolutionary social change. The idea is autonomy. Its most famous proponent is Immanuel Kant. The revolution which it fundamentally shaped was the sexual revolution of the 1960s. Some even argue that the idea of autonomy has shaped modernity itself.[6] "Do your own thing," the mantra of the 1960s, is simply the street version of the philosophical concept of autonomy, a pervasive theme in contemporary society.

Although Kant developed the notion of autonomy to replace theology, the full breadth of autonomy requires an examination of theological ideas as well. While Kant boldly proposes a particular kind of autonomy as the basis for all human dignity, this study looks to a different version of autonomy which sees human striving as part of a divine plan, sometimes called *participated theonomy*, to distinguish it from the Enlightenment model.[7] Participated theonomy places the identity and integrity of the subject within the theological template of creation, redemption, and call to communion as an alternative basis to ground the dignity essential to love, friendship, marriage, communion, and participation in transcendent good.

9

The thesis of this work, which I hope to prove, is that Kantian autonomy is not supple or strong enough to explain and support human love.

Small is beautiful. The famous economist E. F. Schumacher wrote a critique of modern technology to that effect, arguing that what is bigger—technologies, structures, systems—is not always better for human needs. Nevertheless, Schumacher was once walking in Leningrad studying a small map and searching in vain for a famous cathedral. Schumacher later discovered that maps distributed by Soviet authorities deleted any reference to sites having a sign or semblance of religious belief.[8]

Telling this story, Schumacher went on to make the point that an increasingly secular age has tended to omit religious symbols and monuments from its posted sites. Prominent churches may be considered living museums or artifacts from an earlier, more credulous era, but otherwise they disappear from view. There is a troublesome smallness not in the size of the map but in the imagination of the mapmaker. Nothing is more expansive than the horizon of the human soul, extending toward human greatness and divine presence. We need a large map to study the aspirations, needs, desires, and happiness of human beings, a map that includes God and theology.

The job of the Soviet mapmakers was especially difficult in light of the fact that the city, formerly known as St. Petersburg, was brimming with Christian signs and symbols that were part of Tsarist Russia. With the fall of the Communist regime, Leningrad once again became St. Petersburg. New maps had to be made.

The philosophical maps made by the Enlightenment era eliminated two critical themes—transcendence and teleology. Transcendence is the proposition that human efforts can only be understood through the lens of divine origin and destiny; teleology is the proposition that the character and quality of human striving is goal-oriented and purpose-driven. Its inclination toward fundamental goods is not a limitation or heteronomy (to use Kant's term for any influence that opposes the autonomy of the will) but an inherent dimension of human life. As the new mapmakers of St. Petersburg acknowledged great historical monuments that had vanished from official view, so it is the intent of this work to rescue the themes of transcendence and teleology from their ideological exclusion from modern maps of humanity.

Any map of serious philosophical influences in the twenty-first century must reckon with the concept of autonomy, famously associated with the premier philosopher of the Enlightenment, Immanuel Kant. This study will argue that this concept is so important that it has even affected the way in which people understand themselves, their families, their friends, and their God. It will further argue that very divergent and contradictory models of the concept exist and the dominant model, the Kantian notion of autonomy, has not been friendly to the experience of human striving and the innate human inclination toward transcendent goodness and communion with another person.

In many ways, the concept of autonomy, derived from the Greek for "law of self" or self-legislation, meaning freedom and independence, is all over the philosophical map. Its magnitude has forced its Kantian opposite, heteronomy, off the map entirely.

While Kant understood *heteronomy* to mean unacceptable influences or forces from outside the self (*hetero-nomos*, a "law made by another"), his legacy has not provided guidance on how the subject is to relate *to* another. The self is expanded and enlarged almost to the point of absolute sovereignty, but the relation of the self to others and in communion with others has emerged as a most consequential social issue. In Kant's rigid system, all human desire falls into the category of heteronomy, leaving happiness in a confused muddle. All desires must yield to duty, specifically, the duty of obeying "transcendental reason," an abstraction without content. How can a subject experience the desire of love when that desire and love must by definition be subjected to a relentless and unclear demand of duty?

The prodigious size and stature of the monument to autonomy found in the public square of contemporary consciousness conceals underneath its expanse very different and indeed incompatible models and emphases. When examined closely, the colossus of autonomy shows that it has been carved out unevenly from different materials. Some of these are sturdy and hold together well, enduring through various eras. Others have collapsed from structural weakness—retaining some residual mass, but no longer an attractive or salient part of the overall monument of autonomy. These defective parts of the monument of autonomy need to be removed immediately so that a family-friendly model of autonomy can emerge. In chapter four, the freedom-for-excellence model of autonomy advanced by Servais Pinckaers is presented as a kind of freedom or autonomy, a participated theonomy ordered to divine love and human excellence—a model of freedom truly supportive of love, marriage, family, and communion.

Autonomy is *everywhere*, not merely here or there. People everywhere simply take for granted, with the air they breathe, that theirs is the power to choose whatever they wish, defining reality as they please. There is something refreshing and liberating in being free to captain your own ship, to navigate in the waters that you choose at the speed you prefer. Gradually, however, each captain is forced to concede that there are many other ships in the water. Limits begin to appear on the direction and desired location of one's own ship. The captain of the ship learns to pay attention to the charts of the sea known to other sailors, especially when storms arise. Colliding with another captain hardly enhances one's autonomy.

This study is an effort to devise, using Schumacher's phrase, a "philosophical map" of the notion of autonomy.[9] Be warned that it is heavily biased, favoring the view that truth leads to freedom, not vice versa, taking its cue from the wisdom of One who said, "You shall know the truth and the truth shall set you free" (John 8:32). The bias found here includes the proposition that attempts to expand freedom without taking relevant truths into account actually diminish the role and realm of freedom. If we fail to pay attention to maps and charts of human experience already crafted, we can easily get lost ourselves or lose control of our vessel. The captain can hardly afford to be uninformed on the route chosen.

A related bias of this work is that, when talking about freedom, autonomy, and choices, it is necessary ultimately to make love the object of our choices and not simply enshrine choice as the object of our love. This is a love of the good that transcends the immediacy of our circumstances but informs the meaning and texture of those circumstances. The bias here is that eros is not incompatible with goodness, happiness, transcendence, and teleology; it is a building block of each.

By adopting the admittedly biased view advanced here that there are different models of autonomy, leading in different directions, this work also argues that by tracing these different models in history we can arrive at a much better understanding of what has brought happiness to human beings and what has not. While freedom is unarguably a good, enormously valuable in its exercise and potential, the freedom of autonomy does in fact require a map itself if we are to understand it accurately.

Is autonomy principally a matter of freedom *from* something or freedom *for* something? Is it freedom for or from some*one*? Does one's particular model of autonomy see human freedom as consistent with the Christian view of creation and actually part of that view? Is autonomy an end in itself or does it serve another purpose such as truth? These questions have to be identified and answered for human freedom to serve the needs of humanity. We propose to examine these questions and attempt to provide at least the outline of some solid answers.

THE EVOLUTION OF ENLIGHTENMENT AUTONOMY

When we look at our philosophical map to locate clearly the grid of seminal influences that substantially changed history, we can recognize the eighteenth century as pivotal. In the Age of Enlightenment, Kant (1724–1804) developed his view of autonomy by absorbing and redirecting the thought of René Descartes (1596–1650), Thomas Hobbes (1588–1679), John Locke (1632–1704), and Jean-Jacques Rousseau (1712–78). The riptide of change found its way to the work of the philosopher who dominates the eighteenth century, Immanuel Kant, who distilled and transformed their earlier work.

Lewis White Beck provides a quadrant, so to speak, of informative boundaries on the development of Enlightenment thought: "The eighteenth century, unique in so many wonderful ways, is not unique in having vague boundaries. But if, after all, one still wants some dates to mark the opening and closing of the career of the eighteenth-century mind, I may suggest two pairs, which are suggestively close together: 1688 to 1793—from the Glorious Revolution to the Reign of Terror; and 1687 to 1790—from Newton's *Principia* to the last of Kant's *Critiques*."[10]

In taking up Beck's suggestion to look at these two pairs of dates, we recognize first the impact of two Revolutions—the first, British, and the second, French. A thorough understanding of the Enlightenment requires an understanding of the distinctive national peculiarities of British (Hobbes and Locke) and French (Rousseau, Diderot, and the encyclopedists) perspectives that would clearly affect the social and political forces in play.

Looking further into Beck's thematic quadrant, we know that the Glorious Revolution of 1688 sharply limited the power of the English monarch by increasing the role of the British parliament and legally ending the possibility of a Catholic king or queen. It was generally regarded as a victory for democracy and a liberation from religious creeds and codes; it was truly "glorious." Some, however, such as Edmund Burke, while writing favorably of the consequences of the revolution did not think its accomplishment to be a ratification of abstract notions such as the "rights of man" or the "general will." In his *Reflections on the Revolution in France*,[11] written in 1790 (*before* the Reign of Terror and anticipating the mayhem that would follow shortly), Burke sharply contrasted the Glorious Revolution with the French Revolution a century later. Burke held that the first was organic and constructive whereas the French Revolution was imposed by an elite in a destructive fashion.

Jay Winik contrasts Burke's support for the American rebels but opposition to the "new breed of radical, French or English alike": "Actually, for France, he wept. He predicted anarchy, which happened, and then chaos, which also happened, and then dictatorship, which would happen too; for his own England, he soberly warned the English to calibrate carefully any wider expansion of their own liberties. And for the entire world, he condemned a revolutionary dogma premised not on experience and tradition but on ephemeral conceptions of right and wrong, proclaiming instead that each nation and all peoples must rely on their collective history, their own collective character, and their own collective destiny."[12]

Put differently, Burke supported one revolution and opposed the other because, even though they were both descriptive of the Enlightenment era, they had at their core two radically different templates of autonomy.

One century and a year after the 1688 Revolution came the Reign of Terror in France, the bloody aftermath of the French Revolution in which there were mass executions of "enemies of the Revolution." A leader of the Reign of Terror was a thirty-five-year-old lawyer named Maximilien Robespierre who had been imbued with the thought of Rousseau and sought to implement Rousseau's ideas by destroying all who stood in the way. Edmund Burke saw clearly the dangers associated with the social-contract theory of Rousseau which exalted a general will of the people, conferring on the populace a veritable sovereignty and infallibility: "The social contract seemed to lead of its own accord to a tyranny far darker than any monarchical excess: the contract between each of us became an enslavement of all. Enlightenment and the fear of Enlightenment were henceforth inseparable. Burke's attack on the Revolution is a sustained defence of 'prejudice'—by which he meant the inherited store of human wisdom, whose value lasts only so long as we do not question it—against the 'reason' of Enlightenment thinking."[13]

The work of Rousseau, especially the notions of social contract and general will, had an enormous impact on Immanuel Kant: "It is well known that Kant was much impressed by Rousseau's political and practical views. In a sense the rational will of Kant's ethics is a principle higher than the mere elective preferences of the individual man. This *Wille* transcends the interests of the person and indicates the laws of universally good moral activity. To this extent, Rousseau has influenced Kant."[14]

It is intriguing to ask what happens if the will of the subject runs contrary to the general will of the majority. Since autonomy is designed to protect the freedom of the subject, it is difficult to see how a subject who is obligated in the Kantian view to will in conformity with popular opinion can also be considered free. A suspicion may begin to emerge that there are some serious flaws in the Kantian grid of freedom and obligation.

American statesmen studied Rousseau and the French Revolution very closely. John Adams shared with Edmund Burke a horror at the violence of the guillotine but one great American political theorist who was not greatly troubled by the Reign of Terror was Thomas Jefferson, the main drafter, of course, of the Declaration of Independence. One can see in Adams and Jefferson two different models of autonomy. Adams was an Anglophile in substantial agreement with Burke; Jefferson was a Francophile in substantial agreement with Rousseau. Once again, two different narratives of autonomy yielded very different world views.

The French Revolution was quite different from the Glorious Revolution of 1688 and diverged radically and in kind from the American Revolution. Robert Nisbet has highlighted the two different views of humanity in evidence:

> The Jacobin measures in the French Revolution seemed often no more than practical efforts to realize the Rousseauian dream, and it was indeed the effort by the Jacobins to extend their people's state, as they saw their creation, into the minds and hearts of all citizens that gave the French Revolution its totalitarian character. The makers of the American Revolution had been quite content to work with man as he is, shaped by traditional kinship, local, and religious institutions. For the Jacobins, however, nothing would do but the remaking of man through the power of the state. Hence the abolition, commencing in 1790, of the ancient estates, the monarchy, the aristocracy, the communes and provinces, the patriarchal family, the guild, the school and university, and any other structures which, by their long existence, might interfere with the state's work of remaking human consciousness.[15]

To paraphrase Nisbet, the American Revolution championed a model of autonomy that did not seek to recreate human life but was content to work in harmony with "traditional kinship, local, and religious institutions" without any rejection of the transcendence and teleology that inspired those institutions.

The third date offered by Beck to understand the Enlightenment is 1687, the year of Isaac Newton's *Principia Mathematica*. Louis Dupré describes how Newton's mechanistic approach to nature affected the world

of philosophy and, specifically, epistemology—the field of human understanding of truth: "Mechanism functions as a closed system impervious to
any influence from outside, even though all that occurs within it results
from a transcendent source of motion. In the Neoplatonic version, the effect
participates in the divine cause. Moreover it is endowed with a divine teleology that enables the higher spheres to communicate power to the lower
ones. Mechanical philosophy replaced the classical and medieval teleological order by a nonhierarchical world of nature."[16]

Dupré brilliantly describes the death of teleology in the Enlightenment philosophy that sought to implement the closed, mechanical laws
postulated by Newton. By contrast, the transcendent view of human origin
and destiny necessarily meant an openness to a suprahuman or divine communion. The medieval teleology rejected by the closed Newtonian system
of the Enlightenment era had never posited or discerned a passivity in
human identity. The person was not seen as a puppet controlled and driven
by the whimsical purposes of God but rather a subject of creaturely participation in divine life and communion. E. F. Schumacher was successful in
finding a map for this perspective in medieval theology: "As the Scholastics
used to say: 'Homo non proprie humanus sed superhumanus est'—which
means that to be properly human, you must go beyond the merely
human."[17]

This participation will be called by John Paul II "participated
theonomy," a description of human identity and purpose that overcomes
the rigidity and sterility of the Kantian dichotomy between autonomy and
heteronomy where *freedom* from the other ultimately becomes *isolation*
from the other.[18]

The application of Newtonian mechanics to the world of philosophy led to a dramatic difference between classical and Enlightenment metaphysics on a most critical point—whether the entire inquiry is focused on
the grand question of who we are or the more limited question of how we
know things: "If metaphysics be a sort of internal Newtonianism, then its
proper study is the ultimate grounds of knowledge and not the ultimate
grounds of being."[19]

Sadly, the mechanical Enlightenment template of metaphysics was
not an inquiry about the transcendent basis of being itself but a much more
limited and impoverished search for mechanical accounts of how the subject comes to know things. Questions of ultimate purpose (*why*) dropped
to a lower level of the methods of knowledge (*how*). The Newtonian prescription of mechanical action and mathematical formulas prevailed: "With

the enormous effectiveness of Newton's mathematical analysis of nature .
. . the followers of Newton began to believe that only the mathematical
was real. But the constriction of reality to the canons of a reified mathe-
matics brought rebellion with its success. The tidy, heroic couplets of the
eighteenth century clicked by, one after another. People grew restless. And
the Romantics, reacting against the sterile watchmaker view of the cosmos,
mounted a rebellion."[20]

This narrowing of the scope of metaphysical inquiry to the mechanics of gaining knowledge prompted the rebellious Alexander Pope
(1688–1744) to satirize Newtonian metaphysics by beginning his *Essay on
Man* with the "tidy" but barbed couplet "Know then thyself, presume not
God to scan; The proper study of Mankind is Man." But the damage had
been done as the descent into smaller areas of inquiry continued apace. Was
the human being a partner in creation, inherently inclined toward goodness
and endowed with a reasoning power not at all thwarted or hampered by
religious belief? Or, instead, could the subject attain at best to a content-
free, transcendental reason, a world of abstraction divorced from any empirical basis, and aspire to greatness by willing whatever might be
hypothesized as a universal duty, liberated from constraining influences of
tradition, religion, habit, custom, and emotion? Enter Immanuel Kant, the
brilliant proponent of the latter view.

In coming to the fourth date of Beck's chronological quadrant
marking off the Enlightenment, 1790, the publication of the last of Kant's
Critiques, we approach the apogee of the secular foundation for human
dignity, the Kantian notion of transcendental reason and his categorical imperative.

Kant and Autonomy: A Secular Basis for Dignity

Immanuel Kant is at the center of the Enlightenment and the concept of autonomy is at the center of his thought. Since we are intent on
looking closely at the interaction of dignity, freedom, and human love, we
can see in Kant's work the archetype of dignity as autonomy:

> Kant's contribution lies in making human dignity *the* theme of
> philosophy and the centerpiece of liberalism. With so much at
> stake, Kant realizes that a rational justification for human dignity
> must be provided and acknowledges that his whole case comes
> down to one crucial question: Is freedom of the will, which gives
> us our dignity as responsible moral agents, an illusion or a

reality? The problem for Kant is that his commitment to skeptical reason makes positive proofs for the existence of freedom impossible; only "negative" proofs are possible. . . . Despite Kant's best efforts, his negative proofs for freedom and dignity are deeply unsatisfying. They are more like wishful thinking than rational proofs because all they show is that we may act "*as if*" we were free, without knowing if it were really the case.[21]

As an outspoken adherent of the *Aufklärung* or Enlightenment, Kant felt the assault of "reason" (a trope soon to become a narrow and mechanistic abstraction) upon Christian revelation so keenly that he used his formidable talents to develop critiques of reason that allowed religious believers to retain their convictions even though he repudiated any sort of realist metaphysics that would demonstrate or defend the possibility of actually knowing the truth or nature of an object. The mightily murky but believer-friendly nature of his *Critique of Pure Reason* in 1781 could not withstand the impact of this concession to the forces of "reason." The loss of metaphysics meant the loss of realism in theories of truth, the focus of epistemology, and rational consideration of the links between desire and good, the focus of ethics.

If we cannot know the nature of something in itself, not only are we entitled to believe anything we please, but we are also entitled thereby to disavow anything we please. Worst of all, by this epistemological version of unilateral disarmament, people forfeit the medium, context, or common denominator to speak with one another about whether anything can honestly and definitively be considered true. Providing a textbook example of philosopher Karl Popper's Law of Unintended Consequences, Kant clearly sowed the metastasizing seeds of relativism.

By conceding a priori that one could not know the nature or truth of something in such a way that a real correspondence between the mind and the object came to exist, Kant essentially surrendered his religious perspective to the Enlightenment Project. The self-rebutting nature of the Kantian concession to rationalism screams out, "If we cannot know the inherent nature or intrinsic truth of any proposition, what confidence do we have that *this* proposition is true?"

Kant's pursuit of truth was weakened not only by his disavowal of metaphysics but by his separation of philosophy from theology, depriving his reflections of a theological horizon that could complement philosophical templates. For example, the Christian doctrine of the Trinity provides a context for human relationality. Just as the Trinity is a communion of three divine persons—Father, Son, and Holy Spirit—united in a communal bond of love but each distinct in personal identity, so Jesus' teaching in the New Testament proclaims humanity to be a communion of love made up of distinct persons in relationship with each other. Reciprocity provides the guidelines for autonomy. But loss of this Trinitarian focus was surely a factor in the Kantian turn to the subject and the exaltation of individual autonomy without a larger theological horizon that would constitute the anthropological environment of a model of autonomy compatible with communion. Since autonomy and heteronomy are mutually exclusive terms in Kant's system, it means that the subject (that is, the self) is locked into an antagonistic opposition with any "other" (that is, the heteronomous force), including one's own desires and even another person.

David Hume argued that morality and religious beliefs are merely a matter of sentiments, deep and noble feelings that we cannot measure or see through the lens of reason. Nihilists would go much further and deny the very existence of any verifiable truth. Since there are no absolute or universal truths to know, it is fatuous to discuss or debate various theories of knowledge; all is a matter of opinion, conditioning, contingency, and self-interest.

The flawed efforts of Kant to salvage some relevance for religion or a basis for objective truth quickly dissolve from inherent weaknesses and contradictions. Can a proposition be true in science but false in religion? Because truth is fundamentally indivisible, a proposition cannot simultaneously be true and not true in the same way and at the same time. Classic metaphysics describes this as the principle of noncontradiction. Propositions from science and religion cannot contradict each other inherently, indefinitely, or without modification. Either reconciliation or rejection must occur.

Take, for example, the teaching of Genesis that the world came to be in seven days. Reputable science precludes the possibility that the world came to be within one hundred sixty-eight hours. Hence, there must be some modification. It is not a concession but a clarification for believers in Genesis to take the term *day* as a figure of speech. Genesis does not purport to be a scientific manual. It describes the reality of God, creation, and humankind as a theological drama. It is about *who*s and *why*s, not *how*s.

The language of science and religion may entail different orders of discourse, each with its own parameters, logic, and meaning, but truth, radically and powerfully, transcends these different orders and demands some ultimate accounting of inherent and indivisible truth. For the believer, the ultimate truth is the author of creation because it requires a reality of larger compass than the human to account fully for the vectors toward transcendence of the human spirit. There can and must be some reconciliation of the truth claims of science and religion. There cannot be separate, airtight compartments of truth isolated from each other.

Similarly, the reduction of truth to mere sentiment, emotion, or opinion attacks the very meaning of humanity. Can the sketches of Shakespeare, hailed by generations as powerfully accurate accounts of human life, be reduced to sheer sentiment? A light switch will either produce light or not; its operation cannot be considered a matter of mere emotion. If things have objective, verifiable meaning, can we possibly suggest a lower standard for human utterances?

Immanuel Kant wrote that his grandfather emigrated from Scotland to Prussia. Kant was determined to refute the skepticism of the Scotsman David Hume, spending considerable time and effort to show that, in some limited contexts, one could justify the concept of causality. If the Scottish influence of his grandfather was part of Kant's patrimony, the concerns of Hume, the dean of the Scottish Enlightenment, also influenced him to move from empiricism to reason in the hope of making religious belief respectable. But the "transcendental" reason that Kant affirmed was mechanistic and atomistic, leaving the subject or self isolated and uncertain, walking a tightrope between freedom, on the one hand, and a duty, on the other hand, to will something reasonable.

In following the mathematical system of Newton, Kant imposed a deterministic rigidity upon what he sought to protect and expand, namely, human freedom: "Following Newton, [Kant] was committed to the view that everything in nature is caused by mechanical forces. . . . He understood that the task of the natural sciences is to explain the behavior of phenomena, including human behavior, with reference to these forces. He granted, then, that insofar as we seek a scientific explanation of human behavior, we have to work within the deterministic framework."[22]

Despite his brilliance, Kant's position on two other critical issues, the meaning of virtue and the character of love, seriously impede his concept of autonomy from being of help to a subject who falls in love. Kant states that virtue is "self-constraint according to a principle of inner freedom, and so by the mere thought of one's duty in accordance with its formal law."[23] This view of virtue as a duty conforming to a law is a crabbed caricature of the robust scholastic sense of virtue as the capacity for excellence and a human inclination toward the good. In regard to love, Kant says that love "is a matter of feeling, not of will, and I cannot love because I will to, still less because I ought to. . . . So a duty to love is logically impossible."[24]

How can one love an enemy except by willing that love? There is no feeling or sentiment that moves a subject to embrace one who has caused injury; it must be prompted by a will oriented toward union, forgiveness, sacrifice, and reconciliation—agape. Ironically, Kant repudiates the verdict of Saint Paul that love is the greatest virtue when he reduces love to a feeling and virtue to a duty.

Could we consider Kant's salvage effort a success today? The best answer, clearly in the negative, is provided by yet another Scottish philosopher, Alasdair MacIntyre, whose *After Virtue*, first published in 1981, describes the grave damage and disorder that characterize the language of morality today. MacIntyre argues eloquently, if not definitively, that subjectivism and emotivism, the view that morality is nothing but sentiment, preference, and feeling, govern and corrupt all contemporary moral discussion.[25]

One doesn't have to be Scottish (nor is it necessary to consume any Scotch) to say that the great goal of the Enlightenment, *sapere aude* ("Dare to know," the motto of Kant), has not been realized today. Individuals dare to debate and dare to doubt, but much of the world has given up on the idea that one can actually know the truth about anything satisfactorily. We are defined not by what we know or what we believe but by the style and shape of our doubt. The brilliance of Kant and the fiery force of the Enlightenment have essentially led to the cul-de-sac of relativism. Nothing is said to be inherently or absolutely true. Any truth claim is simply a matter of one's preference or feeling, conditioned by one's background and experience.

The bloody upheaval of the French Revolution included the worship of the Goddess of Reason, a nubile young woman, at the altar of Notre Dame Cathedral in Paris. While conceding that the union of altar and throne in Europe did not always produce ethical or edifying conduct on the part of clergy or sovereigns, we still must ask whether human beings have been well served by the replacement of the God of Abraham, Moses, and Jesus by the Goddess of Reason. The Catholic view of religious sacrifice holds that Christ offered himself in sacrifice for the sins of all human beings. This single sacrifice is of divine magnitude and can never be supplanted or duplicated. By contrast, the enthronement of reason as a secularist ideal has demanded multiple sacrifices of realities much needed by humankind.

For an era that loves irony, it cannot escape notice that one of the greatest sacrifices demanded by the Enlightenment notion of reason is the tragic loss of our hard-fought, hard-earned sense of truth, reasonableness, solidarity, and communion. Reason took as its symbol on the altar at Notre Dame the body of a young woman. But in fact reason had become a disembodied abstraction. Since transcendental reason disdained empirical sources, it was forced to borrow the most essential empirical reality of human history, a body. By way of contrast, Catholic liturgy also includes a body on an altar, but it is the body of a Person, not an abstraction. Abstractions and human bodies do not make a good fit.

What happened after Kant? Many philosophers and moralists simply accepted his notion of autonomy as the basis for human dignity. But many bristled at Kant's insistence that the subject had an unalterable duty to will whatever was universalizable as a good—the famous categorical imperative. This insistence on duty encroached upon the supposed freedom that autonomy represented.

Instead of the church, society, or tradition compelling the subject to act in a certain way, now the subject forged his own chains from the iron of the categorical imperative. Those who followed Kant came to be known as the "deontologists," from the Greek word for duty (*deontos*); the largest alternative school of ethical decision-making is the utilitarian approach, eminently compatible with Rousseau's "general will". Saint Thomas Aquinas and the preponderance of the Catholic ethical tradition follow neither deontology nor utilitarianism but a kind of goal-oriented or teleological perspective attuned to creation, participation, realism, and objective truth, as we shall shortly see with Pinckaers.

THE DECLINE AND DIVISION OF REASON

It would surely shock the French encyclopedists such as Diderot and Voltaire, who cheered the French Revolution, to discover that their beloved, newly enthroned Goddess of Reason would be abandoned by a postmodern world totally uncomfortable with any sense of objective, verifiable, or absolute truth. The philosophes of Paris took the point from Thomas Jefferson, writing the *Declaration of Independence* two decades earlier, that some truths are self-evident. This Jeffersonian view, or Jeffersonian truth, we might say, is actually an application of a venerable tradition of reasoning known as the natural law, a topic to be explored at some length very shortly. In the debates and discussions of the twenty-first century, it is difficult to find any consensus about *any* truth deemed to be self-evident. Perhaps the closest that one might come would be the proposition that "everything is relative," or "it all depends," a sad descent into meaninglessness.

Reason as norm and ideal would give way first to rationalism, the narrow insistence that only those claims logically or empirically verifiable can be true, and then to relativism, the view that *no* claim could be logically or empirically proven so as to be inherently or absolutely true. For relativism, all truth claims are up for grabs. Your truth and my truth may not only diverge but be totally unrelated. Truth is merely a matter of feeling, prejudice, conditioning, and opinion.

A related and profound loss that has left a painful impact upon our contemporary scene is the eclipse of virtue, both its meaning and its practice. Virtue as a concept and the particular virtues as modalities of the Judeo-Christian commitment to love both God and neighbor represent an intersection of reason and revelation. Aristotle recognized the reasonableness of virtue in explaining that human well-being comes into existence when a moral agent pursues a virtuous mean between an excess and a defect: the courageous soldier fights for the good while avoiding both foolhardiness and cowardice. The Christian perspective has aligned the human virtues with discipleship in Christ so that Saint Paul in his famous paean to love (1 Corinthians 13) describes the attributes of love (patient, kind, not envious or boastful, and so on) in a way directly analogous to the moral life of the believer.

Few have chronicled the importance of recovering virtue as insightfully as Alasdair MacIntyre. In a work that continues to provoke considerable reaction, *After Virtue*, MacIntyre makes a distinction between internal and external goods:

> When achieved, [external goods] are always some individual's property and possession. Moreover characteristically they are such that the more someone has of them, the less there is for other people. This is sometimes necessarily the case, as with power and fame, and sometimes the case by reason of contingent circumstances as with money. External goods are therefore characteristically objects of competition in which there must be losers as well as winners. Internal goods are indeed the outcome of competition to excel, but it is characteristic of them that their achievement is a good for the whole community who participate in the practice.[26]

Similarly, Charles Taylor contrasts the Romanticism of Schiller and Goethe as a rampart against the domination of a disengaged, objectified scientific worldview. Taylor sees the forces of Romanticism "in standing polemic with the aspirants to rational control and instrumental reason within modern culture."[27]

While I hope to advance the MacIntyre thesis that the recovery of virtue is essential for human flourishing, and to note the extended critique of "instrumental reason" offered by Taylor in his *A Secular Age*, I propose to describe internal or interior goods (best symbolized by the virtues) as the World of Humans and to describe external goods such as power, fame, and money as the World of Things. It is this clash of external, objectified, instrumental reason with the interior compass of natural inclinations to the excellence of good, truth, and beauty that describes the arena of our concern that autonomy does not serve the person very well.

Although the post-Enlightenment legacy of reason slowly dissipated, it did not lose its kingdom entirely; rather its sovereignty was split in two. Reason continues to dominate in the World of Things, but it has virtually no standing in the World of Humans. That is to say that science has made incredible, unprecedented advances, putting an astronaut on the moon, conquering many insidious diseases, and providing an Internet which would revolutionize communications. These admirable accomplishments rest on the attainment, sharing, and operation of countless truths of technology and science.

The late Servais Pinckaers, OP (1925–2008), whose thought we shall shortly explore, identifies the nominalism of the fourteenth century as a precursor of relativism and nihilism. The realist would say that the baseball is round, an instance of the universal "roundness." The nominalist would reply that the baseball is round but there is no such universal reality as "roundness"; it is merely a concept used arbitrarily by conventions of human language. (It is doubtful that a conscientious nominalist who happens to be starving would quibble about whether a ham sandwich is only a name.)

Pinckaers summarizes the nominalist turn toward linguistic confusion and murkiness: "A challenging task faces us today: to get in touch with our natural desire for truth and to restore to the word 'truth' its pristine force. Under the influence of nominalism, truth in philosophy has become abstract and conceptual—in the sciences, depersonalized and constricted. We have confused it with the ideas, formulas, and words we use to express it, and which we think encapsulate it. We are left with mere reflections and imitations."[28]

Sadly, at a time when technology is developing at breakneck speed, the West seems to be seriously adrift on the ethical or personal meaning, value, beginning, or end of the human being treated by medical science. There are internationally accepted standards and axioms to govern the world of things—the metric system, currency exchange ratios, standardized services, software, and hardware—but there are few if any "self-evident truths" about the human beings ostensibly benefited by the World of Things. One could plausibly argue that the quest for human rights is a salutary accomplishment of the Enlightenment. Nevertheless, the achievement of human rights around the globe is hardly universal or consistent; abuses abound on every continent. One could also argue that religious influences (consider William Wilberforce in Britain on slavery and Dr. Martin Luther King Jr. in the United States on civil rights) played a significant role in the attainment of human rights.

Louis Dupré shows what happens when the relationship of a Creator to creatures is reduced to efficient causality: "Christian theologians had always succeeded in maintaining the link between the forms and the realm of the divine through God's eternal image, the divine archetype of all created reality. In late nominalist theology, the form lost this function and the link with the divine became a more external one. Modern thought increasingly defined the relation between the finite and the infinite beings in terms of efficient causality. If form was no more than a construction of the human mind, it could no longer secure the intrinsic union between the finite and the infinite."[29]

Instrumental reason, the mechanical result of efficient causality, has come to govern the World of Things, whereas ambiguity or "exclusive humanism," (that is, a humanism that excludes the divine, in the phrase of Charles Taylor) governs the World of Humans in its philosophical, ethical, anthropological, and cultural dimensions. The World of Humans desperately needs the virtues, and I will argue that the most authentic and humanly fruitful account of the virtues is found in the Judeo-Christian union of reason and revelation, the Old and New Testament, and the traditions supported by the mutual illumination of faith and reason.

Is this an unwarranted indictment of moral discourse in our era? We can find the answer by examining both the macro and micro aspects of the question. Looking at the macro side, we must concede that the twentieth century was the most violent in history, reducing various populations by millions through totalitarian warfare and genocide—Nazi, Communist, and Fascist for starters. History admonishes us that human beings willed the destruction of millions of their peers through war, genocide, ethnic cleansing, barbarism, planned starvation, and holocausts. It is not a record to make either faith or reason proud.

Looking at the micro side, we can say that doubt and disagreement attach to the meaning of a particular human being. I have used the term *human being* intentionally because noted philosophers such as Peter Singer deny that human beings bereft of cognitive skills count as persons. Despite the clear evidence of sonograms and 3-D technology that shows their growth, movement, perception, and choices, debate rages about the very humanity of human embryos and fetuses. Against the overwhelming evidence that an embryo is a human being with a potential (rather than merely a "potential human being"), some who might have a personal interest in obtaining their incredibly rich, pluripotent humanity will claim against logic and science that an embryo or fetus lacks the status of personhood and may not even qualify as a human being. The concept of autonomy or self-legislation is pressed into service to *deny* the humanity or personhood of an embryo or fetus or cognitively disabled patient: since they lack autonomy (rational will), they thereby lack humanity. Autonomy is no friend of those in love or those in danger.

There seem to be few if any "reasonable" claims about the World of Humans firmly positioned above debate and discord. Much of our culture accepts abortion on the view that no one knows for sure when life begins, doubting whether the embryo or fetus truly constitutes a human being, let alone a person. At the other end of the life cycle, many are inclined to end human life that is no longer considered useful. If a subject can no longer communicate meaningfully, a death sentence is considered just, a matter of "mercy killing" rather than murder. Abortion and euthanasia are largely acceptable, done reluctantly and with regret, but done nevertheless. As a matter of logic, however, if these practices are reasonable, there should be no regret. The fact that unease and anxiety continue to surround life issues demonstrates that we can delete files from our computers, but we cannot delete the conscience from our moral choices.

While reason continues to rule in the World of Things, producing ever more efficient machines, laborsaving devices, communications wizardry, and dazzling digital marvels, these wonders are given to people increasingly unsure on matters of fundamental importance—such as the inherent dignity of all human life; our responsibility (to each other) to safeguard human life, especially when it is most frail; and our commitment to pursue a common good that puts some fundamental, critical moral standards above political debate.

But even in the World of Things, reason cannot command with total authority. As powerful inventions and radically new technologies become available to human use, they instantly become available to human abuse as well. The nuclear power that delivers electricity to cities has also delivered death to the cities of Hiroshima and Nagasaki. The medical prowess that powers unprecedented cures and treatments is often used on a highly selective basis, reserved primarily for the wealthy and for the service of socially useful patients, pitting the well-cared-for against the un-cared-for. A disabled fetus, failing to live up to arbitrary standards of well-being or a politically popular quality of life, will be aborted. Lasers, microchips, and fiber optics will be used to produce new generations of weapons, destroying enemies on a scale only dreamed of by an earlier generation of totalitarian oppressors.

The Enlightenment sought to liberate reason from revelation. It succeeded dramatically in doing so. But, as with all revolutions, its success moved much further than the most ardent revolutionary adherents imagined. Not only was reason separated from revelation but it was soon untethered as well from faith, a believer's response to revelation.

This series of separations and divisions reduced the domain of reason to a narrow rationalism—brittle, opinionated, argumentative, and intolerant. No longer the sovereign of human understanding lauded by the Greeks of the fifth century BC or the great scholastics Bonaventure and Thomas Aquinas in the thirteenth century, reason now became technical, essential for making and using things but not in making human decisions. Reason slowly surrendered questions of human purpose to the realm of sentiment and emotion. This was not a good thing because reason traditionally was invaluable in weighing human experiences for lessons learned and tempering the heat and frolic of passion with the moderation of mature logic. Reason now had to seek asylum in the World of Things.

Instrumental reason has become narrow, mechanistic, and deterministic, the domain of science but not suited to the humanities. It is most helpful for the curriculum in a vocational school, but it is of no help in discerning what one's vocation might be. Reason now dominates in making, building, inventing, and repairing things. It provides engineering instructions, blueprints for buildings, and operators' manuals for computers and high-tech gadgetry.

But once we build and buy these things, how do we use them to enhance our humanity? What is the direction in which we need to move to become more authentically human? How do we prevent the World of

Things from dehumanizing the World of Humans? How do humans avoid rattraps of conformity, leading us to work, scheme, and compete endlessly against one another in agitated unease, recklessly and relentlessly pursuing things?

Many believers turned to their faith in religion and revelation to answer these questions. It is still to faith that the devout turn to make important decisions about life, death, family, sex, marriage, love and, yes, God. Secularization does not mean the end of religious belief or practice. Rather, as Taylor demonstrates, *secular* names the social environment in which religious people continue to believe—"a new context in which all search and questioning about the moral and spiritual must proceed."[30]

But faith, separated from reason, cannot provide the answers sought. We cannot even identify correct questions or frame questions correctly without reason. The forces unleashed by the Enlightenment have had the effect of dividing reason and faith and thereby reducing their respective impact. Reason, especially in the format of science, would by default rule the World of Things. Faith, by default, would attempt to answer the big questions in the World of Humans. Both would fail without the aid of each other. Reason has contributed on an unprecedented scale to the things that we have. But humans decide to use things against each other and the things, taking on a life of their own with Frankenstein-like fury, begin to make humans subservient to them. We have more devices than ever to communicate with one another but don't know what to say when we're connected. Instrumental reason has left digital devices connected and human beings disconnected.

AN ETHIC OF ABSOLUTE AUTONOMY

I have used the distinction between a World of Things and a World of Humans to show how reason has come to govern things absolutely but has failed, with the rejection of virtue, in providing any guidance for ultimate questions of human identity and striving. Reason does not provide a compass for the World of Humans. One explanation of how this came to be emerges from a famous passage of Thomas Hobbes, whose 1651 work *Leviathan* describes the state of nature as having "no arts; no letters; no society; and which is worst of all, continual fear and danger of violent death." The "life of man" is famously "solitary, poor, nasty, brutish, and short."[31]

In looking at human dealings as a war of all against all, Hobbes explicitly opposes the scholastic idea that "nature" could stand for the optimal well-being or flourishing of a creature consistent with its goals of proximate and remote goods aimed at happiness. Alasdair MacIntyre describes how the quest for power replaces the goal of happiness: "Hobbes has already said that 'there is no such *finis ultimus*, utmost aim, or *summum bonum*, greatest good, as is spoken of in the books of the old moral philosophers,' and his reason for saying this is his view that human felicity consists in 'a continual progress of the desire from one object to another, the attaining of the former being still but the way to the latter,' and that men are driven on by 'a perpetual and restless desire of power after power that ceaseth only in death.'"[32]

Another pessimistic view of human nature is found in the work of Jean-Jacques Rousseau (1712–78) whose *Social Contract* enunciated the famous verdict in 1762 that "man is born free, and everywhere he is in chains." The social order in short is "corrupted and corrupting."[33] Unlike Hobbes and Hume, Rousseau believed in God and lamented that "everything is good when it leaves the hands of the Creator; everything degenerates in the hands of man."[34]

Jeremy Bentham (1748–1832) formulated and championed a utilitarian approach, holding that "the greatest happiness of the greatest number is the foundation of morals and legislation."[35] John Stuart Mill (1806–73) endeavored to popularize Bentham's notion of utilitarianism by refining the notion of happiness: "The creed which accepts as the foundation of morals Utility, or the Greatest Happiness Principle, holds that actions are right in proportion as they tend to promote happiness, wrong as they tend to produce the reverse of happiness."[36]

As appealing as the Greatest Happiness Principle may appear on first glance, we are left with the dilemma that in trying to quantify pleasure and pain to arrive at a net result of happiness, neither Bentham nor Mill could negotiate around the dilemma that if the pleasure accorded a sadistic torturer surpasses on some arbitrary and subjective scale the pain of his beleaguered victim, it thereby provides a mathematical and moral justification for torture.

Mill states the Enlightenment Ethic with bold eloquence: "The individual is not accountable to society for his actions, insofar as these concern the interest of no person but himself. . . . Liberty consists in doing what one desires."[37]

When we combine Mill's unyielding, absolute, and unfettered defense of individual autonomy with the world view of an Enlightenment figure, John Locke (1632–1704), who strongly influenced the American

founding fathers, we arrive at the Enlightenment ethic of absolute autonomy.

Whereas Thomas Hobbes saw human interaction as the ruthless
pursuit of power by agents whose interests fundamentally conflicted, John
Locke endeavored to highlight the rational possibilities of a social contract:
"Good and evil, reward and punishment, are the only motives to a rational
creature: these are the spur and reins whereby all mankind are set on work,
and guided."[38]

One might suppose that this basic reduction of human motivation
into good or evil, reward or punishment, realistically describes the human
condition. But MacIntyre alerts us to a further narrowing of the social contract even as the realm of reason was narrowed to the World of Things:
"The aim of the contract is to create an authority adequate to safeguard our
natural rights, and for Locke the most important of rights is that of property."[39]

The Enlightenment icons did not always agree on fundamental
matters. Kant and Rousseau believed in God whereas Hume and Hobbes
did not. And indeed their views and versions of God were quite different,
even contradictory. But it is more than a fair summary to say that the mus-
cular, utilitarian individualism of John Stuart Mill, combined with the emphasis on the pursuit of property as the height of rational choice in Locke,
gives us an ethic of absolute autonomy. No force or power from altar,
throne, or marketplace has the right to interfere with the right of autonomy
of the subject. Any limitation from without would be, in Kant's pejorative
term, heteronomy, the imposition of another's will over and against one's
own.

One distinguished philosopher, a decade before he ended his most
fruitful and multi-disciplinary career, traces the roots of post-Enlightenment
confusion back to a Jesuit-trained French philosopher, René Descartes:
"Descartes inaugurated the great anthropocentric shift in philosophy. 'I
think therefore I am' . . . is the motto of modern rationalism. All the rationalism of the last centuries can be considered a continuation and expansion
of Cartesian positions."[40] (The philosopher who saw Descartes at the center
of the troubling, rationalist turn to the subject was Karol Wojtyla, better
known as Pope John Paul II, whose papacy contributed much, as we will
see, to the reconciliation of faith and reason.)

This papal insight summarizes the continuum between the skeptical doubt of Descartes and the inexorable turn to the subject of Kant. The
religious focus on the soul as openness to the divine was replaced by the

secular emphasis on the self, supposedly free but tragically hollow: "[Descartes] increasingly disregarded the self's particularity, moving closer to what Kant would later call a transcendental subject—universal but devoid of a content of its own."[41]

In summary, we have a powerful confluence of hedonism, rationalism, utilitarianism, and materialism that pushes the virtues aside, leaving the World of Things to define what matters in the World of Humans and one might even say, replaces, the World of Humans. Beginning with this new direction, it is hardly surprising that the twentieth century would be marked by unrelenting wars to achieve things at the expense of humans. It was not so much a brave new world as an old conformist world, disgorged upon humankind by an out-of-control Enlightenment ethic that brought little illumination and seriously flawed ethics.

Two

Autonomy and Marriage, Strange Bedfellows

The particular merit of the Enlightenment did not consist, as some have claimed, in abolishing moral or religious absolutes. Indeed, the loss of moral absolutes, whether caused by the Enlightenment or not, lies at the root of the inhumanity of the past century.

— Louis Dupré

A library patron seeking prurient material would not likely go to the philosophy section. Many individuals consider sex and philosophy to be mutually exclusive; nothing, it would seem, could redeem philosophy from a terminal dryness and dullness. Still, the concept of autonomy has shaped the sexual revolution and captivated the imaginations of more people than many realize. Autonomy provided the philosophical justification for the theme of liberation that dominated the 1960s. It proved essential in liberating married couples from their children, their spouses, and their churches.

If we look at the scholarly summation of an erudite couple, Will and Ariel Durant, who spent decades studying what they chose to call "the story of civilization," including of course the shifting sands of sexual ethics, we can find a conclusion that might be surprising: "It was the philosophers and the theologians, not the warriors and diplomats, who were fighting the crucial battle of the eighteenth century."[42]

Why does this matter? The crucial achievement of the eighteenth century, the emergence of an autonomous self as the norm for morality, laid the groundwork for most of our contemporary issues surrounding marriage and sexual ethics. Recall that it was the eighteenth century that gave us both the American and French Revolutions, two demonstrations that ideas, whatever their merit, are not restricted to intellectuals. These ideas are sometimes life-giving and other times deadly. The American Revolution led to President George Washington. The French Revolution led to the

33

Reign of Terror and eventually Emperor Napoleon. Two different templates of autonomy were at work. In both cases, a revolution was fueled by the force of ideas that had consequences, to borrow the language of the American political scientist Richard Weaver. These ideas sometimes converged and often collided, but there is no doubt that huge changes affecting our world today are traceable to the arena of ideas in which philosophers and theologians were the principal gladiators. To an American pragmatist (a phrase likely to be redundant) inclined to be skeptical about the impact of philosophy, one can only point out that skepticism is not a rejection of philosophy but itself a philosophical idea. Moreover, there is nothing more practical than a powerful idea.

A little humor may make a serious point. In his trademark attire of electrified hair, ratty tuxedo, and tennis shoes, Professor Irwin Corey, the American comedian popular in the 1950s, '60s, and '70s boasting the moniker of "The World's Foremost Authority," would gesture dramatically onstage with a faux professorial earnestness. He explained forcefully, "The problem before the Revolution was man's inhumanity to man." Then pausing for effect, he lowered his head and continued with deadpan horror: "But the problem after the Revolution was of course vice versa."

The role of a philosopher–clown goes back to the Greek dramatist Aristophanes lampooning Socrates in *The Clouds*. Despite his comedic venue, Aristophanes did capture a measure of the unhappiness of the citizens of fifth-century-BC Athens with the style of Socrates' relentless questionings, a social discomfort that led eventually to his trial and death. Corey may also have tapped a vein of cynical humor to the effect that revolutions come and go but brutish treatment of one another lasts forever. Still, the effort to understand or even change human behavior through revolution has perplexed minds as great and different as Jefferson and Marx.

We might be tempted to study Bacchus, the Roman god of ecstasy, in order to understand the sexual revolution associated with the 1960s but the one we need is actually Janus, the pagan deity who looks to both the past and the future. In this chapter, we look at how the power of an eighteenth-century idea anticipated and largely precipitated the sexual revolution. We will also ask whether a different model of autonomy might be more usefully pursued today for those who truly seek friendship, love, communion, and, yes, a marriage naturally open to children.

In pre-modern times there was a template of belief based on the conviction that there is a God—"I Am" (Exodus 3:14)—who revealed certain fundamental truths in a blaze of creation, bringing a beloved world into existence with a covenantal bond of eternal union. As faith in God diminished through the secularizing waves of the Enlightenment, love of an absent God would also disappear and love of a present neighbor would change dramatically. Aspects of divine love, such as union and covenant, have given way to a human love searching for fulfillment but unsure if any assurance of that fulfillment can be found. We can speak of this universal searching for love simply as eros, meaning sexual desire and consequent activity.

The efforts of European intelligentsia in the Age of Enlightenment to replace what they deemed to be a repressive and reactionary faith with enlightened reason has failed to destroy faith but has surprisingly succeeded in weakening reason. The Enlightenment ushered into our era a loss of confidence in reason leading to nihilism (the position that nothing can be ascertained with certitude, hence nothing ultimately matters) and relativism (the view that truth is simply a matter of subjective opinion). These philosophical perspectives gradually became political ideologies, holding sway over a considerable sector of the dominant culture. Jettisoned from popular practice, religious desire morphed into sexual desire, the one remaining domain of mystery—eros.

The desire for union with God has often been replaced by a desire for a generic, polymorphous sexual fulfillment. Even the style of worship in many churches has become less the adoration of God than the immersion into a spiritual sauna where all sackcloth is shed and feeling good is the measure of successful liturgy. The satisfaction once given to religious by the knowledge that they were united to a benevolent God now yields to the satisfaction that each individual is liberated to pursue sexual desire unfettered in a secularized culture. For a great percentage of values-free but tech-savvy youngsters, satisfaction is reduced to the sexual while faith is subtly reduced to the erotic. Faith and hope are no longer virtues but sentiments, as Kant proposed, and these youthful yearnings have as their object the confidence that a weekend hook-up will occur.

The problem with this, in the Christian perspective, is not the *existence* of eros but rather its *reduction* to something it manifestly is not, the mere sensation of pleasure unattached to the moral good of self-gift to another. In Christian reflection at its best, there is a close correspondence between human desires (eros) and human needs that, when fulfilled, lead to authentic human experience. The Judeo-Christian vision of creation sees human desires and needs aligned with transcendent goods. When the alignment of angles is toward the greater, toward a realization of what transcends ephemeral experience, then desires will coalesce around and constitute authentic human identity. Passion is at the heart of sanctity, motivating faith, hope, and love toward ever greater vistas.

It is only when the opposite direction is pursued, toward the smaller or the baser, exclusive of an opening toward a limitless horizon, that humanity will be compromised and corrupted. Did the sexual and secular revolution of the 1960s elevate or diminish eros? While expectations of erotic liberation rose dramatically, the evidence of lasting bonds in friendship and marriage is underwhelming. There appears on many fronts to be buyer's remorse for those who championed the sexual Revolution. They embraced the alluring idea of autonomy but perhaps now have none other to embrace.

One author describes succinctly how autonomy has opened the door to an almost unshakeable narcissism in contemporary culture that prevents people from realizing genuine happiness:

> Our time is also marked by an overwhelming degree of subjectivism. If I were to point to one feature of our time which is a problem from the point of view of achieving human happiness, it would be precisely this subjectivism. The presumption that man can only be referring to himself in order to decide on matters in society and politics is the core problem.
>
> By this I mean the common presumption that everything revolves around myself; that I, the ego, am the centre of the universe. Man is in many cases a prisoner of this self. This self-referential life has profound implications for politics. . . . If all there is in the universe is "me," and therefore only my own subjective interests, how can politics exist? How can the term "common good" or "common weal" make any sense?[43]

The 1960s produced an earthquake in sexual behavior. No family or household was exempt from the impact of unprecedented changes. To pursue the image of upheaval, we can profitably look at how earthquakes occur for this vivid metaphor will illuminate our study of sexual upheaval. Ironically, two revolutionary theories converged in the 1960s to explain the origin of earthquakes. The hypothesis of "continental drift," a subject of speculation since the sixteenth century, received serious scientific consideration in the early twentieth century by a German meteorologist, Alfred Wegener. Wegener showed that all of the continents had been connected at one point in the history of the earth. This view seemed plausible enough considering how remarkably similar flora and fauna came to grow on different continents. Still, the creative force and probability of the Continental Drift hypothesis was discounted because there seemed to be no mechanism that might explain *how* the continents actually separated, breaking apart from a single land mass.

A second theory appeared early in the 1960s solving the problem. The mechanism accounting for the creation (that is, separation of) the continents involved plate tectonics. These plates are part of an outer layer of the earth that responds to roiling, increasing heat beneath the surface. As the heat underneath increases exponentially, forming plumes or hotspots, the plates will move in different directions, sometimes colliding violently with one another. The brittleness of the tectonic plates makes it possible for them to move and eventually erupt. The image of a whistling tea kettle finally exploding from the heat of a stove conveys some sense of the formation of an earthquake where fiery forces below the earth's surface generate pressures upward, causing land masses above to move, collide, grind against each other, and produce earthquakes of varying seismic magnitudes.[44]

The discovery of a workable theory to account for the origin of earthquakes in the 1960s paradoxically describes as well the collision of forces long simmering under the surface of American and Western culture. These realities reached the boiling point in this same revolutionary decade of the 1960s, changing the landscape of human culture as surely as any powerful earthquake has altered formerly stationary land masses.

The plate tectonics of the sexual earthquake of the 1960s represented both a consequence and a collision. Sexual ethics changed dramatically in that decade as a consequence of autonomy and related concepts (self-expression, self-determination) long circulating in elite academic and legal circles. By the 1960s, the power of these ideas had acquired a momentum leading them into the popular consciousness of average households: "do your own thing" became mainstream.

The aftershocks of this 1960s earthquake are illustrated by the way in which people use computer technology today. There is an enormous rise in social networking through Facebook pages and Twitter. Baby boomers, as well as their children and grandchildren, are intent upon communicating their every feeling, thought, and sentiment through blogs and texting. This craving for communication is also a craving for communion; it shows the failure of Enlightenment autonomy to satisfy human longings. Blogs appear endlessly in the expectation that someone will read them and understand what the author is valiantly trying to communicate. Lovers and even spouses are identified by computerized services that match personality traits. Computers have replaced churches as the venue where the like-minded meet in search of mystery, love, and meaning. The proliferation of social networking programs demonstrates both the loneliness and the long-ing of contemporary life. From a historical standpoint, there is an analogy to the rise of the Romantic Movement after the Enlightenment era where the needs of the affective and erotic dimension of life rebelled against ra-tionalistic abstractions.

The most important questions have not changed in the focus of eth-ical inquiry: What does it really mean to be human? What choices are most consistent with a good life, that is, a life not simply of material success but one which aims at and substantially achieves happiness? If we consciously eradicate religious meaning from the discussion, it is impossible to answer these questions satisfactorily. Only the trajectory toward the Infinite is wor-thy of finite humans.

What happened in the 1960s was a collision between competing views of humanity. Ideas originating from the Enlightenment—autonomy, the moral duty to submit to universal abstractions, the rule of transcendent reason independent of experience and sensory data, and the rejection of transcendence and teleology—collided with an ethical code distilled from the Mosaic Law and Christian revelation. Autonomy triumphed at the ex-pense of reciprocity.

The secularized tableau of the 1960s sought to define the individual in glorious independence apart from the community. But a view of the sub-ject—and the subjective—that excluded a transcendent horizon ultimately weakened and narrowed the reality of the subject, against the best hopes of sexual liberationists of the 1960s. Autonomy and sexual liberation rati-fied the Law of Unintended Consequences. Today, a subject seeking love is often more adrift than ever, burdened with a hollowed-out self and an empty soul. Marriage and sexuality have been literally disenchanted, trans-formed from a sacred covenant to a secular convenience. Hooking up has displaced the arduous quest for authentic love.

When Italian and other European artists and scholars in the fif-teenth century provided the intellectual candlepower that would be known as the Renaissance, their intent was to recapture in varied expressions all that was authentically human through a "rebirth" of classical greatness, re-turning *ad fontes*—to the sources of their rich heritage:

> The humanism of the Renaissance . . . was deeply religious. The
> Dutch humanist Desiderius Erasmus (1466–1536) wanted to
> read the scriptures in the original languages and translate them
> into a more elegant Latin, and his textual work was of immense
> importance to the reformers. . . . The technical inventions of the
> period helped artists achieve an empirical accuracy and fidelity
> to nature that was unprecedented, based on the depiction of ob-
> jects viewed from a single, objective perspective. . . . But this
> "objectivity" did not mean an abandonment of the transcendent:
> this "scientific art" achieved a numinous vision, just as early
> modern scientists sought a solution that was elegant, aesthetic,
> and redolent of the divine.[45]

New forms, ideas, and expressions were avidly sought with the
idea of recovering ancient beauty and certainly not repudiating it. Countless
artists drew upon the rich tradition of Greco-Roman antiquity, scripture,
the lives of the saints, and popular legends to produce stunning master-
pieces. There were certainly tensions between earlier expressions of Christian faith and Renaissance artists but no gulf separated Renaissance and
Christian sensibilities. In fact, it would be impossible to understand Car-
avaggio, Dante, Leonardo da Vinci, Bernini, or Michelangelo apart from
Christian influences that inspired their greatness by indelibly marking their
sensibilities on the beauty of nature, the artistry of the human body, and
the broad sweep of historic themes allied with the notion of grace—forgiveness, redemption, and resurrection.

In sharp contrast to the overall theme of the Renaissance, the term
Enlightenment refers to the work—beginning in the middle of the eighteenth century—of European intellectuals, who intended not simply to distinguish themselves from traditional Christianity, especially Roman
Catholicism, but to repudiate it and establish reason as the sole standard of
intellectual integrity. Their ideas on the whole were not to express or develop religious faith but to oppose it because, in their view, faith stood
athwart reason, leading the populace into the backwaters of superstition.
But their success in dismantling revealed religion did not take into account
the human need to seek transcendent realities in the realm of mystery and
the infinite. Autonomy pushed to the extreme is confining and distorting,
not liberating.

LIBERATING MARRIAGE IN THE 1960S

> Sexual intercourse began
> In nineteen sixty-three
> (Which was rather late for me)—
> Between the end of the *Chatterley* ban
> And the Beatles' first LP.[46]

Eros did not of course originate in the 1960s, contrary to this spoofery of Philip Larkin, but in many ways its expression has become a rebellion against autonomy as an uncharted mandate for self-expression. Yes, there is more freedom to pursue erotic possibilities unfettered by former moral standards, but the lament of the late Janis Joplin echoes hauntingly: "Freedom's just another word for nothing left to lose."

The rigid force and unclear message of Enlightenment autonomy— "You're totally free but you have an absolute duty to be reasonable"— meant that eros was predestined to fail. If eros is desire seeking communion with another but autonomy demands freedom from all others, then there is no room left for self-gift or self-surrender, the building blocks of an eros that is not merely narcissistic but which finds communion in the life of another.

Partly in response to the Enlightenment ideology, eros has become for a secular society what faith was to Christendom, a quest for relationship and sustaining love. Eros has replaced faith in searching for meaning, fulfillment, and communion but with a difference. Whereas faith had divine love as its trajectory, eros is powerful, a mighty engine of desire yet left directionless. It is denied any claim upon or orientation to transcendence or purpose because these realities extend into the realm of religious meaning.

In the fifth century, Saint Augustine, a scholar who knew something of both faith and eros, recognized that the yearning of the human heart for fulfillment in another was a natural and graced reality. It could not be ignored or repressed but had to be directed through agape—the sacrificial love exemplified by Christ dying for sinners on the cross—to divine fulfillment. Yet the erosion of faith, transcendence, and teleology through the prism of the Enlightenment has left eros without any basis for fulfillment.

Contrary to conventional wisdom, I believe that autonomy has actually threatened and enfeebled eros by robbing it of transcendence and teleology. Evidence for this can be found surprisingly in the work of a proponent of the sexual revolution, a former *New York Times* journalist, Gay Talese, who wrote about the sexual mores of the 1950s and 1960s as an informed, determined advocate of sexual liberation. In his 1980 work of participatory reporting on the sexual scene, *Thy Neighbor's Wife,* Talese wrote admiringly of the work of the Austrian psychiatrist Wilhelm Reich and the founder of *Playboy,* Hugh Hefner. Reich the European intellectual and Heffner the American entrepreneur brought into a popular and commercial setting the practical application of autonomy, illustrating the convenient conduit from European salons to American bedrooms.

Talese writes approvingly that Reich had found "that the God-fixation declined in people who had found bliss in sex." Talese strongly champions the legal battles against censorship and chronicles the commercial success of *Playboy,* starting in 1953 in a Chicago office—directly across the street from Holy Name Cathedral—where Hefner would set up the layout for his monthly centerfolds while listening to the cathedral bells.[47] Writing just before the AIDS epidemic was unfolding in the 1980s, Talese has few cautionary tales in his narrative but reports, somewhat against his own libertarian impulses, the heartbreak that the implementation of sexual autonomy could inflict.

Talese provides a summary of the sexual revolution by describing what Reich, a former clinical associate to Sigmund Freud and opponent of "the antisexual moralism of religious homes and schools,"[48] would have seen after his death in 1957:

> Had Reich lived long enough to witness the radical sixties, he undoubtedly would have seen much that would have confirmed for him his predictions made long ago that society was "awakening from a sleep of thousands of year" and was about to celebrate an epochal event "without parades, uniforms, drums or cannon salutes" that was no less than a revolution of the senses. The churches and governments were gradually losing control over people's bodies and minds, and while Reich conceded that the shifting process would initially produce confrontations, clashes and grotesque behavior, the final result, he believed, would be a healthier, more sex-affirmative and open society.[49]

Talese recounts autonomy in action as married couples, freed from the moral constraint of adultery, must decide on how and with whom to exercise their freedom in the burgeoning practice of 1960s mate-swapping. The sagas of two married couples who went on to found the nudist colony

Sandstone—John and Barbara Williamson with John and Judy Bullaro—are also reported: "The number of mate-swappers in America, most of them middle-class married people with children, were now estimated by some swing-trade periodicals to exceed one million couples; and in a speech to the American Psychological Association, Dr. Albert Ellis, a psychologist and author, said that marriages can sometimes be helped by 'healthy adultery.'"[50]

But the theoretical acceptance of mate-swapping by the Williamsons and Bullaros did not work out in practice. Talese describes the poignant experience of Barbara Williamson listening to her husband make love to another woman in an adjoining bedroom:

> It was confusing, harsh, and frightening, and all the earlier talk on John's part since their marriage about the merits of open sexuality did not now alleviate Barbara's uncertainty; it was one thing to agree with John's theories and quite another to employ them in moments like this, with a woman whom she had just met, and the longer Barbara hesitated the more she knew that she was unable or unwilling to move toward the door.
>
> She felt numb, dizzy, and it took all her resources to stand and walk into the other bedroom. She closed the door. It was after midnight and she was very tired and cold. She realized that she had left her suitcase in the living room but she did not want to get it. Slowly undressing and folding her clothes over the back of a chair, she got into bed and tried to sleep but she remained tearfully awake until dawn, hearing the sounds of their lovemaking.[51]

In an afterword and update included in the 2009 edition of *Thy Neighbor's Wife*, Talese acknowledges a "drastically transformed American sexuality has emerged during this past couple of decades." He also records that the couples described above went their separate ways as relationships at Sandstone led to the breakup of the Bullaro marriage and that "John Bullaro has long been out of touch with his onetime inamorata, Barbara Williamson."[52] The liberation was short-lived. In her 1992 work *Sex, Art, and the American Culture,* Camille Paglia summarizes her own reflections as a baby boomer: "The Sixties revolutionized consciousness, but on the road of excess by which we sought the palace of wisdom, many of us lost our minds, lives, or careers through drugs, sexual orgy, or (my vice) constant challenges to authority. The Sixties, rebelling against Fifties bourgeois conformity and respectability, took life to its extreme and explored the far edges of the possible. . . . Everyone who honestly explored Sixties ideals eventually had to confront the limitations of those ideals. Risk and loss, often permanent, were the price of discovery."[53]

Many affluent and highly educated couples had accepted the practices of sexual liberation in theory but the actual practice was "confusing, harsh, and frightening," leaving an uncertain wife numb, dizzy, and tearful. Her identity descended from spouse to "inamorata." If adultery was "healthy," it was decidedly not happy. I submit that this tearful wife listening to her husband making love to another woman, supposedly in an open, mature, and consensual arrangement, illustrates how Enlightenment freedom miserably failed those who bought into its supposed liberation. Couples were no longer bound by the heteronomous prohibition against adultery, but the norm of autonomy did not equip them to relate to another. A steady descent in relationships led people in the 1960s from covenant to experimentation to convenience. If the verdict on liberation today is that it was a triumph, one cannot ignore the tragedy as well.

Once again, the verdict of the libertarian academic, Camille Paglia on the 1960s is astringent:

> The Sixties attempted a return to nature that ended in disaster. The gentle nude bathing and playful sliding in the mud at Woodstock were a short-lived Rousseauist dream. My generation, inspired by the Dionysian titanism of rock, attempted something more radical than anything else since the French Revolution. We asked: Why should I obey this law? And why shouldn't I act on every sexual impulse? The result was a descent into barbarism. We painfully discovered that a just society cannot, in fact, function if everyone does his own thing. And out of the pagan promiscuity of the Sixties came AIDS. Everyone of my generation who preached free love is responsible for AIDS. The Sixties revolution in America collapsed because of its own excesses. It followed and fulfilled its own inner historical pattern, a fall from Romanticism into Decadence.[54]

Many observers, whether critics or proponents, have documented the seismic sexual changes in the landscape recognizable in the 1960s. In 1989, the philosopher Charles Taylor traced in his *The Sources of the Self* the predominant notions of human identity that flow into a contemporary perspective. Whereas Servais Pinckaers is an unalloyed Thomist, Taylor is more at home with Enlightenment-style autonomy, but his keen awareness of classic philosophical currents from Aristotle to Aquinas to Kant to Rawls gives his largely skeptical outlook a unique value to be taken seriously. The fact that a gifted philosopher of an eclectic bent, Taylor, sees matters in a way largely consistent with an avowed Thomist such as Pinckaers is evidence that in looking at Pinckaers we are not trapped in a narrow scholasticism but are uncovering and recovering classic truths.

Taylor, for his part, sees the 1960s as the culmination of a revolution of ideas, beliefs, and practices long in the making: "The heart of this revolution lies in sexual mores. This was a long time a-building . . . but the development took place earlier among cultural élites. In the 1960s, it was generalized to all classes. This is obviously a profound shift. The relativization of chastity and monogamy, the affirmation of homosexuality as a legitimate option, all these have a tremendous impact on churches, whose stance in recent centuries has laid so much stress on these issues and where piety has often been identified with a very stringent sexual code."[55]

Countless studies, reviews, and works, whether scholarly or popular, have probed the changing contours of sexual ethics in the 1960s.[56] It is necessary to examine the forces and influences *underneath* the shifting tectonic plates of sexual ethics so readily seen in the choices and behavior of both elites and ordinary folks. This is not merely a study of cultural artifacts for it may well be the case that the forces below the surface continue to be active, moving the plates above into new configurations that continue to influence ethical choices for many generations.

Plate tectonics was a revolutionary theory advanced in a revolutionary decade to account for revolutionary events in the earth sciences. It provides a template to examine developments truly consequential in their origin, scope, and results. Like all science, plate tectonics explores both causes and effects. No scientist studying an earthquake would be content to measure only the effects and ignore the causes. In the case of earthquakes, it is impossible to recognize the effects (the shifting movements of the earth's surface) until *after* the earthquake has occurred. If the earthquake is designated, not arbitrarily but scientifically, as an *effect*, then a scientist goes back to look at prior conditions to see whether they can be denominated as cause, condition, coincidence, or clue.

By analogy, if we accept the earthquake as a plausible metaphor for the sexual revolution of the 1960s, we can denominate the changes in attitude and conduct—the earthquake, now visible, showing hugely different configurations on sex, family, marriage, contraception, abortion, and homosexuality—as an *effect* of forces already in action. Just as scientists may disagree on whether some factors are real causes or simply accompany a change, there will not be any unanimous verdict on what specifically caused the sexual revolution. But the work of many scholars indicates that we can rightly stipulate that a sexual revolution occurred in the 1960s and that its contours continue very forcefully into this millennium. By marshalling available evidence, it is possible to identify *some* dominant ideas, both philosophical and theological, as *causes* of the earthquake, the sexual revolution.

Causes and effects shed light on each other. In retrospect, the earthquake alerts the observer to the prior existence and connection of powerful forces. These forces existed and interacted within a context of many geological conditions. A retrospective study of the underlying forces boiling over to generate the earthquake gives us a better understanding of the earthquake itself. It would be very foolhardy simply to look only at surface events. A scientific identification of forces, factors, causes, and effects requires a probing far below the surface which shows the changes most visibly.

Similarly, it is not sufficient for any student of ethics or moral theology simply to look at sociological trends without probing for underlying causes. When human behavior is studied, it is necessary to avail oneself of any number of disciplines and sciences to explain or account for what is happening. To understand, we must turn in large measure to philosophy (most especially ethical theories) *and* theology to explain *why* people have chosen to believe and act as they do. Admittedly, this may be a difficult and possibly divisive path. If it is hard enough to agree on *what* happened, it will be even more troublesome to explain to everyone's satisfaction *how* and *why* important changes have occurred. But the difficulty of the path should not deter us from pursuing it. If we can make any progress in understanding the *whys* of the past in the critical area of sexual ethics, then we have a better chance of understanding the *hows*, the *whys*, and the *whats* of the current and even future scenes.

The pre-eminent laboratory for the social experiments of the 1960s was the institution of marriage, which the Christian tradition also regards as a sacrament, a sacred covenant. The bond between a husband and wife had been consistently protected as a sacred union in which the moral and legal standard was lifelong—"unto death"—open to children and exclusive of any sexual union with someone other than one's spouse. Marriage was accordingly intended to be a bedrock protection for the rearing of children and a union in fact and in law for one man and one woman. It was within this sacred bond that sexual union, itself a sacred experience, would be reserved. As views of the sacred changed, so too did the popular understanding of marriage:

> Those things are sacred in which the spirit of the community has taken residence, and in which *our* destiny is at stake: as it is at stake, for example, in sexual feelings, in attitudes to children and parents, in the rituals of membership and initiation whereby the first-person plural—the "we"—is formed. The sexual revolution of modern times has disenchanted the sexual act. Sex has been finally removed from the sacred realm: it has become "my" affair, in which "we" no longer show an interest. This de-consecration of the reproductive process is the leading fact of modern culture.[57]

The negative formulation of freedom by Kant—freedom from heteronomy—inevitably meant separation as well: the separation of children from marriage through contraception and gay unions, the separation of fetuses from birth through abortion, the separation of spouses through divorce, and the separation of sex from marriage. By contrast, any affirmative sense of autonomy as freedom for consecration, freedom for fidelity, freedom for self-gift lost significant ground. It was freedom of indifference, to use Pinckaers's term, not freedom for excellence.

An extensive survey of the flotsam and jetsam left from the ideological revolution of the 1960s can be found in a powerful indictment by the distinguished social commentator Roger Kimball, publisher of *The New Criterion*:

> That ideology has insinuated itself, disastrously, into the curricula of our schools and colleges; it has significantly altered the texture of sexual relations and family life; it has played havoc with the authority of churches and other repositories of moral wisdom; it has undermined the claims of civic virtue and our national self-understanding; it has degraded the media, the entertainment industry, and popular culture; it has helped to subvert museums and other institutions entrusted with preserving and transmitting high culture. It has even, most poignantly, addled our hearts and innermost assumptions about what counts as the good life: it has perverted our dreams as much as it has prevented us from attaining them.[58]

RESCUING EROS FROM AUTONOMY

The Enlightenment violently rejected faith and then enthroned reason as the operative deity, only to see the domain of reason reduced to the World of Things, no longer functioning as a template for the guidance of human choices in ethical or moral decision-making. Now, if reason is narrowed to rationalism and then is atomized into irrelevance, unable to provide answers for human accountability, what can possibly remain to define, distinguish, and direct human goals? The lofty answer has a pedigree going back to Plato: eros, the search of the human spirit for completion and satisfaction in another, has the potential to move beyond self-love to self-gift. Eros, a craving for meaning and communion, might assume the hard work of faith, searching for mystery, meaning, acceptance, and fulfillment. The difficulty is that the same Enlightenment forces which repudiated the value of faith have also enfeebled the power of eros to move toward agape, a total, sacrificial self-surrender to the beloved. The beloved is the other and hence heteronomous, a foe of autonomy.

Enlightenment-driven makers of the modern mind such as Karl Marx, Sigmund Freud, and Friedrich Nietzsche have focused on power and status, the trappings of autonomy, but have little to say about what matters most in a person's life, namely, personal bonds, communion, and the marital covenant. Relationships are a function of power (independent, over and against) rather than of commitment (with and for) in a covenantal love. Modernity has given us Nietzsche when we need Edmund Burke.

It is hard to find a more authoritative source than Plato for a philosophical avenue such as eros, but the Enlightenment and much of modernity, in its ruthless aversion to any notion of revelation, has forcefully rejected classical philosophy. To accept a template or roadmap created five centuries before Christ would imply a failure of Enlightenment thought to move beyond the captivity of the past. How could modernity regress to classical Greek philosophy and still retain its self-styled, forward-looking trajectory of incessant and inevitable progress? The solution came through a practiced and powerful device of modernity: reductionism. Eros would be kept as an overall theme, but it would be reduced to something tangible and practical, liberated from the purview of classical philosophy—in a word, sex.

Eros, providing the highly respectable banner, would lead the parade of secularized modernity. The new deity atop the float would be as old as Adam and Eve but as new as the latest issue of *Playboy*. Sex would become the ruling template, the monarch of meaning, in the new world of eros where the World of Things could be reunited with the World of Humans.

As the Enlightenment tired of revelation and began to focus on eros as its replacement, it had much work to do, a project, we might say, of intellectual deconstruction. It was one thing to repudiate faith, a goal aided by the human frailty of believers who doubted and sinned on a regular basis. But the daunting task remained of separating sex from any vestige of faith, revelation, or religion. Sex must be endowed with all of the Enlightenment priorities: it must become autonomous, individual, self-expressing, unfettered, and unconfined by tradition.

How could the most obvious, tangible, sensual, and powerful force of human choice be divested of traditional links with religious belief and practice? The task of the secularized, post-Enlightenment era, no longer modernist but now postmodernist, was to separate sex from procreation, to separate procreation from marriage, to separate marriage from the family, and to remove the family (that is, a monogamous unity of one man and one woman, open to children) from its privileged place as the bedrock of society. In each of these instances, autonomy grew at the expense of reciprocity: Sexuality became autonomous but without a reciprocal bond with marriage. Marriage enlarged autonomously, becoming equivalent to cohabitation or a same-sex relationship, but without the reciprocal bond of a marital union of a man and woman constituting the family. Families grew in amorphous and autonomous variety until it became politically impossible to use the singular term *family* since no normative or paradigmatic model still existed.

Only one practical vehicle was available to produce these progressive separations of sex from procreation, children from marriage, and marriage from family: the courts. Because these changes were neither fully understood nor embraced by a majority of citizens, neither state legislatures nor Congress would be responsive, at least initially, to the prospect of massive and radical change. The only engine of substantive social change that could effectively transform a culture existed in the courts, most especially, the Supreme Court of the United States. We will turn in chapter three to several critical Supreme Court decisions in the twentieth century that have rewritten the Enlightenment notion of autonomy as the juridical mantra of privacy.

We have spent some time looking at Immanuel Kant as a Christian and brilliant philosopher who essentially surrendered to the zeitgeist of the

Enlightenment, reluctantly endorsing the claim that no one can know the truth in such a way that an authentic correlation occurs between the life of the mind and the world outside of it. Before we look at a number of Supreme Court decisions that distilled Enlightenment thinking and applied it to popular culture, we can look briefly at the life and work of a brilliant scholar who challenged the American culture to look at eros from a historical perspective.

THE CONTRIBUTION OF ALLAN BLOOM

Few scholars have more effectively captured the loss of the Platonic notion of eros than the late Allan Bloom, a brilliant classicist whose mastery of Greek philosophy and literature alerted him to the decline of eros in the American experience of the 1960s. Profound human desire, the theme of eros, described so movingly and memorably by great writers, ancient and modern, could no longer be found in the popular redoubts of contemporary philosophy or literature, Bloom realized. In the American academic setting of the late twentieth century, Bloom had few rivals to match his scintillating social commentary. Bloom had taught at Yale, Cornell, the University of Toronto, Tel Aviv University, and the University of Paris. I cite this background because it shows, I believe, that a critique of the sexual excesses of the 1960s is not a prerogative simply of conservative Catholics.

Bloom was a legendary teacher at the University of Chicago when he died. He was a partially closeted homosexual whose *The Closing of the American Mind* critiqued with deadly accuracy the relativism of American universities in the 1980s. He argued that academia had to return to the standards and discipline of Greek philosophy for a genuine intellectual flourishing. Sadly, in my opinion, Bloom went immediately in his monumental work from the heights of his beloved Greek antiquity to the nadir of contemporary vacuity without any real reference to an intellectual ally of the thirteenth century, Saint Thomas Aquinas, whose arguments (under different circumstances) he might have found most agreeable. I suspect that Bloom's neuralgia toward religious practice left him averse to a medieval schoolman despite intriguing and impressive points of philosophical convergence.

Bloom died of AIDS at the age of 62 in 1992. His *Love and Friendship* was published a year after his death. The Introduction to *Love and Friendship* is aptly entitled "The Fall of Eros." The opening lines are both a telling critique of the cultural devolution of eros and, in retrospect, a poignant reminder of the loss of a gifted writer and teacher who wrestled with the paths of eros in his personal life:

> This book is an attempt to recover the power, the danger, and the beauty of eros under the tutelage of its proper teachers and knowers, the poetic writers. Against my will I have to use the term "eros," in spite of its alien and somewhat pretentious Greekness as well as its status as a buzzword since Freud and Marcuse. There is an impoverishment today in our language about what used to be understood as life's most interesting experience, and this almost necessarily bespeaks an impoverishment of feeling. This is why we need the words of old writers who took eros so seriously and knew how to speak about it.[59]

Bloom went on to write that eros had been reduced to sex and sex was then reduced to behavior:

> Sex is spoken about coolly and without any remains of the old puritanical shame, as an incidental aspect of the important questions of disease and power. The sexual talk of our times is about how to get greater bodily satisfaction (although decreasingly so) or increasingly how to protect ourselves from one another. The old view was that delicacy of language was part of the nature, the sacred nature, of eros, and that to speak about it in any other way would be to misunderstand it. What has disappeared is the risk and the hope of human connectedness embedded in eros. Ours is a language that reduces the longing for the other to the need for individual, private satisfaction and safety.[60]

I hope to examine in this book what led to the loss of eros that Bloom so painfully yet accurately describes. Like Bloom, I believe that we need to return to the classical roots of eros found in Plato's *Symposium* and in the *Nicomachean Ethics* of Aristotle. Unlike Bloom, I believe that the work of Saint Thomas Aquinas, building upon Aristotle and in the main consistent with Plato, provides us with an anthropology that returns the natural desire of eros to an arc where it can develop into *philia* (friendship) and ultimately be transformed to become agape (sacrificial love). Our Sherpa in this recovery of Aquinas will be the late Rev. Servais Pinckaers, OP. The route we take will scale the intellectual precipices of Aristotle and Plato, so astutely seen and described by Bloom, but it will take us even higher, into the realm of revelation where the love of Christ urges us on to love in a way ordered to divine goodness.

Apart from revelation, it would be hard to state better than Bloom what happened to eros and sex in the second half of the twentieth century:

> The de-eroticization of the world, a companion of its disenchant-ment, is a complex phenomenon. It seems to result from a com-bination of causes—our democratic regime and its tendencies toward leveling and self-protection, a reductionist-materialist science that inevitably interprets eros as sex, and the atmosphere generated by the "death of God" and the subordinate god, Eros. . . . Kinsey contributed to the reduction of eros to sex, a view from the outside utterly destructive of what one feels on the in-side. This perspective, of course does not remain confined to the laboratory, but becomes everybody's way of looking at it.[61]

Bloom's connection between the de-eroticization of the world and its "disenchantment" mirrors the views of Charles Taylor on the replace-ment of the "enchanted world" with a secularized environment not neces-sarily congenial to eros. The eros of Plato understood as a desire for love and fulfillment is no longer present; it has been replaced by a counterfeit, a functional, extrinsic, forensic, and secularized version of sex that absol-utizes behavior, thereby dehumanizing the interior mystery of eros and all authentic forms of human love. There are any number of scholars who have shown that Plato's understanding of eros was not egocentric at all.[62]

The desire for completion and fulfillment in the love of another is a genuine outward-looking phenomenon. One can take this starting point of authentic human desire and show that it is open to transformation into different, possibly deeper, kinds of love, including friendship and self-gift. This approach is the total antithesis of a Puritanism that would see any form of eros as the work of the devil. In fact, one could argue that the devil has been quite successful in disfiguring authentic eros into a cheap alloy of lust by inflating the directionless abstraction of autonomy at the expense of communion and self-gift.

The task before our culture today is not only the recovery of reason but the recovery of eros. In his final work, *Love and Friendship*, Allan Bloom attempted to rediscover or even recreate eros by probing the work of Shakespeare, Rousseau, and the Romantics (Stendhal, Austen, Flaubert, and Tolstoy). Although the term *eros* is not found in the New Testament, I believe that every page of the Gospels addresses the quest and urgency of human desire. One could even argue that authors such as Shakespeare, Jane Austen, and Tolstoy are incomprehensible apart from the horizon of Christian love. Bloom's legacy is one for which anyone who loves culture and civilization must indeed be grateful.

While someone with a Judeo-Christian understanding of the cause of and, especially, the remedy for the unraveling of eros might differ with Professor Bloom on the issue of the relevance of revelation, one can accept entirely and gratefully his description of the current scene—with its successive, reductionist plunge from eros to functional sex to pseudo-scientific behavior—as definitive. One can believe and pray that Bloom has finally found in eternal life the "love and friendship" that he sought so intensely in his earthly existence.

This admittedly bleak assessment of the legacy of the Enlightenment and the loss of eros as a genuinely human good resonant with potential for love and communion does not leave us without hope or options. It is quite possible to reconcile eros, autonomy, and communion in a way truly respectful of these integral aspects of human well-being. At this point, it will be sufficient to point out simply that a different template, respectful of autonomy, truly and excitingly exists. But before we look at the recovery of virtue and the rescue of autonomy from anomie, we must examine in the next chapter how the Supreme Court gradually institutionalized the Enlightenment ethic of absolute autonomy in sexual ethics and embedded it in the dominant cultural paradigm of the United States.

THREE

AUTONOMY BECOMES *PRIVACY* IN THE COURTS

DEFINING RIGHTS AND LIVES: NO RULES, JUST RIGHTS

"At the heart of liberty is the right to define one's own concept of existence, of meaning, of the universe and of the mystery of human life."[63] When Supreme Court Justice Anthony Kennedy wrote this holding in the 1992 case of *Planned Parenthood v. Casey*, he summarized a century of jurisprudence that had moved inexorably toward fulfilling the Enlightenment ethic of absolute autonomy. The somewhat rapturous and global aspects of Kennedy's manifesto on liberty seem to echo Lord Byron or a Lake District poet, giving voice in prose at the end of a long day to the proposition that life is whatever we choose it to be. This is autonomy on steroids.

Outback Steakhouse, the popular restaurant chain, has a well-known slogan on its menus: "No rules. Just right." The endearing and enduring attraction of this slogan leads countless customers to relax in a pleasant setting and enjoy some great beef. But we know, their slogan notwithstanding, that there are rules even at Outback. Even this appetizing formula has some inherent limits. For one thing, it is necessary to order something listed on the menu. If you order a steak well-done and it comes out rare, some rule of resolution must be found in either your revised preference or another offering from the kitchen. At the end of the glorious feast, the customer is expected to pay the bill. When Outback entices a libertarian customer with a "No rules–Just right" message, it is indulging what a true Lake District poet, Samuel Taylor Coleridge, referred to as a "willing suspension of disbelief," which constitutes a poetic faith. It is enjoyable to suspend disbelief at a favorite restaurant and share in a light-hearted spoof, abetted perhaps by some tasty, mood-altering beverages. But is it wise to treat as cavalierly a formula of the Supreme Court that appears to provide a philosophical justification for the Outback "No Rules" adage?

Perhaps the best way to attempt an answer is simply to look at the words and take them in their plain meaning. To what genre of thought, language, or literature does this passage belong? It is not a frivolous question because this assertion is not the musing of an armchair philosopher but the *ruling* of a Supreme Court decision that has teeth with life-and-death consequences. The scope of this proposition must be determined to ascertain whether it claims to be a moral norm, aesthetic ideal, or legal standard. Are we dealing here with a mantra or a mandate?

It is Justice Kennedy himself who answers the question by quoting his own adage eleven years later in *Lawrence v. Texas* in a decision striking down the sodomy law of Texas.[64] Let us give a fuller context for the now famous adage to show how powerful its impact has become. Justice Kennedy writes this:

> Two principal cases decided after *Bowers* [a Supreme Court decision in 1986 upholding a Georgia statute imposing criminal sanctions for consensual homosexual behavior] cast its holding into even more doubt. In *Planned Parenthood of Southeastern Pa. v. Casey* . . . the Court reaffirmed the substantive force of the liberty protected by the Due Process Clause. The *Casey* decision again confirmed that our laws and tradition afford constitutional protection to personal decisions relating to marriage, procreation, contraception, family relationships, child rearing, and education. In explaining the respect the Constitution demands for the autonomy of the person in making these choices, we stated as follows: "These matters, involving the most intimate and personal choices a person may make in a lifetime, choices central to personal dignity and autonomy, are central to the liberty protected by the Fourteenth Amendment. At the heart of liberty is the right to define one's own concept of existence, of meaning, of the universe, and of the mystery of human life. Beliefs about these matters could not define the attributes of personhood were they formed under compulsion of the State."[65]

Justice Kennedy is assuredly not seeking the post of Poet Laureate by quoting again his axiom on one's right to define one's own concept of existence, the universe, human life, and meaning itself. He may write as a philosopher, but he rules as a Justice of the Supreme Court, handing down a binding decision affecting the critical areas he describes: marriage, procreation, contraception, family relationships, child rearing, education, and homosexual behavior.

Kennedy adds with dubious coherence that "beliefs about these matters could not define the attributes of personhood were they formed under compulsion of the State." But it is the State here, promulgating the Law of the Land, that is defining critical attributes of personhood—its existence or not, its protection or not—with the compulsory force of law whereby individuals who choose to disregard or disagree with the Court-mandated definitions of the most intimate matters are subject to criminal prosecution. In striking down one state enactment after another, the Supreme Court has for several decades been *removing and restricting* the right of citizens—through their elected representatives—to define their family relationships.

The twentieth century became the bloodiest in human history. It took an enormous number of lives to stop Hitler and Stalin from exercising their ostensible right of defining the universe and human life in the most odious fashion. This axiom of Justice Kennedy announcing a supposed right of universal definition of meaning is neither the musing of a Romantic poet nor the satire of Lewis Carroll but the formidable and potentially frightening language of a judicial locomotive moving at full speed. The question remains whether it is on the right track, going in the right direction.

In the same 2003 *Lawrence* decision, Justice Antonin Scalia refers to the notoriety of Kennedy's maxim as the "famed sweet-mystery-of-life passage." But, as he continues, Scalia's point is far from rhetorical: "I have never heard of a law that attempted to restrict one's 'right to define' certain concepts; and if the passage calls into question the government's power to regulate *actions based on* one's self-defined 'concept of existence, etc.,' it is the passage that ate the rule of law."[66]

Scalia captures the breathtaking scope of the Kennedy maxim. His pungent critique recognizes that the implications of a universal define-meaning-as-you-want model are so powerful as to destroy the carefully calibrated rule of law enshrined in the Constitution. If anyone is entitled to justify potentially lethal actions on the grounds that these actions are warranted by a right to define one's own universe, meaning, life, and existence, then all boundaries of behavior have vanished. If I can legally justify my definition of the meaning of my fist so that it encroaches upon the meaning of your nose, you can see beyond a bloodied nose that the consequences are immediate.

THE RIGHT TO PRIVACY AS COURT-APPROVED AUTONOMY

Justice Scalia's warning—that the "define your own universe" language, repeated verbatim in two major Supreme Court decisions on pivotal sexual ethics (abortion and homosexual behavior), can essentially do away with the rule of law, the confluence of common sense and common law—is one that cannot be ignored. The effect of the language is to grant the concept of eros an imperial sway over any would-be adversaries. It may be amusing to have everything just right without rules at a good restaurant, but it is hardly funny when moral decisions must rest on time-tested rules that are in place to protect human beings from the mistakes of judgment, excess, and abuse in which everyone is vulnerable.

The crowded intersection of philosophy, medical ethics, and jurisprudence has aligned to generate a perfect storm of unbridled fury. While the overall legacy of the Enlightenment reduced scholarly confidence in the ability of people to discern or articulate any objective, let alone absolute, truths, the Supreme Court, in Kennedy's language, did its best to validate the one remaining socially acceptable absolute truth: we are each of us empowered to define whatever existence means, whatever meaning itself means, whatever the universe means, and whatever life means. A few years after *Casey* upheld *Roe v. Wade*, the 1973 decision legalizing abortion, a United States President was roundly ridiculed for responding in a deposition that "it all depends on what the meaning of is, is." But as a matter of intellectual consistency, is it not the case that this embattled politician merely illustrated the grandiloquent declaration of the Law of the Land? Do we not have the authority, right, and power to define what "is, is" on our own terms? Looking at the sexual revolution of the 1960s, its philosophical origins and continuing cultural implications, one can connect some important dots. Those dots must be recognized before they are connected. Some legal precedents or ideological antecedents such as the 1927 case of *Buck v. Bell*, approving of eugenics, have largely been overlooked by legal scholars who, for one reason or another, were not disposed to link ethical theories with legal decisions. Only a combined study of ethical and legal history can adequately explain how and why massive changes in public opinion occurred on issues of sexual ethics. We have tried in the preceding two chapters to show how the concept of autonomy powered the sexual revolution and how the 1960s sharply modified the institution of marriage as a sacred covenant. In this chapter, we will identify how the philosophical premises undergirding autonomy became the legal paradigm of privacy.

This happened through the instrumentality of the law (and, specifically, the United States Supreme Court). The Court translated an intellectual abstraction, autonomy, into a constitutional standard, privacy.

A reputable study of any ideological context—left, right, center, religious, or secularist—is likely to see the 1973 Supreme Court decision on abortion, *Roe* v. *Wade*[67] as the best known litmus test of divergent views of the sexual revolution. But *Roe* did not occur in a vacuum. Two Supreme Court decisions preceded it—*Buck v. Bell* (1927) and *Griswold v. Connecticut* (1965)—setting the stage for the *Roe* justification of abortion, virtually on demand, first by legitimizing eugenics (*Buck*) and then discovering a constitutional right of privacy (*Griswold*) to confer upon abortion a constitutional protection. Since an enormous body of legal analysis already attends *Roe v. Wade*, we will try to advance the discussion by contrasting a theological template, to be developed in the next chapter, with the agenda of eugenics, contraception, and abortion now embedded in the American culture. The define-your-own-meaning view of "the universe" found in *Planned Parenthood v. Casey* (1992) exemplifies and consolidates the Enlightenment ethic of absolute autonomy. It did not arise in a vacuum but emerged as the predictable consequence of earlier decisions. This ethic of absolute autonomy is essentially a variant of substantive due process, a perspective with roots in the bloodiest period of American history—slavery and the Civil War.

THE RISE OF SUBSTANTIVE DUE PROCESS

A skeptical reader is assuredly entitled to ask just how a constitutional system famous for its checks and balances could lapse into an ideological pattern that would consistently promote an agenda of sexual autonomy. How could a framework renowned for its checks and balances become so unbalanced? The answer lies in a pernicious theory or legal philosophy known as substantive due process whereby a judge will for presumably benign but nonetheless personal reasons create or insert a political view into a judicial decision that should be immune from the prejudicial insertion of political theories or preferences. It is substantive due process that becomes the judicial vehicle for implementing the Enlightenment ethic of absolute autonomy.

The best-known, indeed infamous, decision of the United States Supreme Court is the Dred Scott decision,[68] handed down in 1857. A Missouri slave, Dred Scott, argued that while the slave of an army doctor, he had lived as a free man—both in Illinois, a free state, and in Minnesota, a free territory where slavery had been banned by the Missouri Compromise. Scott argued that he remained free upon his subsequent return to Missouri. The sweeping opinion of Chief Justice Roger B. Taney held that Dred Scott lacked jurisdiction to bring any suit because neither slaves nor free blacks were citizens of the United States. Generalizing about African-Americans, Taney wrote this:

> They had for more than a century before been regarded as beings of an inferior order and altogether unfit to associate with the white race, either in social or political relations; and so far inferior that they had no rights which the white man was bound to respect; and that the Negro might justly and lawfully be reduced to slavery for his benefit. He was bought and sold and treated as an ordinary article of merchandise and traffic whenever a profit could be made by it. This opinion was at that time fixed and universal in the civilized portion of the white race[69]

Taney went on to rule that the Missouri Compromise of 1820 was unconstitutional, striking at the very foundation of legislative compromises that had held the Union together for several decades. This explosive decision of the Supreme Court aroused enormous fury in the northern states, contributing to the election of the Republican Abraham Lincoln in 1860 and, eventually, the Civil War.

Why is it necessary to study the *Dred Scott* case when our primary focus is on the link between the Enlightenment notion of autonomy and the American jurisprudence of the sexual revolution? The answer is that in *Dred Scott* we find the first application of substantive due process, that is, the application of a political or social judgment to the legal issue under consideration in the absence of any textual basis to support the judgment. The majority opinion of Chief Justice Taney misrepresented the Constitution on slavery and substituted a personal opinion for the fragile patchwork of compromises worked out by Congress over decades.

A distinguished legal scholar, Cass R. Sunstein, has summarized what is remarkable about the *Dred Scott* case: "*Dred Scott* was the first Supreme Court case since *Marbury v. Madison* invalidating a federal law. Since *Marbury* created judicial review in the context of a denial of jurisdiction, *Dred Scott* might plausibly be said to be the first real exercise of the power of judicial review . . . . *Dred Scott* was the birthplace of the controversial idea of 'substantive due process' used in *Roe v. Wade*, in many important cases endangering the regulatory/welfare state, and in the recent cases involving the 'right to die.'"[70]

Professor Sunstein, who currently serves as the Administrator of the White House Office of Information and Regulatory Affairs in the Obama administration, describes *Dred Scott* as a clear case of "judicial hubris": "There was no basis for the Court's conclusion that freed slaves could not count as citizens. In fact, some freed slaves participated in the ratification of the Constitution itself; and freed slaves were allowed to vote in at least five of the colonies. The Constitution does not suggest that free citizens do not stand on the same ground as everybody else."[71]

The denial of legal rights to African-Americans by Justice Taney is chilling in its scope and impact. Here is his reasoning:

> The words "people of the United States" and "citizens" are syn-onymous terms, and mean the same thing. They both describe the political body who, according to our republican institutions, form the sovereignty and who hold the power and conduct the Government through their representatives. They are what we fa-miliarly call the "sovereign people," and every citizen is one of this people, and a constituent member of this sovereignty. The question before us is whether the class of persons described in the plea in abatement compose a portion of this people, and are constituent members of this sovereignty? We think they are not, and that they are not included, and were not intended to be in-cluded, under the word "citizens" in the Constitution, and can therefore claim none of the rights and privileges which that in-strument provides for and secures to citizens of the United States. On the contrary, they were at that time considered as a subordinate and inferior class of beings who had been subju-gated by the dominant race, and, whether emancipated or not, yet remained subject to their authority, and had no rights or priv-ileges but such as those who held the power and the Government might choose to grant them.[72]

There is a troubling analogy in the logic and structure of Taney's exclusion of blacks from citizenship with a twentieth-century exercise of substantive due process in the judgment of Justice Blackmun in the 1973 case of *Roe v. Wade* "that the word 'person,' as used in the Fourteenth Amendment, does not include the unborn."[73] In each instance, a class of human beings is excluded from the legal rights and protections that would otherwise flow from citizenship and personhood.

It is a small historical consolation that Taney's thunderbolt did not go unchallenged. Justice John McLean wrote this in his dissenting opinion in the *Dred Scott* case: "A slave is not mere chattel. He bears the impress of his Maker, and is amenable to the laws of God and man; and he is destined to an endless existence."[74]

A congressman from Illinois with a distinguished reputation as a trial lawyer, citing a dissenting opinion in the case, pointed out in a speech shortly after the Dred Scott decision that in five of the original thirteen states existing when the Constitution was ratified, "free Negroes were voters, and, in proportion to their numbers, had the same part in making the Constitution that the white people had."[75] It would become the sacrificial work of this Illinois congressman, Abraham Lincoln, to overturn Dred Scott.

Michael McConnell, a former federal judge on the U.S. Court of Appeals for the Tenth Circuit, and currently director of the Stanford Constitutional Law Center, has quoted the very same dissent of Justice Benjamin R. Curtis cited by Lincoln: "When a strict interpretation of the Constitution, according to the fixed rules which govern the interpretation of laws, is abandoned, and the theoretical opinions of individuals are allowed to control its meaning, we have no longer a Constitution; we are under the government of individual men, who for the time being have power to declare what the Constitution is according to their own views of what it ought to mean."[76]

We shall see—a century later and with comparable harm—how this phenomenon of a judge substituting his own personal or political opinion has imported the Enlightenment ethic of absolute autonomy into the American culture.

In reducing Dred Scott to the status of property, Chief Justice Roger Taney gave short shrift to the argument that Scott's extended residence in free territory changed the conditions of servitude that had existed before. Nor did he apply Article IV of the Constitution to the case so that "all needful Rules and Regulations" would have recognized the legality of the Missouri Compromise under which Scott would have been freed. Taney simply assumed, to quote McConnell again, that "a statute can be unconstitutional because it violates unenumerated rights."[77]

Judge Robert Bork has argued brilliantly that the *Dred Scott* decision marks the first appearance in American jurisprudence of what has come to be known as substantive due process. The author of the controlling opinion, Chief Justice Roger Taney of Maryland, a strong proponent of slavery, purported to discover a constitutional right to slavery in the United States Constitution:

> How . . . can there be a constitutional right to own slaves where a statute forbids it? Taney created such a right by changing the plain meaning of the due process clause of the fifth amendment. . . . The substance Taney poured into the clause was that Congress cannot prevent slavery in a territory because a man must be allowed to bring slaves there.
>
> How did Taney know that slave ownership was a constitutional right? Such a right is nowhere to be found in the Constitution. He knew it because he was passionately convinced that it *must* be a constitutional right. Though his transformation of the due process clause from a procedural to a substantive requirement was an obvious sham, it was a momentous sham, for this was the first appearance in American constitutional law of the concept of "substantive due process," and that concept has been used countless times since by judges who want to write their personal beliefs into a document that, most inconveniently, does not contain those beliefs.[78]

Along with Sunstein and Bork, the doyen of liberal American legal theory today, Lawrence H. Tribe, an ideological opposite of Bork, agrees that substantive due process can be traced back to *Dred Scott*: "In any event, the practice of treating the due process of law guarantee as a central source of substantive limits on state governmental authority has a long pedigree and seems unlikely to be abandoned in the foreseeable future. Indeed, the practices dates at least to 1857, when the phrase 'due process of law' in its Fifth Amendment incarnation was first applied to invalidate an act of Congress in the infamous *Dred Scott* decision, in which the phrase was taken to encompass a set of *substantive* limitations on the permissible *content* of government's commands or penalties."[79] (Italics in original)

Tribe indicates here and elsewhere in his *The Invisible Constitution* that he is comfortable with substantive due process. While acknowledging the obvious verdict of history that *Dred Scott* was an infamous abuse of power, Tribe argues that its importation of substantive content into its review of statutes was never repudiated. Indeed, he argues that some substantive values (such as life, liberty, or property) have properly been retained by courts:

> Neither the War Between the States nor the Fourteenth Amendment was thought to have altered *Dred Scott*'s importation of

> substantive content into the notion of "law" as it appeared in the
> Fifth Amendment's prohibition against federal action depriving
> any "person . . . of life, liberty, or property, without due process
> of law." Put otherwise, those who wrote and ratified the Four-
> teenth Amendment's Due Process Clause were using the same
> language that had appeared in the Fifth Amendment at a time
> when the Supreme Court had plainly understood that language
> substantively, albeit in a *particular* substantive manner that the
> authors and ratifiers obviously chose to repudiate in the opening
> words of the Fourteenth Amendment.[80] (Italics in original)

When Tribe emphasizes that a *particular* court will *import* its own
substantive interpretation of "law," he implicitly recognizes at least two
major problems with the phenomenon of substantive due process. First, a
particular court unfettered by a requirement to interpret a text in fidelity
to the intent of its drafters or enactors, will obviously be subject to the
volatile ideological pressures that swirl around any significant case or con-
troversy in that *particular* time. This means that the value of the law as a
break against ideological excess is surrendered, a point that Tribe shortly
concedes, as we shall see. The entire purpose of the first ten Amendments
to the Constitution, the Bill of Rights, was to restrict the exercise of power
by the state in a way that would reflect the imposed will of the majority at
the expense of the legitimate and urgent interests of a minority. Freed from
the need to interpret existing law in accord with recognized standards, a
particular court will indulge in *particular* prejudices, ideologies, and forces
that govern at a *particular* moment. The second problem that arises when
a court *imports* substantive values or meaning is, simply, from where is
this substantive meaning *imported*? In all likelihood, a judge will import
substantive views from an ideology, those ideas, values, or prejudices (of
whatever merit) held by the judge. This means in practical terms that the
raging storms of a particular era will prevail and the law will be of no help
in protecting minority interests against prevailing ideology and prejudice.

These problems inherent in substantive due process of importing
ideology and falling prey to the whirlwinds of particular prejudice are not
merely hypothetical. Tribe describes the exact problem by citing two cases
that, he argues, have employed substantive due process. In the first case,
Bolling v. Sharpe, the Court promoted the cause of racial integration in
public schools but in other cases where substantive due process was in play,
namely, cases dealing with the imprisonment of innocent Japanese civilians
in California during World War II, Tribe acknowledges the degree to which

substantive due process can be stretched to become indistinguishable from ideology and prejudice:

> In order to impose an equality requirement on Congress parallel to the equality requirement that the Fourteenth Amendment's Equal Protection Clause imposes on the states, the Supreme Court found it necessary, in *Bolling v. Sharpe*, to hold that Congress deprives public schoolchildren of their "liberty" without "due process of law" when it forces racial minorities to attend schools of their own and forbids racial mixing in the public schools of the nation's capital. That is, the Court had to read "due process of law" to include a purely substantive, and not merely a procedural, component—something it had been doing with respect to the Fifth Amendment's Due Process Clause ever since the 1940s, although in a way most people now would criticize as tragically insensitive to the realities of racial discrimination, as when the Supreme Court decided the Japanese curfew and relocation cases *Hiribayashi v. United States* and *Korematsu v. United States*.[81]

Tribe has described cases which used substantive due process in racially charged contexts. But the actual results of these cases could not be more contradictory: one promoted racial integration (*Bolling v. Sharpe*) in Washington, DC, and the other (*Korematsu*) remains notorious for its invidious racism. One dissenting justice in the *Korematsu* case, Frank Murphy, accurately described it as having descended "into the ugly abyss of racism."[82] When a particular approach—substantive due process—can account for diametrically opposite results, including the continued forced detainment of innocent civilian citizens in internment camps, is it not time to re-examine that approach?

When we look more closely at *Korematsu*, we can see how controversial and dangerous the Court's ruling was. Oral argument took place one month before the presidential election of 1944 when wartime emotions in the United States were at fever pitch against Japanese individuals. The distinguished legal historian Lucas A. Powe Jr. describes the wartime paranoia in California: "The relocation of 112,000 people of Japanese descent, most of whom were American citizens, was the biggest single blight on civil liberties in America in the twentieth century. Spurred by public fears after Pearl Harbor, long-standing prejudice against Asians, as well as national newspaper columnists, Roosevelt and then Congress authorized the War Department to declare certain areas military zones, and thereafter the commander of the area could impose curfews and travel restrictions, and even order people excluded entirely from the area."[83]

Pursuant to this congressional mandate, the War Department issued an order excluding Japanese-Americans from the West Coast: "Forbidden to leave, forbidden to stay, they had no other legal option but to leave jobs, homes, and possessions behind (or unload them at distress prices) and report for internment, mainly in the arid West, in one of ten god-forsaken, dust-blown, barbed-wire-fenced camps."[84]

With this description of barbed-wire internment camps in mind, it defies belief that such a distinguished legal scholar as Lawrence H. Tribe could simply describe the *Korematsu* case as "tragically insensitive." This case was an outrage. The indiscriminate internment of American citizens along with Japanese aliens was accomplished through mass relocations carried out in 1942. Motivated by fear and racism, it was still popularly supported by California voters as the 1944 presidential election and the *Korematsu* case were being decided.

Another distinguished jurist present at *Korematsu* was Justice Robert H. Jackson. His description of the "crime" of Fred Korematsu in his dissenting opinion is as chilling today as when it was written. Korematsu's offense was "being present in the state whereof he is a citizen, near the place where he was born, and where all his life he has lived."[85]

If we agree that *Korematsu* was the most egregious judicial violation of civil liberties in the twentieth century and concede as well that *Dred Scott* was the worst judicial infamy of the nineteenth century, then we have to conclude that the common denominator of these two cases—a reliance by the Court on substantive due process—is at the very least subject to enormous abuse. By *importing* a *particular* prejudice, to use Tribe's strangely innocuous language, the Supreme Court disenfranchised African-Americans and upheld the detention of innocent Japanese-American citizens.

Why does Professor Tribe go to such lengths to defend substantive due process? Sadly, it is because he agrees with the ideology of reproductive rights embedded in Supreme Court jurisprudence of cases of the last three decades protecting sexual autonomy. The alternative path to achieve desired results is a Burkean appeal to the citizenry through the legislative process. This method of enacting laws is clearly constitutional and reflective of popular sentiment. But it apparently would not yield the results that Professor Tribe and other proponents of sexual autonomy desire. Hence the courts become the chosen instrument of radical change.

Professor Tribe recognizes the power of Bork's critique of substantive due process given above and seeks to blunt it:

> It is fairly common for opponents of judicial declarations that "substantive due process" protects individuals with respect to one or another particular claim of right, such as reproductive freedom, or a right to die with dignity, or the right to control the upbringing of one's children, to invoke the ghost of *Dred Scott* as ammunition against such protection. They typically argue that sticking to the Constitution's text would have prevented the travesty of *Dred Scott* and that, more generally, sticking to that text would prevent judicial usurpation of what should be state (and sometimes federal) legislative authority. Even setting aside the complex debate over whether *Dred Scott*'s profound misstep was overdetermined by the antebellum Constitution itself, this argument overlooks the cataclysmic consequences that would result from "sticking to the text"—which, in this context, would mean sucking all substance (as opposed to procedure) out of the Due Process Clauses of the Fifth and Fourteenth Amendments.[86]

But in *Dred Scott, Lochner* (to be considered later in this chapter), and *Korematsu*, the clear abuses and outrages resulted from the very opposite situation. It was the "substance" of prejudice, bigotry, paranoia, and laissez-faire ideology that sucked the oxygen out of the procedural protections of the Bill of Rights (the fifth amendment) and a constitutional amendment (the fourteenth) designed to safeguard equal protection and due process.

Substantive due process is basically a matter of legislation—that is, enacting desired public policy. But enacting public policy is the work of elected legislators who must engage in debate with other elected legislators in order to craft suitable legislation. When policy has not been forged in the crucible of debates and elections, it is not difficult to see how personal opinion can quickly become public policy. What could be more malleable than a strategy or approach—substantive due process—that can promote the contradictory policies of racial desegregation (*Bolling v. Sharpe*), a laudable goal, and the maintenance of race-based internment camps (*Korematsu*)? How does substantive due process differ from a judge acting as a legislator? If Lawrence Tribe is correct when he asserts that the interests of life, liberty, and property found in the Fifth Amendment have a legitimate substantive dimension, then why must the substantive due process of the Supreme Court in the 1960s and beyond ignore the substantive interest of human life?

We have examined the philosophical legacy of autonomy that stems from the eighteenth century and have looked at the concept of substantive due process that originated in the nineteenth century case of *Dred Scott*. These forays have been necessary to show the roots of the judicial activism that would graft the Enlightenment ethic of absolute autonomy onto the branch of American government that Alexander Hamilton had classically but too optimistically described as the "least dangerous."[87] Regardless of where one stands on the political spectrum today, everyone has an interest in assuring that the courts steer clear of the dangers recognized by Hamilton and the other Founders who worked tirelessly to limit the power of officeholders, elected and unelected.

If the Supreme Court simply enacts sexual autonomy or reproductive rights as the law of the land apart from constitutional constraints, indulging in the substantive due process that by all accounts has done so much harm, then we are in great danger. But before we look directly at several Supreme Court cases from 1927 to the 1960s and beyond, we have to face a question that proponents of substantive due process such as Professor Tribe have raised.

IS NATURAL LAW A CATHOLIC VERSION OF SUBSTANTIVE DUE PROCESS?

Where does natural law fit into this debate? This might be described as the tale of two Thomases, one classic and one contemporary. The term *natural law* is given its definitive articulation in the *Summa Theologica* of Saint Thomas Aquinas, but it was another Thomas whose occasional musings on the topic led him to be critiqued not as a doubting Thomas but as one who may have believed too ardently in this recovered body of thought.

When President George H. W. Bush nominated Clarence Thomas to the Supreme Court in 1991, an extended debate over the meaning of natural law erupted because Judge Thomas had given speeches in which he referred favorably to this frequently misunderstood perspective of philosophers and jurists. The chairman of the Senate Judiciary Committee (and future Vice-President), Senator Joseph Biden, immediately challenged Judge Thomas with an op-ed column in the *Washington Post*.[88] Thomas was grilled at length on his understanding of natural law, a historical perspective closely linked with Catholic moral theology; both Biden and Thomas are Roman Catholics.

Judge Thomas had cited the view of Dr. Martin Luther King Jr. that the U.S. Constitution could only be intelligibly construed in light of the Declaration of Independence, a founding document that declared some truths to be self-evident, among them, life, liberty, and the pursuit of happiness. The laws of segregation and racial discrimination began to tumble because they were repugnant to a universal sense of human dignity and decency. As Dr. King, among others, pointed out, the glaring contradiction between the dignity of every human being and the state-enforced prohibition from having a meal at a segregated lunch counter, people of all races and religions united in affirming transcendent and inviolable truths before which laws offensive to human dignity would fall.

Legal scholars quickly joined the fray in the Thomas nomination hearings. The dean of the liberal judicial commentariat, Professor Lawrence Tribe of Harvard University, instantly attacked Thomas for holding a view that Tribe considered to be obsolete, reactionary, and dangerous.[89] But Thomas received powerful, analytical support from a universally praised legal scholar, the previously cited Michael McConnell.[90]

Since we have cited legal scholars such as Judge Robert Bork to the effect that the most infamous Supreme Court decision of all, *Dred Scott v. Sandford*, was the beginning of a misguided effort to create or defend a right not found in statute or precedent, we must face the question of whether judges such as Justice Thomas, who show deference for what is termed natural law, are themselves guilty of harboring views consistent with a largely discredited substantive due process. Is natural law simply a form of substantive due process?

First, there is a debate, even (or perhaps especially) among conservative philosophers and legal scholars about what natural law is and whether or how it applies to judicial review. Great differences of informed opinion exist about the content of the natural law and the degree to which it can be discerned or applied by courts. An examination of the pre-eminent authority for natural law, Saint Thomas Aquinas, demonstrates that far from being an ideological prejudice or religious relic, the perspective of natural law can be a liberating use of reason to extend almost beyond limit the quest for human excellence.

Let us examine two different texts from Saint Thomas in which he describes what is meant by natural law. First, he states this in his encyclopedic *Summa Theologica*:

> Since all things subject to Divine providence are ruled and measured by the eternal law, as was stated above . . . it is evident that

all things partake somewhat of the eternal law, insofar as, namely, from its being imprinted on them, they derive their respective inclinations to their proper acts and ends. Now among all others, the rational creature is subject to Divine providence in the most excellent way, insofar as it partakes of a share of providence, by being provident both for itself and for others. Wherefore [the rational creature] has a share of the Eternal Reason, whereby [the rational creature] has a natural inclination to its proper act and end: and this participation of the eternal law in the rational creature is called the natural law.[91]

Several remarkable things emerge here. First, Saint Thomas does indeed subscribe to the belief that there is a God, who has promulgated an eternal law, but this God is hardly the adversary of human aspirations seen by Nietzsche and the powerful tributaries of modern atheism allied with him. God is understood by Saint Thomas as the author or exemplar of divine providence, a reasoned and reliable intent to foster human excellence. Whatever limits attach to excellence are inherent or intrinsic; they are not mandated from outside. (To use the catchphrase of the Enlightenment, any rules or laws are not "heteronomous," that is, imposed extrinsically, but intrinsically oriented toward the end of excellence of the rational creature.)

Our contemporary Thomist mentor, Servais Pinckaers, OP, whom we shall study in chapter four, builds upon the distinction between a freedom of indifference and a freedom of excellence. Pinckaers illustrates this difference simply but brilliantly by distinguishing between a child indiscriminately pounding on whatever piano keys he wishes (freedom of indifference) from a student playing a Mozart concerto.[92] The student is in theory free to select any key she wishes but only a particular one at a particular time and in a particular way will faithfully capture the genius of Mozart.

Second, there is a communal dimension to the natural law. Saint Thomas has in the previous question (I-II, 90.4) defined law as "an ordinance of reason, promulgated by one who cares for the community, for the benefit of the common good." Any rule offensive to reason simply fails to qualify as a law, and any rule injurious to the common good must be dismissed as unreasonable.

Third, the natural law for Saint Thomas is not a matter of imposition from without, as shown above, but a participation of the rational creature in a larger plan of excellence. It is implicit in this vision that no individual can fully achieve excellence in isolation. Excellence is both communal (a dimension of a realized common good) and personal (for example, the happiness of a friendship arising from shared goods and mutual integrity). This sketch of excellence flatly contradicts the Enlightenment ethic of absolute autonomy that tends to separate individuals from each other, conferring on each individual a plenary authority to define one's universe, in Justice Kennedy's view, and of course one's rights.

This is not to say that excellence precludes autonomy but rather that autonomy takes its cue from an ordered liberty or freedom aligned with the natural or optimal goal of a human being. The student playing Mozart is still autonomous even though some piano keys cannot be selected if one is to realize the concerto in an authentic, truly excellent fashion.

But does any of this answer the question of whether natural law is simply a religious, right-wing version of substantive due process? Permit an idiosyncratic Celtic response: it does and it doesn't. Quoting Saint Thomas on the meaning of the natural law does not specifically address the issue of whether natural law provides content or context for a judge substituting a personal opinion for a defined field of legal parameters. Nevertheless, a fair reading of the *Summa* does demonstrate that this classic exponent of the oft misunderstood phrase gives no quarter to any concept or claim inhospitable to reason. By natural law is not meant an ossified body of obsolete prejudices harmful to the human community but a conviction that everyone participates in ultimate goods consonant with their best interests in a rational way.

Moreover, as natural law emerges as a shorthand expression for communal, human participation in a plan brought into existence by a loving God for the benefit of His creatures, ourselves, it discloses the premise that the human and divine are not on a collision course. There is a covenantal partnership in creation. Natural law is not a club to beat heretics into conformity or a code emanating from religious councils to impose belief on infidels. These invidious caricatures of the natural law are on par with a yahoo reduction of evolution to the proposition that we are simply descended from the apes. Critics of evolution must be held accountable for bad science; critics of natural law must be held accountable for bad philosophy.

We must be content at this point with dispensing from caricatures of the natural law. To plunge further into the murky and fast-moving waters of scholarly debate on the issue of applicability of natural law to judicial decisions would distract us from the central question of what exactly constitutes natural law. We can at least show what it is not. It is not a tailor-made list of particulars automatically to be implemented, ratified, or confirmed. It is not a mechanical or ideological construct that in any way substitutes for precedents, statutes, or the common law tradition even though the common law and natural law display a ready resonance.

If natural law represents the conviction that all propositions can and must be tested by the inherent capacity for reason of human beings, the exercise of that human reason leaves open the possibility that reason may not be able to answer every question to the satisfaction of each inquirer. As a necessary but not necessarily sufficient component of human understanding, reason has throughout history been seen as correlative with faith or revelation. The Judeo-Christian world view considers some propositions to be true (such as the existence of a God Who is all good) but in some critical way inaccessible to the furthest reach of reason. The province that is not unreasonable but transcends the limits of human reason is theology. Most important in this theological tableau is the arena of theological anthropology—the meaning of the human, as critiqued by reason yet open to transcendent realities of mystery, creation, and the infinite.

Saint Thomas's brief but telling account of natural inclinations cited above provides a preview and suggestion of how eros can be understood not as an individualistic, entirely autonomous right of unfettered expression and action but as a deeply personal desire for love and completion, shared universally but differently by fellow rational creatures, and oriented toward an excellence of human love totally consistent with the common good. Our goal in this study is to move from a rigid abstraction of autonomy, isolated from the reciprocity of mutual goods and human needs, to an existential reality of generous communion that embraces love, friendship, eros, and agape far more favorably, while preserving autonomy as a good informed by these other real goods.

We are now ready to look at Supreme Court jurisprudence that has relied on substantive due process. In 1927, the Court legitimized involuntary sterilization. In the 1960s, the ideology of reproductive rights, the judicial enactment of sexual autonomy, began to change and challenge the institution of marriage. Ask yourself, as we look at these cases, whether the result is autonomy or anomie.

BUCK V. BELL (1927): DARWIN IN THE BEDROOM

A well-know jurist, not an enthusiast of organized religion, wrote that "a page of history is worth a volume of logic." Wounded three times in the Civil War and the son of a famous physician and poet who had applied the term "Brahmin" to New England aristocracy, Oliver Wendell Holmes Jr. intended this pithy *obiter dictum* to be a vote in favor of experience and common sense over scholarly abstraction. It corresponded with the pragmatic Yankee ideals championed by the elite of which he was a part. The snappy, attractive quality of the adage should not blind the reader, however, to a certain not so subtle bias against any systematized view that might qualify as logical—or even theological. Nevertheless, Holmes's preference for the daily laboratory of experience soon itself became a philosophy of empiricism, having both strengths and virtues. While a certain mistrust of any grandiose system is healthy, one finds in *Buck v. Bell* that the magisterial Justice Holmes did not shrink from providing an open-ended philosophical credo to justify involuntary sterilization, resting his decision on a logic that truly appalls when the facts from this "page of history" are fully known.

Americans are enamored of pragmatism, the view that something can be defined by whether and how something works. Serenely disregarding David Hume, about whom they may never have heard, Americans thrill to connect cause and effect, picking those actions that can produce the fastest and most desired consequences. A bent toward pragmatic approaches fits snugly with an empiricism that relies far more on practical experience than theory. But the case of *Buck v. Bell* quickly shows us the limits of pragmatism and empiricism in establishing social policy.

Buck v. Bell is a page of history that demonstrates beyond cavil the victory of Enlightenment ideas in U.S. courts and citadels of elite opinion. A "feeble-minded white woman" by the name of Carrie Buck was committed to a state mental institution in the Commonwealth of Virginia in 1924. Her mother, Emma, had been declared feebleminded in 1920 in Charlottsville, Virginia. In 1924, the State Colony for Epileptics and Feebleminded in Lynchburg, Virginia, declared Carrie to be feebleminded. Shortly thereafter, Carrie's daughter, Vivian, whose pregnancy resulted from a rape, was also declared to be "defective" even though she was only seven months old. The local proponents of eugenics felt it was advantageous to pinpoint three generations of alleged feeblemindedness among the Bucks to bolster the argument that Carrie was a biological threat.[93] Carrie Buck became the test case for a Virginia law that provided for the involuntary sterilization of "mental defectives"[94] if the superintendent of an institution believed that it would promote "the health of the patient and the welfare of society."[95]

When Oliver Wendell Holmes Jr. penned the *Buck v. Bell* decision, he had been on the Supreme Court for twenty-five years. He was, in a legendary way, legally and politically astute, and his enormous experience was intimidating. Legal scholars often point to a 1905 dissent that Holmes wrote in just three paragraphs to be his most famous constitutional contribution. The case was *Lochner v. New York*,[96] and the issue before the Supreme Court was whether a statute enacted by the New York legislature restricting working hours at a bakery to ten hours a day was constitutional. Biographers of Holmes make clear that he was profoundly skeptical of economic reformers who were introducing legislation in many states to restrict child labor, remove sweatshops, and provide safer working conditions for laborers.[97] Nevertheless, he recognized the implausibility of relying on a grand theory of "sanctity of contract" to put the brake on humanitarian reforms. He wrote in a trenchant, biting, and widely cited dissent that the U.S. Constitution "is not intended to embody a particular economic theory. . . . It is made for people of fundamentally differing views, and the accident of our finding certain opinions natural and familiar or novel and even shocking ought not to conclude our judgment upon the question whether statutes embodying them conflict with the Constitution of the United States."[98]

The "sanctity of contract" theory that the majority of the Court invoked to strike down the reformist labor legislation in New York rested on the grinding efficiency envisioned by the ideology of economic laissez faire: government had no business stepping into the marketplace, a world of *sacred* contracts, supply and demand, winners and losers. This view held that the government should absolutely not intervene in labor disputes where the parties to a contract were bound by its terms with unbreakable finality. The effect of the ideology was to preclude the court from looking at traditional areas of safety and health governed by, inter alia, tort law. Instead, the grand theory of economic laissez faire, held as a political or economic opinion by several jurists, dictated the inevitable outcome of the case and delayed needed labor reforms until the 1930s, well into the New Deal. A contract was considered sacred whereas the well-being of working minors was not.

We have seen that the British political theorist John Locke (1632–1704) introduced a sociological reading of virtue and proposed a social contract to tame "state of nature" selfishness and antagonism by individuals and forces that recognized their interests to clash. We might consider Locke to be Hobbes Lite. Locke exercised an enormous effect on the American founders, but his "law of nature" idea of individuals working out a social contract based on enlightened self-interest is often confused with natural law, the context and content of Pinckaers's "natural inclinations" also described in chapter one.

The theory of economic determinism that the majority of the Supreme Court endorsed in *Lochner* (and for decades thereafter) is a precise laboratory setting for Locke's emphasis on property. The "sanctity of contract" that the Court enshrined as substantive due process, that is, voting for an economic theory of laissez-faire determinism—the economically smarter and stronger will inevitably prevail, a good thing for society—as opposed to permitting reformist legislative statutes or precedents, is an exact formulation of Lockean contract theory. It is worth recalling that in his original draft of the Declaration of Independence, Thomas Jefferson, reflecting his adherence to a Lockean view, wrote of "life, liberty, and the pursuit of property." Jefferson reluctantly changed *property* to *happiness* at the direction of Benjamin Franklin, for whom happiness was no laughing matter and whose name, ironically, would later become slang for big money, the ultimate prize of those intent on crafting a social contract to acquire and protect property.

The *Lochner* decision and its judicial progeny, favoring a laissez-faire theory in support of supposedly unstoppable engines of economic progress, came at the expense of poor workers who often risked both health and safety in dreadful conditions. The real needs of the poor were sacrificed to a theory endorsed arbitrarily by the Supreme Court.

At the turn of the twentieth century, proponents of eugenics were making considerable headway in promoting their theories:

> Beginning in the early years of the twentieth century and spanning the decades of the 1910s, 1920s, and 1930s, eugenicists in the United States called for programs to control human reproduction. They urged legislatures to pass laws to segregate the so-called feeble-minded into state colonies, where they would live out their lives in celibacy; they supported compulsory state sterilization laws aimed at men and women whose "germplasm" threatened the eugenic vitality of the nation; they led the drive to restrict immigration from countries whose citizens might pollute the American melting pot. Their science filtered into popular culture through eugenics advice books and child-rearing manuals, eugenics novels, plays, and films, and scores of magazine and newspaper articles.

Americans avidly embraced arguments about hereditary determinism; at its zenith, eugenics enjoyed the support of a broad range of intellectuals, reformers, and political leaders.[99]

Private correspondence of Holmes indicates clearly that he believed in eugenics, that he considered it a positive, scientific contribution to serious social problems. Holmes was keenly aware that any endorsement of eugenics would be directly analogous to the Supreme Court's embrace of the laissez-faire "sanctity of contract" ideology from which he dissented in *Lochner*. His *Buck v. Bell* opinion that allowed Virginia to sterilize individuals involuntarily was consistent in jurisprudence with his opinion in *Lochner* whereby he likewise allowed the state of New York to legislate reforms. In both cases he struck out against an economic version of substantive due process but the ideology in play in *Buck* was not really the social Darwinism of Herbert Spencer but the eugenics agenda of individuals such as Margaret Sanger.

The frosting on the cake of a disingenuous approach is the dismissive sentence with which Holmes concludes his three-paragraph dissent: "The Fourteenth Amendment does not enact Mr. Herbert Spencer's *Social Statics*."[100] Several points make this sarcastic conclusion almost incredible. First, Holmes was privately most sympathetic with the nineteenth century version of social Darwinism espoused by Herbert Spencer. Second, no legislator or lawyer at any point in the record leading to the Court decision in *Lochner* had invoked Spencer. This was a gratuitous, purely pre-emptive strike by Holmes to inoculate himself publicly from any association with a particular school of thought that would claim to be "logical" as opposed to "historical," in the dichotomy of his famous quote, and to separate himself as a jurist from economic and sociological theories that he privately held.

It is instructive to examine the exact language by which Holmes provided a sweeping justification for involuntary sterilization. Even without invoking by name the ideology of eugenics, *Buck v. Bell* left the door open in principle for any number of coerced "sacrifices" from poor unfortunates who did not measure up to an arbitrary quality-of-life standard, "imbeciles" who might "sap the strength of the state":

> We have seen more than once that the public welfare may call upon the best citizens for their lives. It would be strange if it could not call upon those who already sap the strength of the State for these *lesser sacrifices*, often not felt to be such by those

concerned, in order to prevent our being swamped with incompetence. It is better for all the world, if instead of waiting to execute degenerate offspring for crime, or to let them starve for their imbecility, society can prevent those who are manifestly unfit from continuing their kind. The principle that sustains compulsory vaccination is broad enough to cover cutting the Fallopian tubes . . . Three generations of imbeciles are enough.[101] (Emphasis added)

Here in bold bravado is the agenda of eugenics. Consider the premises upon which Holmes's declaration above rests: (1) The welfare of the state is superior to the interests of the individual. (2) A scale of "sacrifices" exists which a citizen must be prepared to forfeit, the greatest being the surrender of one's life as a soldier. But what other "lesser sacrifices" might be identified by the state? Would not the care of any infirm or disabled individual—child, handicapped adult, chronically, or terminally ill citizen— qualify as a loss to the "public welfare" that "saps the strength of the State?" (3) Strictly speaking, a sacrifice is voluntarily made; in this instance, a coerced action, sexual sterilization, is deemed to be a "sacrifice" and the suggestion is made that "the imbecile" won't even miss it (. . . often not felt to be [a sacrifice] by those concerned"). (4) Citizens can be divided into "the fit" and "the unfit." (5) No crime or act of violence is imputed to any of the "imbeciles," it is simply their condition that offends the public welfare. (6) Unless the birth of children is likely to meet a quality-of-life standard, no right for that child to come into the world can be said to exist.

A recent, highly critical, study of Holmes's jurisprudence[102] shows that serious factual doubt exists about the supposedly "defective" condition of Carrie Buck and her family. Albert Alschuler cites several studies from prestigious law school journals that directly challenge the accuracy or sufficiency of evidence purportedly showing Carrie Buck to be "feebleminded."[103]

What happened to Carrie Buck after the decision?

Shortly after the Court's opinion was announced, Carrie Buck was sterilized. She was eventually discharged from the Virginia Colony for Epileptics and Feebleminded. She married twice— her first husband died after twenty-four years of marriage—sang in the Methodist Church choir, and took work helping a family in Front Royal, Virginia, to care for an elderly relative. She died in a state-operated nursing home near Waynesboro, Virginia, in 1983, at the age of seventy-seven.

Considerable doubt surrounds her imbecility today. In fact, she was said to display substantial intelligence as well as kindness, to be an avid reader and a lucid conversationalist, even in her last days. Her daughter, Vivian, lived only eight years, but she too contradicted institutional and judicial estimates of her mental capacities. She went through the second grade in school and was considered by her teachers to be "very bright."[104]

Did Holmes feel regret about his callous decision? Quite the contrary, he wrote to his young British friend, a lifelong correspondent and hagiographer, Harold Laski, of what he considered to be the *reformist* nature of the historic decision: "I wrote and delivered a decision upholding the constitutionality of a state law for sterilizing imbeciles the other day—and felt that I was getting near the first principle of real reform."[105] Alschuler also details the "pleasure" that Holmes experienced, described in a letter to his friend Lewis Einstein, in sanctioning the involuntary sterilization: "Establishing the constitutionality of a law permitting the sterilization of imbeciles . . . gave me pleasure."[106]

The noted legal analyst and historian Lucas A. Powe Jr. uses the *Buck v. Bell* case to make a larger point: when the justices agree with a particular law, they are likely to uphold them regardless of other considerations. Powe summarizes Holmes's approach in *Buck*:

> Holmes needed but two paragraphs to reject the Fourteenth Amendment claims. He dismissed due process by noting: "We have seen more than once that the public welfare may call upon the best citizens for their lives. It would be strange if it could not call upon those who already sap the strength of the State for these lesser sacrifices." . . . He gave even shorter shrift to equal protection, which he dismissed as "the usual last resort of constitutional arguments." . . . Just as with the Court's rulings on the scope of federal powers, there is no getting around the fact that the Court chose to uphold these laws because it agreed with them on the merits.[107]

This is precisely what occurred in the 1960s when justices who favored the ideology of reproductive rights (that is, rights language used in isolation from basic human goods or countervailing rights and responsibilities), drawn essentially from the Enlightenment model of autonomy, relied on substantive due process to arrive at conclusions that had no constitutional or textual warrant. An ideology became the law of the land regardless of countervailing decisions from federal and state courts and statutes enacted by a majority of American legislatures, which is where the Founders believed divisive issues could best be handled.

EUGENICS AND THE INCARNATION: A CLASH OF WORLD VIEWS

It is not an accident that most of the opposition to *Buck v. Bell* came from the Catholic establishment in the United States. Christine Rosen spends an entire chapter describing historical Catholic opposition to eugenics in her brilliant *Preaching Eugenics: Religious Leaders and the American Eugenics Movement.*[108] The single dissenter on the Court, Pierce Butler, was known as a devout Catholic and friend of many Catholic Bishops. Unfortunately, he did not write an opinion to explain his solitary dissent.

Aside from historical or political reasons for Catholic opposition to eugenics, as documented by Rosen, we need to consider the radically antagonistic world views of eugenics on the one hand, and the Incarnation—the mystery revered by Christians that in Jesus Christ there is the reality of God assuming human flesh—on the other.

Eugenics claims to be scientific, proudly declaring that populations need to be filtered so that the unfit or less promising are eliminated at either the beginning or end of their life. There is but a single yardstick—a social calculus of utility. By contrast, the view of Christian revelation provided in the sixth chapter of Saint John's Gospel is that Jesus Christ gave to His disciples His very flesh and blood. This account of the Eucharist whereby believers "give thanks" that they can participate intimately, personally, and communally in the reality of enfleshed Divine Love emerges directly from the mystery of the Incarnation. Derided by critics as adherents of virtual cannibalism, Christians such as Roman Catholics who believe that Christ is really present when they receive the Eucharist, see a direct correlation between the mystery of the Incarnation, God becoming flesh in the person of Jesus Christ, and the sacrament of the Eucharist (that is, the sacred sign pointing to the actual and real presence of Christ).

This correlation between Incarnation and Eucharist flows directly from *Gaudium et Spes*, n. 22 (cited in the first chapter) which sees Christ as the radical measure and meaning of all humanity. As God is enfleshed in Christ (the Incarnation), human beings are elevated to a unique relationship with Christ through the reception of the Eucharist. The meaning of human life is immeasurably transformed by the capacity to receive Christ in His body and blood. Such a reception does not at all mean that the devout who receive the Eucharist are thereby morally superior to their neighbor, Christian or non-Christian. It simply means that there is an intimate bond between Christ and those who devoutly seek to receive Him. We have seen that the force of *Gaudium et Spes*, n. 22, is that *everyone* is transformed by Christ or the Christ-event of the Incarnation. Since the person is a unity of body and soul, this transformation of meaning affects the entire person—body, soul, flesh, mind, spirit—and marks human beings as unique in the eyes of God, distinct from the rest of creation, truly the image of the Divine (*imago Dei*).

Such a sacramental vision has immediate practical moral consequences. It means that no person can simply be defined, measured, or valued as a matter of social utility. Every person has a fundamental, inherent meaning and value beyond price or description. This inherent human meaning or value is distinct from the moral value of a subject's achievements and virtues. Human worth is not dependent upon the moral characteristics of the subject; the same truth applies to Adolph Hitler as to Mother Teresa. There is an inherent moral significance present simply by virtue of being human. This assuredly strikes many individuals as stupid or incomprehensible. John's Gospel records that many contemporaries of Jesus found His teaching on the Eucharist impossible to accept.[109]

But for those who accept a Eucharistic vision of humanity, namely a gratitude for the very being of any person and the sacramental link with Christ, no mere quality-of-life standard is acceptable in moral issues. Saint or sinner, hero, zero, or Nero, every human being has been touched by the grace of the Incarnation. There is no human good so meritorious as to earn this bond with God. There is no human evil so depraved as to lose the intrinsic capacity for the divine brought about by the life of Christ on earth.

There could not be a more direct conflict in world views. Those who hold and advance a utilitarian calculus of human worth have a discernible, quantifiable standard of human life, its usefulness to the subject and society. Those who see all human life as sacred, rendered inherently valuable first by creation and then by the redemptive presence of Christ, are prepared to discover incomparable value in every AIDS patient, Down syndrome baby, chronically or terminally ill patient, disabled or cognitively challenged individual in existence. Justice Holmes wrote in 1927 that "three generations of imbeciles are enough." The Christian who believes that Christ's life has radically changed the measure and meaning of humanity would conclude today that three generations of ideologues are enough.

EUGENICS: BACK TO THE FUTURE

The distinguished author of our "page of history" quotation, Oliver Wendell Holmes Jr., the Brahmin epitome of Harvard Law School who served as Associate Justice of the U.S. Supreme Court for thirty years, played a pivotal role in the development of a jurisprudence that would change the legal and social context of sexual ethics forever.

Holmes is a logical choice—to credit the other side of his history-logic equation—to start our inquiry of the impact of Enlightenment philosophy upon the law because he ranked as the very embodiment and voice of the American establishment in the first third of the twentieth century. The "Yankee from Olympus"[110] mightily influenced not only law but also social policy through his meticulously crafted judicial opinions. Adoring journalists and law professors point to their eloquence. I hope to identify one crucial example of a horrendous *misanthropy*—understood in the root sense of an anti-human bias—in the ideology of eugenics.

The legal historian Liva Baker documents the longtime commitment that Holmes held for eugenics, as he fully accepted the theories of the Rev. Thomas Malthus whose *Essays on Population* predicted impending disaster as a result of overpopulation, and considered eugenics to be a "true beginning, theoretically, of all improvement."[111]

Eugenics is the pseudo-science or ideology that divides human beings into the fit and the unfit, working hard to reduce the number and influence of the "unfit." Its ugly track record is finally receiving the attention it deserves in the work of Rosen and other scholars. Its philosophical underpinning lies in the proposition that not all human beings are worthy of civil or legal protection, including life; only those whose lives conform to a "reasonable" standard are entitled to life and legal protection.

No doubt Holmes considered his disdain-dripping conclusion—"Three generations of imbeciles is enough"—to embody Yankee virtue at its finest: "Let's be practical, this mother and her children cannot take care of themselves, let's put an end to this practice of bringing imbeciles into the world."

History has not looked kindly upon Holmes's *Buck* opinion. In addition to the documented skepticism about whether Carrie Bell was in fact mentally challenged, it did not help that totalitarian forces later in the twentieth century drank deeply from the same poisoned well of eugenics that Holmes had drawn from atop Olympus. The opprobrium that Hitler and his Nazi horrors visited upon the mad scheming of eugenics was more than deserved. But the roots of eugenics preceded Hitler by at least half a century. Nineteenth-century efforts of Nietzsche and others to divide humanity into the weak and the strong, the unfit and the fit, laid the groundwork for the belief that not all human life has dignity nor does every human being have an inherent, inviolable dignity deserving of legal protection.

Catholic social teaching has long insisted on the importance of solidarity—the shared commitment to a common good—as a duty that society has toward those in need. No disability nullifies the mutuality of love.

Buck v. Bell marked the approval of eugenics at the highest level of American society. Its justification of involuntary sterilization did not prompt any mass outcry or opposition. All but one Supreme Court Justice (Pierce Butler, the sole dissenter, did not write an opinion) said that a state possessed the legal power to sterilize a woman against her will: upon any adjudicated pretext of "feeble-mindedness" or mental retardation, she would find surgeons treating her not as a patient but as a threat to the community. The state effectively replaced the family as the provider of care and arbiter of behavior.

Buck v. Bell had an enormous impact on state legislation, as Rosen records:

> The Supreme Court's decision in *Buck v. Bell* unleashed a torrent of new compulsory sterilization laws. In the two years immediately following the decision, eleven states passed new legislation that incorporated the safeguards (outlined in the *Buck* decision) necessary to withstand constitutional challenges. Between 1925 and 1935, with the avid support of physicians and reformers, these laws resulted in the quadrupling of the number of men and women sterilized in state institutions. The increase is even starker when a broader span of time is examined: In 1917, approximately 1,422 people in institutions were sterilized; by 1941, that number had reached 38,087.[112]

If this is the misanthropy shown toward the mother, what of the status of the child? The implication is that it would be better for the child not to live. First, we can stipulate the benign intent of Margaret Sanger and her fellow founders of Planned Parenthood who advocated the mass production and distribution of contraceptives to reduce the number of "unwanted" children. Margaret Sanger formed the American Birth Control League (ABCL) in 1921, designed to serve as an educational effort and to lobby for legislative "reform." Concerned about the care of poor women,

Sanger had opened the first birth control clinic in the United States in Brooklyn in 1916.[113] The road to moral infamy, including racism and involuntary sterilization, was being paved with good intentions.

Clearly Sanger and her allies were alarmed at the poverty to which pregnant women and their children were subject. But their solution—fewer children—was tragically and terribly distorted.

While Karl Marx pushed for class warfare among adults, the Sanger agenda was implicit class warfare among infants. Only the better class of children, well-bred infants generated and raised by parents who approved the progressive nostrums of Charles Darwin and took seriously the alarmism of such thinkers as Thomas Malthus (who warned that the world would soon be overwhelmed by overpopulation), could be admitted to the human club. All others, sadly but forcibly, would be shut out. Eugenics essentially transforms *Homo sapiens* from a community in which all human beings are welcomed to a club where respectable genes are required as dues.

A great contradiction occurs in Justice Holmes's *Buck* decision that will loom large in subsequent Supreme Court decisions on sexual ethics. As a pillar of Yankee individualism and self-reliance, Holmes might be expected to champion the rights and needs of an individual, especially an impoverished or disabled mother. Yet he opts, callously and imperiously, to increase the power of the "State" over and against the rights of indigent women. How can an icon of individualism cede such coercive power to the state?

Later, in 1965, in the *Griswold* decision appraised below, the Supreme Court will discern in the Constitution a right to privacy unrecognized since 1789, and begin the process of expanding privacy as an all-justifying right in sexual matters. Strictly speaking, *Griswold* and *Buck* are fundamentally inconsistent on whether such a right to privacy exists. Had Holmes in *Buck* found that Carrie Buck had a privacy right, she would have prevailed against the Commonwealth of Virginia. But *Buck*, *Griswold*, and *Roe* are all consistent on the bottom line: inconvenient human life has no entitlement to legal protection. *Buck* defends the right of the state to prevent inconvenient human beings from coming into existence. *Griswold* (as we will see) defends the right of a married couple to prevent inconvenient human life from coming into existence and *Roe* (as we will see) defends the right of anyone to terminate inconvenient human life even after it has already, incontrovertibly, come into existence.

So Holmes does not find for Carrie Buck any "privacy right" (to use the subsequent language of *Griswold* and *Roe*) to have children, but his holding is consistent with *Griswold* and *Roe* insofar as it does not discern any state interest in safeguarding the existence or well-being of children whose lives will be affected by the court rulings. In *Buck*, the interests of children are seen as antagonistic to the state. In subsequent decisions, those interests are seen as antagonistic to parents and society at large. Indeed, the state or parents may have an interest in children *not* coming into existence. For the public welfare, their *nonexistence* is preferable to their life.

Those who argue that eugenics does the community a favor by reducing the number of individuals at risk miss the central point: the common good is never truly achieved at the expense of family bonds. Conformity to abstract standards of social utility—this class of healthy infants deserves to live and that class of handicapped infants has no right to live—coercively imposed by police power, is not in any way compatible with the real needs of human beings. The common good of society rests on principles that must remain inviolable. Such a principle is the freedom of a family from punitive, harmful, or dehumanizing measures.

It was, of course, the 1857 *Dred Scott* decision that, by perpetuating the yoke of slavery, hastened the Civil War. And it was the overturning of the 1896 justification of racial segregation (*Plessy v. Ferguson*) by *Brown v. Board of Education* in 1954 that toppled the "separate but equal" standard that had effectively disenfranchised African-American citizens from the fruits of public education. An entire society looks back in shame at these harmful decrees once enshrined as the supreme law of the land. Even people notoriously short on familiarity with history usually have an awareness of the enormity of *Dred Scott*. But average citizens today would be hardpressed to make reference to a Supreme Court decision, written by a judicial giant in sparkling prose, which stood for the rights of the state to intervene coercively in the lives of truly innocent people and thwart them through surgery from seeing another human being (literally their flesh and blood) come into existence.

Why isn't *Buck v. Bell* a case as well-known and notorious in the public mind as *Dred Scott*? Is it shame at the failure of a mind usually regarded as a legal genius to grasp a fundamental right—the right to share family life and love unfettered from the coercive force of the state? Is it a sort of Victorian decency that refuses to speak of such awful things as calling human beings "imbeciles" and forcing women to be sterilized? Perhaps one explanation lies in the ambivalent status of eugenics today.

Is *Buck v. Bell* a spent force or a predictor of the future? Evidence accumulates that it is the latter. The distinguished libertarian theoretician Richard Posner has written that "belief in human eugenics was a staple of progressive thought in Holmes's lifetime," adding that "with the renewed interest . . . in euthanasia, and with the rise of genetic engineering, we may yet find those [eugenic] enthusiasms prescient rather than depraved."[114] As depressing and appalling as this conclusion is, I believe that Posner, senior lecturer at the University of Chicago Law School and judge on the U.S. Court of Appeals for the Second Circuit, is exactly right. Holmes's opinion in *Buck v. Bell* is a harbinger of growing social movements for eugenics and euthanasia. Far from being a universally scorned embarrassment, the Holmes decision stands as a historic justification for those who would apply a utilitarian standard to populations. Essentially, *Buck* and its ideological adherents argue that only those who have social utility are entitled to life.

Those who are sympathetic to eugenics today in the form of genetic engineering and who prize logical consistency cannot reject *Buck v. Bell*, a court case after all that comes down squarely on the side of having the "right" kind of children. In his 1973 opinion in *Roe v. Wade*, Justice Harry Blackmun is constrained of course to cite this "precedent" enshrining the right of the state to police private bedrooms. He dutifully does so in a single sentence, citing it as an example of limits on the privacy that he will go on to extol as a constitutional right.[115]

Buck v. Bell, never overturned by the Supreme Court, is a horror for all who have grasped the misanthropic antagonism toward children that has become dominant in elite circles. To understand the "logic" of this anti-child bias, we must look further at the triumph of the Enlightenment ethic of absolute autonomy in several landmark cases of the Supreme Court from the 1960s to the present.

PRIVACY, REPRODUCTIVE RIGHTS, AND SUBSTANTIVE DUE PROCESS

1. *Griswold v. Connecticut (1965): The Birth of Privacy, Not Children*

In 1651, Thomas Hobbes described the condition of the world as a war of all against all in his *Leviathan*: "During the time men live without a common power to keep them all in awe, they are in that condition which is called *war*; and such a war as is of every man against every man."[116]

The 1960s would modify this dire and pessimistic scenario of Hobbes by providing eros as the common power to keep everyone in awe. Religious faith no longer delivered the kind of awe required, so eros stepped up to serve as the omnipotent successor of faith. But since altar and throne were gone or discredited, the awe must be promulgated by the one remaining force capable of commanding the society, the state, specifically, the judicial branch of the state.

In 1965, the majority of the "brethren" who succeeded Oliver Wendell Holmes on the Supreme Court substituted a sexual theory for a capitalist theory as the engine of the stalled juggernaut of substantive due process—politics replacing the law—revved up for even more adventures. With *Lochner* and its laissez-faire progeny, the Court saw to it that anything goes in the sweatshop. With *Griswold* and its progeny, the Court has replaced an economic version of substantive due process, the *Lochner* laissez-faire ideology resulting from the Industrial Revolution, with a social variant of substantive due process, the ideology of privacy or sexual autonomy that has emerged from the sexual revolution.

Specifically, the Court ruled in *Griswold v. Connecticut*[117] that contraceptives must be commercially available to married couples. While writing ironically and at length about marriage as a sacred bond, the Court discerned within the U.S. Constitution an implied right to a zone of privacy that would guarantee the private use of contraceptives by spouses. Justice William O. Douglas argued that this privacy is based on a "penumbra" tracing its source of light to the First, Fourth, and Fifth Amendments, prohibiting the legislature of the state of Connecticut from restricting the sale of contraceptives. Justice Potter Steward stated in his dissent to the Douglas opinion that he believed the Connecticut statute to be "uncommonly silly," voicing his personal opinion that contraceptives should be generally available to the public. But Stewart (and Hugo Black, usually an ally of Douglas) saw no reason to deny a state legislature's right to enact a law, albeit one that might be silly or "asinine," provided the statute did not violate any traditional constitutional safeguards.[118]

As a well-known mountain climber, Douglas was able to apply his talents to the U.S. Constitution, discovering hitherto unknown meanings that radically changed contemporary sexual ethics. The language used by Douglas is so nebulous as to invite parody. It is as though script writers for *Saturday Night Live* suddenly clerk for the Court. The infinitely creative Douglas wrote this: "Specific guarantees in the Bill of Rights have penumbras, formed by emanations from those guarantees that help give them life and substance. . . . Various guarantees create zones of privacy."[119]

Commenting on this imagery worthy of the *Twilight Zone*, Mark Levin writes, "Don't be embarrassed if you don't know what emanations from penumbras are. Young lawyers across America had to pull out their dictionaries when reading *Griswold* for the first time. A penumbra is an astronomical term describing the partial shadow in an eclipse or the edge of a sunspot—and it is another way to describe something unclear or uncertain. 'Emanation' is a scientific term for gas made from radioactive decay—it also means 'an emission.'"[120]

Can anything better illustrate the bizarre labyrinth that results when the Supreme Court uses technical scientific language, drawn from astronomy and geology, to discover legal justification for a novel, free-floating "right," the exercise of which separates the primal human expressions of sharing love and giving life?

Judge Robert Bork makes the point that *Griswold* was at its core not really about contraception. "The protection of marriage was not the point of *Griswold*. The creation of a new device for judicial power to remake the Constitution was the point."[121]

And remake the Constitution it did. With *Griswold*, the tools of substantive due process are put in place. Penumbras and emanations will work their magic to allow an ideology of reproductive rights, a sad separation of claimed rights from real goods, to gain judicial ascendancy. Genuine enactments of state legislatures restricting or outlawing abortion will be struck down by a single judicial fiat of *Roe v. Wade*. The Court has imported ideology from the Enlightenment and now enacts it with a radical force. The sacredness of marriage described in *Griswold* will quickly be forgotten in *Eisenstadt* as a slippery slope from contraception to abortion to gay marriage and euthanasia becomes judicial reality. The ideology of autonomy, designed by Kant to guarantee human dignity, will ironically insure that there will be fewer humans.

Perhaps the most telling comment about the sea change in jurisprudence signaled by the *Griswold* decision was Justice Hugo Black's adamant dissent. Black was the first New Deal appointment of President Franklin D. Roosevelt to the Supreme Court in 1937. He was a staunch opponent of substantive due process in any form. A mere two years before *Griswold*, Black spoke out forcefully against the notion of the Court as a legislature. Writing in *Ferguson v. Skrupa*, Black provides an eloquent defense of judicial deference to the legislative branch: "We have returned to the original constitutional proposition that courts do not substitute their social and economic beliefs for the judgment of legislative bodies, who are elected to pass laws. Whether the legislature takes for its textbook, Adam Smith, Herbert Spencer, Lord Keynes, or some other, is no concern of ours. . . . [R]elief if any be needed lies not with us but with the body constituted to pass laws."[122]

Professor Stanley Morrison, a sharp critic of Justice Black's approach to the Fourteenth Amendment, paid him a great compliment on his consistent opposition to substantive due process in an otherwise hostile article: "When he thus seeks to abolish substantive due process, he is on solid ground historically. If the clause is to be interpreted in accordance with the meaning it had to the framers and others in 1868, the doctrine cannot be justified. It is . . . a later excrescence derived from natural-law sources."[123] Morrison provides here the very valuable insight that substantive due process may well owe its historic origin to a Lockean version of natural law far more at home with legal rights than with moral goods.

We have seen how Justice Taney purported to follow the Constitution in discovering a right to own slaves in *Dred Scott* even though, as Professor Sunstein has pointed out above, the Constitution actually limited the role of slavery. Unlike Taney, Black is a consistent textualist or originalist who requires a basis in the Constitution for any claimed right, whether economic or social.

2. Eisenstadt v. Baird (1972): The Bridge to Roe

For all of Douglas's pious pronouncements about the sanctity of marriage in *Griswold* (when in fact the plaintiffs were not even married), the Supreme Court in just seven years ruled that contraceptives were to be commercially available to everyone, married or single. Striking down a Massachusetts statute that was never enforced, the Court in *Eisenstadt v. Baird* ruled that the "right to privacy" discovered among penumbras by *Griswold* belongs to everyone. Marriage, so solemnly established as the predicate in *Griswold* for spouses opting to practice contraception, was now entirely irrelevant to the use, sale, and availability of contraceptives. Sexual autonomy is for the masses, not merely the married.

Justice William Brennan in *Eisenstadt* declared that "whatever the rights of the individual to access contraceptives may be, the rights must be the same for the unmarried and the married alike."[124] The linkage of privacy and marriage in *Griswold* by William Douglas, an unlikely and awkward apostle of holy matrimony, is now shoveled into the dustbin of history.

The decision is notable for its language, ingeniously crafted by Justice Brennan, laying the groundwork for *Roe v. Wade*, then making its way through countless conferences and debates among the justices at the

Supreme Court level,[125] and establishing autonomy now as not merely a marital right, but as an individual prerogative: "It is true that in *Griswold* the right of privacy in question inhered in the marital relationship. Yet the marital couple is not an independent entity with a mind and heart of its own, but an association of two individuals each with a separate intellectual and emotional makeup. If the right of privacy means anything, it is the right of the individual, married or single, to be free from unwarranted governmental intrusion into matters so fundamentally affecting a person as the decision whether to bear or beget a child."[126]

Anyone skeptical about the impact of the Supreme Court on the cultural understanding of marriage in the United States today need only look at Brennan's description of marriage as "an association of two individuals each with a *separate* intellectual and emotional makeup." How sharply this contrasts with the New Testament view of a married couple as having a two-in-one-flesh unity. As quoted in the Gospel of Mark, Jesus teaches, quoting Genesis, that a husband and wife have a unique unity: "'For this reason a man shall leave his father and mother and be joined to his wife, and the two shall become one flesh. So they are no longer two, but one flesh.' Therefore what God has joined together, let no one separate."[127] The common law recognized this unity in many ways, respecting the bond of husband and wife as a unity of common interest in matters of civil, criminal, and property rights. Brennan's description of separate interests runs directly contrary to the Judeo-Christian perspective found biblically in the Jewish scriptures of Genesis and the parallel Gospel texts of Matthew and Mark.

But Brennan doesn't restrict himself simply to reversing the biblical paradigm of marriage; that task is necessary but not sufficient for absolutizing the right to privacy as a plenary prerogative. He proceeds to separate the *Griswold*-created right to privacy from any link with marriage, moving far beyond the anomalous sermon of Douglas a mere seven years earlier. Brennan describes this right as a freedom from "unwarranted governmental intrusion," but this formulation of the newly discovered right, cloaked in the attractive mantle of libertarian freedom, actually conceals the fact that it is the government that at critical times provides a defense against intrusion from other forces that would harm us. If a robber stops you on a dark alley, you would be delighted to see a policeman exercise some highly warranted intrusion on the thug with a gun at your head.

The implications of this high-sounding yet lethally arbitrary phrase become totally clear in the next passage when Brennan helpfully identifies the matter at hand: "matters so fundamentally affecting a person as the decision whether to *bear or beget* a child."[128] Whether a child will come into the world or not is the question at hand. The power to give life, continue life and end life are what Brennan is talking about. The libertarian language suggests a shell game where the right of a child to have a birthday is irrevocably lost.

Is *Eisenstadt* the inverse of *Buck v. Bell*? In *Buck*, Justice Holmes granted power to the state to sterilize Carrie Buck because her family failed to measure up to an arbitrary standard of acceptable genetic identity. Now *Eisenstadt* confers a comparable right of sterilization upon any woman facing pregnancy. Can we say that *Eisenstadt* has valorously reversed the wrong of *Buck* by putting the right to end human life where it belongs, in the hands of the mother rather than the state? Only a superficial reading of the two cases would see *Eisenstadt* as the exact inverse of *Buck*. Yes, the power to contracept, sterilize, or abort is not now limited to the state, but in entrusting this potentially lethal power to a single individual, there is still fully present the Enlightenment ethic of absolute autonomy in matters of sex, marriage, and procreation. It is simply given to a different party as a baton would be handed to a runner for the next leg of a race.

The cases of *Eisenstadt* and *Buck* are entirely consistent in their embedding in the law the right to terminate human life at its embryonic, fetal, and even infant stages. All that changes is the party given the authority to exercise the right. For Justice Holmes in *Buck*, it was the state that would referee who might measure up to the eugenic expectations of the time. For Justice Brennan in *Eisenstadt*, it is the mother who becomes not simply the referee but the judge, jury, and possible executioner in regard to the child's right to live. C. S. Lewis in his classic *The Abolition of Man* foresaw this transition in 1949. Lewis warned that when objective morality, or what he referred to as the Tao, was abandoned by society, the only determinant of morality would be political power. Morality becomes simply a function of the will and whim of the majority. The superficial contrast of *Buck* and *Eisenstadt*—where in the first case it is the state that decides the right to life, and in *Eisenstadt* it is the call of the mother—merely shows the advance of the political agenda of the Enlightenment ethic of absolute autonomy. Any right independent of objective, transcendent morality will devolve into a political football, thrown about a large field and captured by the most powerful player.

The proponents of the sexual revolution may consider Holmes, Douglas, and Brennan to be prophets, way ahead of their time in using the law to promote sexual maturity and responsible intercourse. The problem is that a political theory of "privacy" far removed from a traditional constitutional context such as the Fourth Amendment right against unreasonable search and seizure or the Fifth Amendment protection against self-incrimination has become settled law with only the shakiest of foundations.

These amendments from the Bill of Rights connect privacy with governmental intrusion—unreasonable state action that can unduly restrict personal and property rights. Tort law has governed individual issues of where or whether the privacy of one's basic human needs would trump the right of another's arguable claim. But the language of "penumbras" and "emanations" originated by Justice Douglas and cleverly expanded by Justice Brennan became what might ironically, if painfully, be called the "mother" of all sexual autonomy cases, *Roe v. Wade*.

3. *Roe v. Wade (1973): Abortion as Sacred Right or Eros as Sacrament*

In a brilliant critique of the judiciary, Max Boot explains how the Supreme Court, eight years after *Griswold*, seized upon the "right to privacy" and enshrined abortion as a constitutionally protected choice:

> This nebulous explanation [of *Griswold*] became the basis for the Court's famous ruling in *Roe v. Wade* and its companion case, *Doe v. Bolton*, which turned abortion into a constitutional right on a par with free speech and the right of assembly. The seven-justice majority in *Roe* was not greatly troubled by the fact that at the time the Fourteenth Amendment was enacted, thirty-six states and territories either prohibited or limited abortion and that twenty-one of those laws still remained on the books in 1973. Justice Harry Blackmun, writing for the majority, nevertheless decided that the Due Process Clause protected abortion, though he conceded that other parts of the Constitution, such as the Ninth Amendment, might just as well accomplish the same ends; he wasn't picky, as long as the results were correct.[129]

The comparisons between *Dred Scott* and *Roe* could not be more compelling. In both cases, the Court ruled that a particular class of individuals (African-Americans in *Dred Scott*; unborn children in *Roe*) did not enjoy a constitutionally protected right to life or liberty. In each case a "right" is arbitrarily announced that is indistinguishable from a political, personal opinion. Chief Justice Taney had any number of reasons to strike down slavery on purely legal, not moral, grounds, as Abraham Lincoln was among the first to point out. But Taney was politically committed to the notion of a "right to slavery" and would not waver or budge from this *idée fixe* any more than the majority in *Lochner* would abandon their commitment to "the sanctity of contract." When substantive due process is involved, as in *Lochner* and *Roe*, the role of the justices becomes legislative: they consider and approve theories, embedding them in their decisions.

In *Roe*, Blackmun devised an artificial trimester template to justify state interest in protecting abortions: the mother would begin the pregnancy with an unlimited right to abort, a right remaining for at least three months. The interest of the state in preserving the life of the child only comes into existence upon proof of viability, the capacity of the child to exist outside of the womb. A human being would now be dismissed as "potential life," an Orwellian phrase breathtaking in the boldness of its distortion. This legal fiction has become more untenable with each passing year as the test of "viability" has changed dramatically with the appearance of technology raising the odds of survival outside the womb for an embryo or fetus. The ability of science to treat the embryo and fetus as a patient within her mother's womb means that viability can even occur within the first trimester.

One doesn't have to be a doctor to see huge problems with the faulty medical approach of *Roe* and the arrogance of depriving state legislatures, laboratories of democracy, from having any meaningful say regarding abortions. Even pro-choice legal scholars such as Justice Ruth Bader Ginsburg, Archibald Cox, and John Hart Ely have recognized how deeply flawed was the legal rationale of *Roe*.[130]

Ely was a former law clerk to Chief Justice Earl Warren and professor of law at Harvard University who penned a critique of *Roe* so powerful in its analytical acumen that it set the standard of law review articles on *Roe*. In an absolutely damning judgment, Ely wrote about *Roe*: "It is bad because it is bad constitutional law, or rather because it is not constitutional law and gives almost no sense of an obligation to try to be."[131]

Ely's characterization of *Roe* as bad constitutional law or something that falls short of constitutional law left proponents of abortion with a dilemma. They liked the outcome of the case which legitimated abortion on demand since the health interest of the mother was construed with such latitude that any perceived inconvenience could legally justify an abortion.

Nevertheless, the legal establishment recognized early on that the legal reasoning upon which this desired outcome rested was not only fragile but suspect. Ely brilliantly made the point taken up by critics of right and left that *Roe* moved from judicial review into the thicket of legislative enactment, striking down the debated and voted upon conclusions of dozens of state legislatures, substituting the judgment of seven unelected individuals for that of the duly elected legislators. Madison and Hamilton would not have approved.

Mark Levin succinctly summarizes the legislative, as opposed to judicial, nature of Blackmun's work in *Roe* in striking down the Texas statute that prohibited Norma McCorvey, a pregnant resident of Texas, from having an abortion:

> Not satisfied to strike down the Texas law, Blackmun began to write what seemed to be a new federal statute. According to Blackmun's opinion, a woman's right to abortion could only be abridged by a compelling state interest. In effect, Blackmun argued that there was an inverse relationship between a woman's interest and the state's interest that ranged across a spectrum from conception to birth. Therefore, the state's interest at conception was minimal but increased as the pregnancy progressed, reaching its peak at the end of the pregnancy. A woman's interest, paramount at conception, began to give some ground to the state's interest in protecting the fetus as it matured toward being able to live outside of the mother. But Blackmun specifically declared that the unborn child was not a "person" under the Fourteenth Amendment, and thus had no equal protection rights.[132]

Enacted after the Civil War to protect the rights of a class of people, African-American slaves, the Fourteenth Amendment was now used by several unelected justices to disenfranchise another class of people, unborn humans. It was a chilling reversal of the clear legislative intent of Congress, perpetrated by a court acting as a super-legislature.

I argued in the first chapter that the ultimate effect of the Enlightenment was actually to *decrease* scholarly confidence in discovering the truth. This net decrease in perceived awareness and self-confidence in certifiable truths applied to both science and the humanities. Perhaps the most telling and tragic evidence of this loss of nerve about reality can be found in Justice Blackmun's abandonment of the effort to ascertain when life begins: "We need not resolve the difficult question of when life begins. When those trained in the respective disciplines of medicine, philosophy, and theology are unable to arrive at any consensus, the judiciary, at this point in the development of man's knowledge, is not in a position to speculate as to the answer."[133]

The unvarying premise and practice of society has been to give the benefit of the doubt to the possibility that human life exists when there is the potential for harm. Rescue operations are immediately launched in cases of a mine disaster or air or sea mishap on the possibility that human life may be in jeopardy. The presumption favors life just as criminal law enshrines a presumption of innocence. Yet here, in the most intimate and ordinary of circumstances, the conception of a baby in her mother's womb, the Court turns agnostic.

Similar scruples about knowledge have not bothered the judiciary in arcane matters of economics, finance, housing, and education, where courts are known to arrive at draconian solutions in apparent ignorance of critical facts. How often housing units for prospective purchasers or tenants in big cities are subject not simply to economic forces of supply and demand but judicial edicts on rent-control, zoning, development, and taxation where facts are genuinely not known but courts are determined to be activist.

All medical evidence before *Roe*, and most decidedly after *Roe*, has pointed in the clear direction of human life beginning when the sperm fertilizes the egg: DNA appears onstage from Act One. As technology has increased the means available to study intrauterine life through ultrasounds and MRIs, showing motion, breathing, and even expressions of apparent emotion by a fetus, there can be no doubt that a fetus is a human being. It is not "potential life" but human life with a potential. For Justice Blackmun to ignore what any doctor who has delivered babies knows—the slow but steady path of human life—and the ever more specific findings of embryology and neonatology, calling the use of this scientific data "speculation" is as potent an example of the failure of the Enlightenment as one could find.

Legal writers such as Robert Bork and Mark Levin have explored with great effect the inherent contradictions of *Roe* whereby the Supreme Court not only ignores but invalidates legislative judgments of various states about when and how human life should be protected. My point is to establish that judicial excess did not occur overnight or independently of powerful philosophical currents.

It is important to note that a moral opposition to abortion does not translate into a lack of concern for pregnant women. As the pro-life movement grew after *Roe*, volunteers have paid increasing attention to the often heart-wrenching circumstances of women who become pregnant. Issues of rape, domestic violence, poverty, and the breakdown of the family cannot be ignored. There is a tremendous need for social capital—human resources mobilized on behalf of the vulnerable and marginalized.

It is true that a pregnancy can often bring medical peril when a woman has serious health issues for which a pregnancy would increase the risk. There are no easy ethical answers. Dilemmas, discussions, and debates are inevitable. But *Roe* and its offspring[134] did not simply defer to the health of a mother, an honest, honorable, and necessary concern. It went much farther in legally dehumanizing the life in the womb. Performing an abortion to safeguard the health of the mother became the standard exception to any state interest in preserving fetal life. Indeed, "health" has been construed so elastically by the Supreme Court and federal circuits that it would include psychological and personal factors to the point where the medical or even social inconvenience of fetal life would suffice for its killing, sometimes by the grisly practice of partial-birth abortion in which the brains of the fetus are literally vacuumed out of the mother's body. Pro-choice proponents are absolutely correct that, as popular attention has turned to the barbarous practice of partial-birth abortion where the body of the baby is partially outside the womb prior to its killing, American voters tend to see it as a practice indistinguishable from infanticide and, as a consequence, look upon abortion with even greater abhorrence.

In the United States, nearly fifty million infants have been aborted since *Roe v. Wade* in 1973. But their lost lives have not been the only tragic consequence of this horrendous decision. The truth has been contorted and distorted into falsehoods and euphemisms. One overwhelming untruth is the claim that *Roe* and abortion in the United States are all about protecting the health of the mother. There are some tragic but rare instances where the health or life of the mother and the life of the baby are directly at loggerheads, but medical practice over many decades has established procedures and protocols to reduce dramatically the instances where a Solomonic either–or decision must be made. *Roe* is instead about *elective* abortion, that is, abortion-on-demand, when for some personal, social, economic, or generic health reason (for example, the possibility of depression), the mother decides against bringing a child into the world. The language of Planned Parenthood and the highly lucrative abortion industry is plain: No unwanted children are to be brought into the world. The banner of all who recognize the sanctity of human life is just the opposite: No child brought into the world must ever be unwanted.

Another example of obscuring the truth lies in the euphemism about being "pro-choice." Invariably, politicians will speak grandiosely about protecting a woman's "right to choose." They will never conclude the sentence. Every student is taught in elementary school the difference between transitive and intransitive verbs. A transitive verb such as "choose" takes an object. The subject is to choose something. A waitress serving a customer in a restaurant would be quite frustrated if, instead of ordering something, the customer simply glanced at the menu and kept repeating, "I'm pro-choice." Well, the choice is beef, chicken, fish, or shut up.

When the consequences of a choice are shown to be grisly and de-humanizing, the putative open-mindedness of a pro-choice position vanishes. It is especially sobering when it becomes clear that what is involved is the terminating of a human life. It is not merely "the pregnancy" that is terminated; it is the innocent fetus whose life is snuffed out. Whatever euphemism is chosen or sidestepped, the operative meaning is to kill, a reality intuitively present for all, an image which naturally produces squeamishness. It is part of our humanity that we recognize threats against it.

This in itself provides a lesson that we will explore in our next chapter: human beings are naturally inclined toward basic human goods such as the truth. When ordinary language conveys clearly and simply that choices violate basic human goods, such as the life of an innocent party, our patterns of speech become convoluted. We are not comfortable in speaking the truth to one another. Euphemisms, fig leaves, circumlocutions, and, ultimately, silence will become the manner and content of our discourse with each other.

FROM EUGENICS TO GENETICS TO "NEWGENICS": THREE GENERATIONS OF IMBECILES

We began this chapter by looking at the horrendous case of *Buck v. Bell*, legitimizing the involuntary sterilization of a harmless woman in the Commonwealth of Virginia who enjoyed the ordinary pleasures of domestic life with a religious and loving family. We have seen the research of legal scholars detailing how accusations of feeble-mindedness against Carrie Buck and her family were trumped up, ideologically fueled drivel to create a test case legitimizing eugenics. A recent study of eugenics by

Eugene Black, suitably entitled *War against the Weak*, summarizes the awful impact of *Buck:*

> By the late 1920s, the Carnegie Institution had confirmed by its own investigations what many in the scientific world and society at large had long been saying: that the eugenic science it helped create was a fraud. Nevertheless, Carnegie allowed its Cold Spring Harbor enterprise to supply the specious information needed to validate Virginia's legal crusade to sterilize Carrie Buck. Relying on . . . pseudoscience and his own prejudices, U.S. Supreme Court Justice Oliver Wendell Holmes had established the law of the land. . . . With Holmes' decision in hand, Carnegie's Cold Spring Harbor enterprise had unleashed a national campaign to reinforce long dormant state laws, enact new ones, and dramatically increase the number of sterilizations across America. Sterilizations multiplied, marriage restrictions were broadened. Hundreds of thousands were never born. Untold numbers never married. The intent had been to stop the reproduction of targeted non-Nordic groups and others considered unfit.[135]

Holmes clearly agreed with the ideology of eugenics and ratified its ghastly practice. He had decried the ideology of "sanctity of contract" imposed through substantive due process in *Lochner* but sanctioned the ideology of eugenics in *Buck v. Bell*, ignoring the pertinent constitutional safeguards of the Fourteenth Amendment—equal protection and due process—readily applicable to Carrie Buck's impoverished, vulnerable condition. With juridical legerdemain, Holmes attempted to conceal his ideology but laid the groundwork for the ideology of reproductive rights in future decisions of the Supreme Court. The jurisprudence of *privacy* brought to a new century and a new millennium a radically different paradigm of marriage, family, sex, reproduction, contraception, sterilization, and abortion. Our homes are deeply influenced by the culture of eugenics and the legacy of *Buck v. Bell*. In fact, the desire to regulate offspring in conformity with subjective, arbitrary standards has never been greater.

The same author of this exhaustive study coins the term *newgenics* to draw stunning parallels to the present and suggest what lies ahead:

> Today's headline is tomorrow's footnote. In 1978 Louise Brown became the world's first test-tube baby and a braver new world shuddered. Since then, *in vitro* fertilization has become common

reproductive therapy. In 1997, Dolly the cloned Scottish sheep captured cover stories and stirred acrimonious debate across the world. Shortly after that, several cows were cloned in Japan. . . . In 1998 the Chinese government launched a program to clone its pandas. . . . Virginia scientists cloned five pigs. Entire menageries are in various stages of being cloned, from monkeys to mastodons to family pets. . . . Human clones are next.[136]

As scientists and prospective parents discuss genetic preferences for offspring, settling not only on sex selection but, as technology increases, with the power to suppress harmful genes and reconfigure genetic material to maximize desired outcomes, a strange thing has happened. The world is experiencing a global baby bust. That is exactly the title of a recent scholarly article in *Foreign Affairs* which describes how the rate of world population growth has decreased by nearly 50 per cent since the 1960s. The incidence of birth rates is in free fall. As the population of countries age in a setting where fewer and fewer young people exist, the quality of life of entire civilizations is very much at risk.[137] The paths of sterilization, contraception, and abortion have led the United States and much of the West to what the distinguished jurist and Harvard Professor Mary Ann Glendon rightly terms a demographic winter. Holmes imported an ideology and ignored constitutional safeguards of human rights. From a purely analytical standpoint, his egregious work was the ideal prelude to the reasoning of *Korematsu* and *Roe v. Wade*, substantive due process in its rawest form.

Justice Holmes famously justified his 1927 *Buck* decision with the acid remark that three generations of imbeciles are enough. It is now approximately three generations since the Supreme Court legitimized and virtually institutionalized involuntary sterilization as a part of the ideology of eugenics. At the risk of breaching a compact of civility, one can only ask, who are the real imbeciles in all of this?

FOUR

THE RECOVERY OF VIRTUE: FROM AUTONOMY TO THEONOMY

Debates over autonomy and heteronomy, faith and reason, are ultimately an argument over God—God's existence and impact upon humankind. The contemporary proponents of a humanism exclusive of the transcendent are as forceful today as were Hume and Hobbes during the Enlightenment. Atheism has not only captured a significant niche in the media but essentially claims that science has refuted any reputable claims of religious belief. And yet, religious belief is not without its own scholarly adherents as well.[138]

What matters for our discussion is that in our critique of Enlightenment-based autonomy we not neglect the very legitimate sense of inherent autonomy proposed and supported by the disciplines of philosophy, religion, and theology. When autonomy is formed and focused in correlation with basic human goods it can reflect human striving in and for excellence. But if there is a divorce of subjective from objective, of faith from reason, of individual from community, of sex from marriage, and of marriage from family, the reciprocity of subject and object, faith and reason, marriage and family will leave one aspect of the configuration—namely, autonomy—inflated and unfocused. Autonomy is only a problem when it leads to anomie. Autonomy cannot simply be a claim of power but rather a value at the service of personal identity and human communion. Understood fully, autonomy is a value at the service of virtue.

Cardinal Christoph Schönborn, the archbishop of Vienna and general editor of the *Catechism of the Catholic Church*, has written helpfully on the issue of causality as traditionally understood by philosophy and the distortion of that understanding by imperious and unfounded claims that purport to be scientific:

> Modern science first excludes *a priori* final and formal causes,
> then investigates nature under the reductive mode of mechanism

97

(efficient and material causes), and then turns around to claim both final and formal causes are obviously unreal, and also that its mode of knowing the corporeal world takes priority over all other forms of human knowledge. Being mechanistic, modern science is also historicist: It argues that a complete description of the efficient and material causal history of an entity is a complete explanation of the entity itself—in other words, that an understanding of how something *came to be* is the same as understanding *what it is*. But Catholic thinking rejects the genetic fallacy applied to the natural world and contains instead a holistic understanding of reality based on all the faculties of reason and *all* the causes evident in nature—including the "vertical" causation of formality and finality.[139]

When the role of God is reduced to that of prime mover or uncaused cause through the lens of efficient causality, the wonder of creation and the adventure of being human are irreparably lost. Karen Armstrong summarizes the profound scholarship of Bernard Lonergan that connected the subtlety of human inquiry with its ultimate target, the divine:

In *Insight: A Study of Human Understanding* (1957), [Lonergan] argued that knowledge required more than simply "taking a look." It demanded *in*-sight, an ability to see into an object and contemplate it in its various modes: mathematical, scientific, artistic, moral, and finally metaphysical. Continually we find that something eludes us: it urges us to move on further if we wish to become wise. In all cultures, humans have been seized by the same imperatives—to be intelligent, responsible, reasonable, and loving, and, if necessary, to change. All this pulls us into the realm of the transcendental, the Real and Unconditioned, which in the Christian world is called "God."[140]

CREATION, REDEMPTION, AND COMMUNION: A CHRISTIAN TRIFECTA FOR HUMAN DIGNITY

Lonergan's point has direct application to the highly charged issues of morality and social policy on which a great deal of polarization exists. There is for all mortals a pull into "the realm of the transcendental, the Real and the Unconditioned." This pull—that is, attraction, inclination, yearning, eros—points to a much firmer foundation for human dignity than a hollowed-out autonomy. We have seen that proponents of a robust theory of autonomy such as Kant have seen Enlightenment autonomy as the key to promoting human dignity: the more autonomy, the more dignity. But if Lonergan and the Judeo-Christian tradition are right, this pull toward transcendence must at the very least be included in the framework of human dignity. To go even further, an exclusion of that pull will distort or diminish the framework of human dignity. It is not reasonable simply to assume that *any* assertion of autonomy thereby advances or grounds the dignity of the person. Lonergan's "pull" suggests that a participated theonomy—the human participation in the providential plan of God—is the surest and richest basis for human dignity at its fullest.

The late Pope John Paul II, a leading participant in and subsequent interpreter of Vatican II, described "the dignity of *the person*" as "the most precious possession of *an individual*."[141] This language resonates with the contributions of the Thomistic philosopher Jacques Maritain who distinguished between *individual* and *person*. A subject can be understood as an individual in those categories that are properly quantifiable such as calculating the per capita payment of taxes by citizens. But a subject is truly a person in regard to all topics that cannot be reduced to calculation or quantity. Dignity is such a category. It is a qualitative reality, often intangible, that defies calculation. When an affront occurs to someone's dignity it is the entire being of the *person* that is affected, not merely a part.

Is autonomy the only real basis for the dignity of the person? The post-Vatican II development of Catholic teaching holds that the ultimate foundation for the dignity of the person is not merely a philosophical concept such as autonomy but a theological identity: "The dignity of the person is manifested in all its radiance when the person's origin and destiny are considered: created by God in his image and likeness as well as redeemed by the most precious blood of Christ, the person is called to be a 'child in the Son' and a living temple of the Spirit, destined for eternal life of blessed communion with God."[142]

The three points that define the plane of dignity for every person are thus creation, redemption, and a call to communion with God. J. Brian Benestad notes that this threefold foundation means that the perfection of human dignity must always be sought:

> This threefold foundation for human dignity (creation, redemption, and the call to communion with God) is both unshakable and instructive. No act of the human person can remove this

foundation. Even when people commit the worst sins and crimes and suffer diminished physical and spiritual capacities they retain human dignity. While informed Christians often acknowledge and emphasize this Christian teaching about the permanent character of human dignity, rarely do Catholics hear that human dignity is also a goal or an achievement. But this perfection of human dignity is the clear implication of the threefold foundation of human dignity.[143]

Clearly the destiny of human dignity must be linked with its origin. It is not sufficient to ascertain a basis for dignity without identifying a direction toward its completion or perfection. The Catholic trifecta of creation, redemption and communion with God provides an intelligible and powerful explanation of where human dignity can be said to begin (in the creation of the human being who bears the image of the divine) and find its fulfillment (in eternal communion with God).

While freedom is inarguably a good, enormously valuable in its exercise and potential, the freedom of autonomy requires a map itself (to recall Schumacher) if we are to understand it accurately. Is autonomy principally a matter of freedom *from* something or freedom *for* something? Is it freedom for or from some*one*? Is autonomy an end in itself or does it serve another purpose such as truth? These questions have to be identified and answered for human freedom to serve the needs of humanity.

To put some flesh on the bones of Lonergan's pull, we will now look in depth at the theological template of natural inclinations. It remains to be seen whether autonomy, through its champions of science and instrumental reason, provides a sufficient basis for human desires of love, friendship, and communion. If eros summarizes the restlessness of the human heart, we must consider with Saint Augustine whether that restlessness can be resolved apart from God.

SERVAIS PINCKAERS: A THOMISTIC *RESSOURCEMENT*

A distinguished Catholic moral theologian, Servais Pinckaers, OP, wrote eloquently about the possibility and indeed the need for an authentic Christian humanism. Pinckaers, a Belgian theologian and emeritus professor of moral theology at the University of Fribourg, Switzerland, has identified two stages in the elaboration of theology: "To affirm and defend the superiority of the wisdom of God, communicated through faith, over all human knowledge and wisdom, particularly by resisting the autonomy and anthropocentrism they inculcate; [and] . . . to work in the pure light of faith joined to reason, for the forming of a Christian wisdom, which will be the fruit of the believing mind and will witness the truth of the Gospel to all people and all tenets. This is what we may call authentic Christian human-ism."[144]

It was a profound hostility to the Catholic Church and Catholic theology that fueled the Enlightenment, especially in its French variation. Similar and perhaps even greater suspicions abound about faith—and the Catholic Church in particular—today. But in attempting, following the path of Pinckaers and others, to identify an authentic Christian humanism that succeeds in reconciling faith and reason while establishing a truly life-giv-ing, love-affirming appreciation of eros, it is not necessary to ask the reader to check reason at the door. Quite the contrary, insofar as an authentic Christian humanism can be found, one also discovers that it contains self-correcting components, alerting us when the fragile balance of faith and reason is in jeopardy. The Catholic sensibility, as evidenced by Gothic cathedrals displaying both gargoyles and saints, is always both–and; there is a need for both faith and reason, both scripture and tradition, both con-science and Church teaching.

Pinckaers makes the point throughout his groundbreaking study of Catholic moral theology, *The Sources of Christian Ethics*, first published in French in 1985, that a full account of humanity requires consideration of the divine. A standard greater than the human is needed to understand and take the measure of humanity. Pinckaers is not making a novel point here. Countless Christian theologians, especially the spiritual and intellec-tual mentor of Pinckaers, Saint Thomas Aquinas (1224–74), have elabo-rated classically and brilliantly on the point that the path to full discovery of our human nature requires a Godward trajectory.[145] It may be that Pinck-aers's greatest contribution is not the novelty of his approach, since it rests on thirteenth-century foundations, but on the timely imagination of his *ressourcement*, that is, a return to time-tested sources and engagement of classic wisdom with contemporary concerns in a setting where classical wisdom—the secular teleology of Aristotle and the theological anthropol-ogy of Aquinas—are desperately needed.

This affirmation of the divine as essential to comprehending the human flows directly from the affirmation of Vatican II in the *Pastoral Constitution on the Church in the Modern World* (a document readily and more easily known by its Latin title, *Gaudium et Spes*, "Joy and Hope"), n. 22, often cited by scholars as the key to Pope John Paul II's understanding of Vatican II: "In reality it is only in the mystery of the Word made flesh that the mystery of man truly becomes clear."[146]

Is not such a statement offensive to non-Christians? How could a church be so arrogant as to suggest that it is Christ who provides the template for understanding *all* human beings? When Christian tradition is allowed to speak at its best, it is clear that neither arrogance nor condescension is present. Yes, the Christian tradition believes that God becoming incarnate in the person of Jesus Christ has changed history and provides the ultimate narrative of authentic human life. If it is arrogant to say that Christ has affected the life of all, regardless of whether individuals believe in Him or not, then by analogy it would also be impertinent to say that the sun affects every living person, regardless of their opinion on sunlight.

This text from Vatican II (1962–65) finds its way into nearly every magisterial document of Pope John Paul II because he was convinced of the need to link ethical issues with a theological anthropology, a bonding of identity with teleology (goal-driven choices) in human beings.

Gaudium et Spes, n. 22 states that Christ the Lord "in revealing the mystery of the Father and his love fully reveals man to himself and makes clear his supreme calling."[147] Again, we can concede that some are stunned by what might be perceived as the arrogance of this claim—Christ changes the life of everyone. But any Christian, Catholic or otherwise, can go nowhere else but toward this truth. Either Christ is the Son of God, intimately involved in our very creation, redemption, and call to communion, or He is something less and other than divine. This is an affirmation not about the power of the Church, the struggling and hurting body of Christ, but about the power of Christ.

Note the implicit premises of this declaration from Vatican II. Human beings not only have the capacity but the desire for self-knowledge and this self-awareness leads to the discovery of a calling or vocation based on divine love. It is this vocation to love that marks off the proper boundaries of authentic autonomy, its limits and also its possibilities.

This ringing restatement of the Christian tradition—that it is impossible to comprehend the full scope of humanity without taking God into account—represents the exact antithesis of the "God is dead" view of Friedrich Nietzsche in the nineteenth century that demanded the "death" (conceptually) of God as a prerequisite for understanding humankind. Because of erroneous philosophical presuppositions, Nietzsche believed that the interests of the divine and the human were on a collision course. To borrow a quotation from Winston Churchill, never has the opposite of the truth been stated with more precision. The Enlightenment project of separating reason from faith and revelation proves the point. The fulminations of the encyclopedists against religion led to the events and excesses of the French Revolution, such as the September Massacres and the Reign of Terror. The rise of a survival-of-the-fittest brand of social Darwinism, laying the groundwork for the eugenics movement and Nietzsche's theory of the superman, were ruthlessly exploited by Hitler to inflict incredible harm upon millions of innocent people in the Holocaust and World War II.

Can we say that the world is more intelligible or decipherable since the Enlightenment and Nietzsche or that the concept of autonomy has safeguarded the dignity of the individual? "At the end of the nineteenth century, philosopher Friedrich Nietzsche provided the West with the most ruthless account of the meaningless universe. Taking both Schopenhauer and Darwin to heart, Nietzsche proudly declared that all philosophy, all religion, all science, all literature, all art were only so many desperate attempts to paint meaning on a meaningless cosmic canvas. We must 'recognize untruth as a condition of life,' he explained, and all attempts to portray truth are merely fictions masking the will to power."[148]

The effort begun in the eighteenth century to elevate reason and separate it from faith, revelation, or theology has failed dramatically to deliver on its promise of greater freedom and meaning. A return to and recovery of classic fonts of wisdom on the meaning of human beings could not be more urgent today. It is this *ressourcement* that we begin.

PINCKAERS, NATURAL INCLINATIONS, AND A THEOLOGICAL ANTHROPOLOGY

Drawing from and distilling the classic work of Saint Thomas Aquinas, Pinckaers identifies five inclinations or tendencies that characterize all of humanity. These tendencies or dispositions did not happen by accident but reflect the benign will of a loving Creator. These inclinations not only describe the optimal goals of human life but serve as principles for practical reason, that is, they are foundational for making practical judgments about worthy ends and suitable means in everyday human choices. They could be understood as hard-wired in humanity, inscribed universally in human consciousness.

It must be emphasized that all of these inclinations describe the person as a rational agent with free will. The subject of creation, *Homo sapiens*, is not a puppet of a disembodied deity but truly and fully a partner in creation. Insofar as the person shares in the *imago Dei*, the very image of God, he or she bears an understanding and capacity for wisdom consonant with humanity at its most profound and authentic. A great saint, Irenaeus of Lyons (c. AD 200), put it well: "The glory of God is humanity fully alive." Humanity does not need Prometheus to steal fire from the gods, as in Greek mythology, because a loving God has already endowed humankind with the awareness to discover and use fire. The Creator has also given to humanity the ability to use fire either for constructive or destructive purposes. We are rational creatures with free will, to our honor or shame.

The five natural inclinations found in Aquinas and distilled powerfully by Pinckaers are listed by him in his *The Sources of Christian Ethics*:

1. The inclination to the good
2. The inclination to self-preservation
3. The inclination to sexual union and the rearing of offspring
4. The inclination to the knowledge of truth
5. The inclination to live in society

> These inclinations, serving as principles for the practical reason, were comparable to the first principles of speculative reason. According to St. Thomas they were self-evident to all human beings, before any research and formulation had taken place; they were known intuitively, as it were. They served as premises, on which all reasonings and questionings about human goods were based. Doubtless not everyone managed to formulate these principles explicitly; some might even deny the propositions they expressed. Nonetheless, the inclinations existed and were active even when denied, for their profound influence was unaffected by the surface agitation of ideas.[149]

This Thomistic template provides us with a theological anthropology that highlights the unity, rational nature, and self-transcending capacities of the person. When Pinckaers, drawing from the Thomistic tradition, speaks of "natural inclinations," it is important to note that *natural* means pertaining to the nature, essence, or being of an individual, a subject, and, in particular, a person. Many otherwise knowledgeable scholars have confused the Hobbesian "state of nature" ugliness sketched in *The Leviathan* with natural law, as though natural law were somehow a description of life in the raw. We will shortly look further at what *natural law* means in a Thomistic context, but for the moment our task is to identify the meaning of *natural inclinations*.

If, for Pinckaers, *natural* means pertaining to the very being of a person, it is by definition ontological. It is not incidental, accidental, or contingent but resides at the very core of a human being, the being of a person. As such, this natural or ontological quality transcends any physical, biological, ethnic, racial, gender, cultural, or other demographic divider. These natural inclinations constitute together a constant of human well-being. By way of example, a blind person is naturally inclined toward the basic human good of sight. Indeed, the person without sight probably values the importance of vision more than those who are sighted. But the physical incapacity in no way invalidates the natural inclination to a basic human good.

For someone with a handicap, which really includes everyone in the last analysis, the fifth natural inclination described by Pinckaers, to live in society, has direct application to the quest for communion that characterizes all of humanity, the eros or craving for meaning, acceptance, and fulfillment. True communion of life and love (a theological view) or solidarity (an ethical view) is the complete antithesis of the Enlightenment ethic of absolute autonomy. Apart from self-interest, the Enlightenment could specify no reason to love. Kant considered love to be a mere emotion.

What is the force of *inclination* in the term under consideration? As with *natural*, it is ontological, having a realism and purposefulness that pertain to the very core or essence of a person. The trajectory of the inclination points toward a destiny descriptive of one's identity. If we are naturally inclined toward the good (that is, whatever is morally good and the whole range of basic human goods), it means that we are beings who fundamentally and interiorly aspire to genuine good. It means that we cannot be radically corrupt if we are naturally inclined or disposed toward what is good. It means that this inclination toward the good is apparently shared as a human aspiration, meaning that we cannot divide humanity into two categories of good and evil, saintly and depraved. We are not Manichaean. Calling it an "inclination" implies that we have a distance to go before we can reach it but that we are *ab initio* oriented toward the right goal.

This concept of inclination necessarily imports the reality of God. If the Thomistic template of Pinckaers is correct, and both logic and experience have classically validated it, then our inclinations are not accidents but the result of a Supreme Being causing all human beings to be naturally inclined to excellence, the good in its varied forms. This is a quality of human nature that resides at the core of all human desire and aspiration.

It is virtually self-evident that all of us are inclined toward basic human goods. How did this happen? Granted, we have not yet attempted a definition of the good, but we have a sense that sight is a good and blindness is not; hearing is a good and deafness is not; friendship is a good and loneliness is not. Contrary to Nietzsche's view, human needs, desires, and aspirations are not on a collision course with a sense of the divine but aim for a fulfillment that actually transcends human limits. Creation, redemption, and the call to communion are a story of human searching and divine responsiveness, not futility.

Moreover, the sense of good that Pinckaers, following Aquinas, puts first on the list of natural inclinations is inherently a signal of the transcendent. If we reach a point at which we say, this is all the good we can have, and go no further, then it ceases to be a good. Having been confined or curtailed, the good in question is no longer unbounded or open-ended. The boundary or limit may actually oppose a genuine growth of change and transformation. An exclusively human good would not be *capax Dei*— open and receptive to God. The transcendent, essentially shorthand for God, is necessary for individuals to orient their choices in a direction fully consonant with their well-being, which is, in a sense, also unbounded because it is *capax Dei*.

The political philosopher Leo Strauss linked the importance of discovering the good with divine revelation: "Man cannot live without light, guidance, knowledge; only through knowledge of the good can he find the good that he needs. The fundamental question, therefore, is whether men can acquire that knowledge of the good without which they cannot guide their lives individually or collectively by the unaided efforts of their natural powers, or whether they are dependent for that knowledge on Divine Revelation. No alternative is more fundamental than this: human guidance or divine guidance."[150]

Pinckaers and Thomistic realism argue that the philosophical quest for the good requires the assistance of divine revelation because the good touches on the transcendent—grace and mystery—realities that cannot be fully understood apart from revelation.

Is this claim—that revelation is needed—simply an appeal to the "God of the gaps" to supply or complete arguments otherwise unavailable? Once again, Leo Strauss provides an elaborate and intricate argument not only that revelation can never be dismissed but also that the very possibility of revelation refutes the sufficiency of philosophy or science in the broadest sense:

> All arguments in favor of revelation seem to be valid only if belief in revelation is presupposed; and all arguments against revelation seem to be valid only if unbelief is presupposed. This state of things would appear to be but natural. Revelation is always so uncertain to unassisted reason that it can never compel the assent of unassisted reason, and man is so built that he can find his satisfaction, his bliss, in free investigation, in articulating the riddle of being. But, on the other hand, he yearns so much for a solution of that riddle and human knowledge is always so limited that the need for divine illumination cannot be denied and the possibility of revelation cannot be refuted. Now it is this state of things that seems to decide irrevocably against philosophy and in favor of revelation. Philosophy has to grant that revelation is possible. But to grant that revelation is possible means to grant that philosophy is perhaps not the one thing needful, that philosophy is perhaps something infinitely unimportant. To grant that revelation is possible means to grant that the philosophic life is not necessarily, not evidently, *the* right life. Philosophy, the life devoted to the quest for evident knowledge available to man as man, would itself rest on an unevident, arbitrary, or blind decision. This would merely confirm the thesis of faith, that there is no possibility of consistency, of a consistent and thoroughly sincere life, without belief in revelation. The mere fact that philosophy and revelation cannot refute each other would constitute the refutation of philosophy by revelation.[151]

The five natural inclinations proposed by Aquinas proceed along the course of a typical human life. As the subject matures, he or she realizes the difference between good and evil. A fundamental awareness arises that good is to be done and evil to be avoided. It is good to be alive. Secondly, it is good to do everything to preserve one's existence, health, and well-being. Third, the awareness of a fundamental difference of male and female coincides with a desire for sexual union and the realization that human life is transmitted through this sexual union, itself an inclination to something good, whereby children are understood irreducibly to be a blessing and benefit regardless of costs or sacrifices that may be involved in rearing them. Fourth, one is inclined to learn as much as possible about these realities, discovering that mistakes can profitably yield truths to take to heart so that mistakes need not be repeated. Fifth, the natural inclination to live in society means that our inherent social identity asserts itself; it is not good for anyone to be alone. If we are to live together, it is better to do so in peace and harmony, working together for the goods to which all peoples are "naturally inclined," so that shared truths about a common good can inform individuals, families, neighborhoods, communities, and nations about human well-being.

The ultimate instance of goodness is divine goodness, a reality found in the definitive disclosure of divine identity and love in Jesus Christ, as affirmed by *Gaudium et Spes*, n. 22 cited above. It was a former opponent of Christ, Saul of Tarsus, who came to the conclusion that if Christ were not truly raised from the dead, then all faith in Him would be in vain (1 Corinthians 15:12–14). No Christian could possibly depart from this hard-earned wisdom of Saint Paul. It is a matter of both faith and reason, working together in harmony, that one life has redefined the meaning and measure of all lives.

The five natural inclinations provided by Saint Thomas Aquinas, recovered and renewed through the contemporary scholarship of Servais Pinckaers and others, present a philosophical portrait of human striving, singly and communally. Together they describe what all of us seek and need—a natural inclination to life renewed by love. The Christian tradition affirms that this urgent necessity arises only in the context of an encounter with Jesus Christ, an encounter of reason and faith, without prejudice to either, and with the fruitfulness of a friendship that overcame both sin and death, a friendship that makes it possible for human beings to enjoy authentic communion beyond the atomism of a desiccated autonomy and to be transformed by the transcendent—grace and mystery.

PERSONAL IDENTITY, LAW, AND HAPPINESS

Is there something more to one's personal identity than our sexual desire or behavior? To ask the question is to answer it: of course there is. In looking at the Thomistic template of natural inclinations, we can discover how admirably eros or sexual desire and the yearning for completion can be integrated into a life of authentic striving for the true, the good, and the beautiful, all of which are transcendental realities that lead powerfully to God.[152]

The reader can best understand the richness of Pinckaers's

ressourcement of natural inclinations by reading his *The Sources of Christian Ethics*. It is a truly masterful, magisterial synthesis of Catholic moral theology in a way that will engage the intellectual interest of anyone serious about ethics. The brief effort in the following pages to summarize the work of Pinckaers and then appropriate it to specific issues of sexual ethics may fail either to summarize or characterize Pinckaers correctly, that is, as according to the intent and meaning of Pinckaers himself. Accordingly, I must take responsibility for any unintended divergences from his incredibly powerful reflection.

Pinckaers is especially concerned to show that a love and pursuit of what is truly good exemplifies human freedom at its best. The moral law is not coercive, for we have the ability to pursue evil and avoid good, the opposite of the primary principle of the natural law: we are not *forced* to seek good. Nevertheless, any violation of the moral law does have consequences: a husband who fails to love his neighbor or his wife will have neither a happy neighborhood nor a happy home.

Perhaps a popular tale of human foolishness will illustrate, in a pedestrian way, what Pinckaers details with scholarly precision. Two rubes in a truck came to an overhead bridge. A sign said, "Height Limit: 10' 6"." The two got out and measured the truck's height, which came to twelve feet. They contemplated their dilemma. Then the driver looked at his buddy and said, "Come on, we can make it. Nobody's watching."

The natural law is not a barrier mandated by an outside source to prevent us from driving our vehicle where we wish. Instead, the natural law is a measure of whether a worthy goal, moving from point A to point B, can be achieved with the particular means chosen. The moral dynamism flows from within the subject's need rather than from some external command. The natural law does not fall afoul of the Enlightenment demand for autonomy, but, reflecting authentic human goods, it shows a different model of autonomy, a participated theonomy or freedom for excellence open to the divine—an identity linked with needs, reciprocal or mutual goods, and the larger community.

It is necessary to situate Saint Thomas's concept of law in general, and natural law in particular, within his overall theological framework. Recall that the famous definition of law given by Saint Thomas—"an ordinance of reason, promulgated by one who cares for the community, for the benefit of the common good"—is found in the section of the *Summa* that directs the believer toward happiness. Saint Thomas is here taking a path already traveled preeminently by Aristotle five centuries before Christ. We begin to discern that law is not an end in itself but an instrumental good designed to lead one to happiness. Happiness can never be reduced to conformity to a code, as some uninformed critics claim Christianity professes. It is truly the total ensemble of all available goods for the person, the *totum bonum* of human flourishing.

While Thomas draws happily and heavily upon Aristotle as a philosophical mentor, the Christian understanding of happiness developed by Saint Thomas and the Christian tradition locates the *totum bonum* of human realization squarely within the beatific vision, the encounter of the believer with God. This notion of happiness is sharply at variance with hedonistic conceptions of happiness that reduce it to a psychological condition. For Thomas, happiness is fundamentally a spiritual reality that embraces the entire person. It includes the psychological and physical dimensions of well-being but can never be reduced to them.

Saint Thomas first follows and then develops the work of Aristotle on happiness:

> Now the first principle in practical matters, which are the object of the practical reason, is the last end: and the last end of human life is bliss or happiness. . . . Consequently the law must regard principally the relationship to happiness. Moreover, since every part is ordained to the whole, as imperfect to perfect; and since one man is a part of the perfect community, the law must regard properly the relationship to universal happiness. Wherefore the Philosopher [Aristotle], in the above definition of legal matters mentions both happiness and the body politic, for he says (*Nicomachean Ethics*, v. 1) that we call those legal matters "just, which are adapted to produce and preserve happiness and its parts for the body politic": since the state is a perfect community, as he says in his *Politics*, i, 1.[153]

Several themes emerge from this approach to natural law. There is an awareness that any rule, to qualify as a genuine law, must be an ordinance of reason. Since a law is considered a rule or measure of human acts, it is intrinsically linked to practical reason, the template of ethical choices. Any expression or articulation of a rule that purports to be a law, if shown to violate reason, fails in fact to qualify as a law.

In addition to the theme of reasonableness, there is the link of the law with happiness. It is a reasoned and reasonable measure of human acts oriented toward the happiness of the subject. In this sense, the law is an interior reality, connecting the nature or core being of the subject with the *totum bonum* or ensemble of basic human goods the realization of which produces happiness for the creature.

The law has a communal dimension to it. As an ordinance of reason it is oriented toward the common good and promulgated or made known by one who has the responsibility of caring for the community. If we apply this perspective on law to sexual ethics, we must conclude that all moral activity, including sexual desire and actions, has a communal dimension. Again, this is not to say that human behavior is automatically or mechanically to be in conformity to a communal ideal or construct. It is to assert, however, that only those actions will bring happiness that are not inconsistent with the common good.

All moral activity is inherently relational. This is especially true in the case of sexual choices where a relationship to another individual is at the core of moral meaning. Even in the case of masturbation there is an image of another that prompts the quest for sexual pleasure. When Genesis states that "it is not good for man to be alone," it is a moral prescription applicable to all sexual activity. The pursuit of isolated pleasure through pornography, masturbation, or any form of self-gratification leaves the subject in a worse situation because an action which is inherently relational has been reduced to an isolated and isolating event.

A telling example of how the Enlightenment standard of autonomy has failed is the addiction to pornography made possible by the Internet. Here happiness is reduced to a psychological or physical level of pleasure that momentarily relieves stress or provides escape through fantasy, but because there is a discontinuity between authentic, inherently relational, other-directed happiness versus a self-centered, isolating act that seeks happiness in a solitary way, something less than and different from real happiness is the result.

Instances of self-gratification through pornography and masturbation are not only isolated acts; they are *isolating* acts. They leave the subject with a false sense or counterfeit of a basic human good. This explains why individuals are so often troubled by feelings of hollowness, guilt, and shame after actions of solitary self-gratification. To those who say that pornography or masturbation are harmless, suitably private phenomena, there is the sad but indisputable rebuttal that individuals who persist in patterns of solitary sexual self-gratification have the experience of relating to others in a troubled way. No spouse can measure up to a sexual ideal fantasized by hypersexualized erotic images. Moreover, evidence abounds that spouses who spend considerable time in Internet chat rooms fail to communicate as often or as effectively with their mates. Pornography illustrates how autonomy becomes anomie, destroying the relational dimension of eros.

Carefully consider the works of Saint Thomas as he cites Aristotle's *Nicomachean Ethics* and the *Politics*. Ever the wise and empathetic commentator, Saint Thomas simply states Aristotle's view, expressed in the *Politics*, that the state is a "perfect community," which doesn't mean for Aristotle that it is flawless, but that it has the potential to complete or perfect the goals and desires of its subjects, the citizens of the *polis*. Saint Thomas writes eighteen centuries later in a much different setting than fifth-century-BC Athens. The impact of Christ and His revealed truth have broken forth into the consciousness of the Christian community. But Thomas doesn't scruple to "correct" Aristotle on his claim that the state is a "perfect community," even though Thomas knew full well that the Greek *polis* of Aristotle's era would not have been aware of Christ and would in fact have paid some kind of obeisance to the Greek deities. What matters to us is that Saint Thomas does not accept unreservedly the philosophical perspective of Aristotle, but he refrains from making gratuitous criticisms or pointing out readily apparent disparities between the pagan and the Christian view.

Why is this important to note? Many critics of Saint Thomas claim that he blindly or slavishly follows Aristotle, confusing philosophy with theology and mixing paganism with Christianity. The truth is quite different. Like the master of the household described by Christ (Matthew 13:52), Thomas brings out of his treasure the best of the old, reason as yet unaided by revelation, and the best of the new, a sense that communion rests in Christ and far transcends the limits of any state. Aristotle was certainly not a theocrat, nor is Thomas. Both were aware that we ignore the common good and the communal dimension of sex at our own peril.

In speaking of the last end of human beings, happiness, and ordering his treatment of morality and law toward that last or all-encompassing end, we can productively make reference to a medieval dispute that bears directly on our contemporary concerns. Simon Tugwell describes the clash of viewpoints within the Dominican order on what exactly constituted the content of happiness:

> The point was raised formally in a medieval controversy about
> the essential content of heavenly bliss. Durandus of St. Pourçain,
> a Dominican noted for his opposition to orthodox Thomism,

maintained that what the blessed enjoy immediately and directly
is not God, but their own vision of God. He suggests a compar-
ison with a man's love of wine: it is not the wine, as such, that
satisfies him, but his drinking of the wine. This view is very
firmly refused by Meister Eckhart, who is followed and, indeed,
quoted on the matter by Blessed Henry Suso. The reflex movement of self-consciousness would be a distraction from the beatitude of simply knowing God. According to the text in St. John
(17:3), eternal life is in knowing God, not in knowing that we
know God. It is not that we are unconscious of our own knowledge of God or of our own bliss; but the consciousness of ourselves is not the actual object of our bliss, it is not that that
actually makes us happy.

   The danger with our good works, our spiritual accomplishments, and all the rest of it, is that we shall construct out of them
a picture of ourselves in which, effectively, we shall situate our
happiness. Complacency in ourselves will then replace delight
in God.[154]

Both Aristotle and Saint Thomas run through a long list of candi-
dates for happiness that ultimately fall short—including sex, power, fame,
fortune, and health. Saint Thomas holds to the view that only union with
God will suffice to provide authentic happiness for human beings. But Tugwell identifies an insidious counterfeit of this genuine proposition in bringing to our attention the notion that real happiness consists of our being
aware of our happiness, a feeling that replaces the presence of God. There
is nothing medieval about this beguiling error. With the disappearance of
faith in God found in a secularized world view, eros is expected to do the
heavy lifting of search, yearning, seeking, and loving. But eros, as Allan
Bloom described, has been reduced to physical sensation. It is left to do
something vital—the quest for love and communion—but is not empowered for the task. Even devout Christians have forgotten the insistent point
of Saint Thomas and the Judeo-Christian tradition: only the presence of
God generates human happiness.

INCLINATIONS, ENDS, AND GOODS

   The whole point of the natural inclinations is that they rest upon
and flow from an anthropology in which the divine presence is essential.
It is not demeaning to speak of human beings as creatures for that is what
we are. It is a relationship, not merely a status. We are limited, frail and fi-

nite, and dependent upon a Benevolent Presence who does not share our mortal limitations. Those who believe that Jesus of Nazareth is indeed the incarnate expression of that Benevolent Presence and that Jesus reveals this Presence to be his and our Father, take the point that any purported content of happiness, short of the presence of God, will fail as miserably as all of the other flawed contenders. It takes God to make humans happy.

The moral methodology of Saint Thomas and the Catholic tradition is fundamentally teleological or focused on a desirable end—*telos* in the Greek—the pursuit and realization of which provides an instance of a real or basic human good. This is made clear at the very beginning of the section of his *Summa*, the *Prima Secundae*, which begins the study of moral theology. Saint Thomas links anthropology and human choice: "The object of the will is the end and the good. Therefore all human actions are done with an end in view."[155]

These goods or ends are coterminous with our needs. Something that we really need is really good. Something that is really good is probably what we really need, though not in every case. T. S. Eliot gave classic voice to the teleological approach to morality in his *Four Quartets* when he wrote: "What we call the beginning is often the end. And to make an end is to make a beginning. The end is where we start from." The end—good, goal, need—is indeed where we start from as we begin to plan our activities, weigh our choices, and make practical decisions about the linkage of worthy ends and suitable means. It is always wrong to choose directly against an end—good, goal, or need—which is essential to human well-being. For example, I cannot choose to kill my landlord even if I believe him to be cruel and unfeeling. This is not reductively a mandate of church, state, or any external authority but a verifiable proposition of reason: to choose against a good is thereby to choose for an evil—as a defect, excess, or contradiction—and one cannot logically (or morally) choose evil.

Suppose it is said that my landlord is so callous that he does not *deserve* to live, that his life is so tainted by selfishness that the world is a better place without him? A variety of problems are embedded in that possibility, all of which coincide in demonstrating that I cannot murder my landlord. First, and most philosophically, the Latin adage, *Ens et bonum convertuntur*, "Being and the good are interchangeable," reminds us that every instance of being, whether saint or sinner, fool or scholar, is in some way good. The famed transcendentals of Aristotle are convertible: in some way the good, the true, and the beautiful are linked with being. An aspect of each can be found in the other. So to remove that human life is to choose against the good.

Second, even if I am convinced that my wicked landlord does not deserve to live, I have to ask what competency or authority do I have to make such a determination? In stipulating that all human beings are creatures, I must acknowledge as a fellow creature that I lack the moral competency to end a life that I was not responsible for starting.

Third, for those who reject the conclusive wisdom of both philosophy and theology, it is sufficient to point out that in choosing to take the life of another, I am signaling approval of and actually abetting the chain reaction of chaotic, lethal human violence. Gang warfare in major cities is a tragic example of Thomas Hobbes's *Leviathan*, a war of all against all. The remedy for violence cannot be found only in a social contract, whether of Rousseau or Rawls, because that secular contract still entertains the spurious and emotionally charged claim that some lives deserve to be protected while others do not. All life is sacred, without exception.

There are instances where it may be necessary to sacrifice a real good to be faithful to our spiritual identity. Life, for example, is a basic human good but a fire fighter who enters a burning building to save lives is risking his or her life—*not* committing suicide, for the fire fighter desperately wants to live as well—in order to be faithful to an honorable profession and vocation. The same holds for a physician who treats patients in the midst of an epidemic or a soldier who jumps on a hand grenade in battle to save the lives of comrades.

This means that in order to understand or identify the morality of a particular action—a deed or choice or possibility—we must look at the goal or good, the *telos*, involved. For what purpose are we proposing to do this? To what good or goal is the proposed choice or deed oriented? These questions are pivotal in answering not only the question of what deeds may be done but what kind of person do I propose to be. So much of popular ethical analysis revolves around hard cases and triage hypotheticals with no consideration given to the most important search of all—how we define ourselves as moral agents. What kind of people do we fashion ourselves to be? What truly matters is not a label that someone else attaches to us but our self-definition by way of our moral choices that clearly and unmistakably mark us as good or not, honorable or not, authentic or not.

For Saint Thomas and the Thomistic template of natural inclinations that is part of his theological anthropology, several propositions emerge as conclusively true: (1) A moral law is a measure of human action; it must be reasonable, that is, not in opposition to the real goods to which human beings aspire. (2) Freedom consists in the capacity to pursue a goal or good, a *telos*, that is compatible with the optimal well-being of a subject and ultimately contributes to the subject's happiness. (3) Happiness can be found ultimately only in God. Any claim or candidate for real happiness short of God or incompatible with God will fail.

That is to say, happiness *requires* the friendship of God because any purely human source of happiness is by definition finite and thereby incapable of satisfying human yearnings that are constantly moving beyond a merely human horizon. An example is found in the propensity to forgive. While some may never be inclined to forgive another for an offense, the attractiveness of the chance of forgiveness and reconciliation is never absent from the imagination of even the most hardened or vindictive soul. To forgive is indeed divine; to yearn for forgiveness or to offer it as a gesture of magnanimity is something that moves beyond any rational calculation of self-interest. Forgiveness and reconciliation are rightly regarded as good in themselves and necessary for a truly, fully human experience of transcendent happiness. In this sense, forgiveness is a path that leads toward both transcendence and transformation.

Sexual pleasure has become the runaway secular candidate for happiness. It will provide exactly that—pleasure—but its effect will fall short of authentic happiness if its acquisition is incompatible with the divine plan of sex within a lifetime marital covenant of two individuals of the opposite sex in a union open to the possibility of children. Pleasure is a marvelous, legitimate human good when it is attached to a morally responsible deed. Still, stealing someone else's ice cream cone on a hot July afternoon will taste good for a brief while, but the aftertaste of guilt abbreviates still more the short-term pleasure of the experience.

THE LANGUAGE OF FREEDOM

Because it is a *theological* anthropology in which our consideration of nature, inclinations, and goods occur, we have the freedom to consider larger themes that flow from and touch upon revelation. When Genesis teaches that the human bears the image and likeness of the divine, a truth is proclaimed: in some mysterious way human life is in relationship with the divine. We have seen the teaching of Vatican II that the full measure of humanity is known only in reference to Christ, the enfleshed reality of the divine in earthly experience. Christ personalizes the link between human and divine identified in Genesis when He says in the Gospel that what we do for our neighbors, especially those most vulnerable and at risk, is what we do for Him (Matthew 25:45). The freedom of human beings is a freedom of excellence, the liberty of the children of God. This is the very opposite of Enlightenment Deism.

The final chapter of Servais Pinckaers's *The Sources of Christian Ethics*, is entitled "Natural Inclinations at the Source of Freedom and Morality."[156] Pinckaers is intent on showing that Christian morality is neither static nor legalistic, and that the natural inclinations summarized by Saint Thomas Aquinas in his *Summa Theologica* provide evidence that authentic morality aims at the happiness of both subject and community with a dynamism well-ordered to the respective needs and goods of every human being. It is especially important to look at the foundational inclination to the good insofar as the entire moral enterprise of human beings depends on this starting point. The other four natural inclinations—toward self-preservation, truth, society, and sexual union—depend on the bedrock capacity to know what is true, distinguishing real and apparent goods, and identifying evil as in some way the privation or distortion of what is truly good.

Pinckaers is greatly distressed with Catholic moralists who have subscribed, often unwittingly, to mistaken notions of freedom originating in the nominalism of the fourteenth century. Its impact was not only upon Catholic theology; it influenced the duty-centered views of Kant. Law and obligation have replaced happiness and virtue as the focal point of inquiry in both Catholic and secular spheres. A review of the birth and development of nominalism and philosophers subsequently reliant on Kant, including the Scotsman David Hume, finds that dominant ideas can operate over centuries, growing in importance or application while affecting daily practices on a grand scale.

Pinckaers specifies the problem with nominalism:

> Nominalism instigated a veritable revolution in the structuring
> of moral theology in the fourteenth century, to such a point that
> it created a real break between the preceding centuries and our
> own. . . . Nominalism produced a new concept of freedom as a
> choice between contraries that emanated from the will alone,
> known as freedom of indifference. It removed from the realm
> of freedom every natural inclination, including the desire for
> beatitude as our ultimate end, so essential in St. Thomas. Henceforth this inclination was to be subject to choice between contraries. Nominalism also broke the bonds between freedom and

what could, outside of itself, be based on natural inclinations: reason, law, sensitivity, and other people, even God. Freedom became an enclosed atom, an isolated island, a monad. From that time on, it best affirmed itself by claiming independence of everything other than itself. . . .

For Aquinas, freedom was rooted in the natural inclinations which animate the spiritual human faculties: the inclination to truth for the intellect, to beatitude and goodness for the will, the inclination to live in the society of other persons, the natural desire for God, and so forth. According to Thomas, the human person was not free in spite of these natural inclinations, needing to resist them in order to rule them, but was free precisely because of the natural inclinations to truth, beatitude, and goodness, which opened the mind and heart to infinite dimensions and conferred the ability to freely transcend every limited good.[157]

The separation of freedom from its intrinsic ordering to truth, beatitude, and goodness has greatly impoverished the moral life by removing the rudder from the ship. What is left is a directionless freedom drifting in conformity with changing currents. Nominalism is closely connected with autonomy, maximizing freedom but removing its inclination toward truth, beatitude, and goodness.

Roger Scruton emphasizes how the nominalist turn ultimately destroys clarity in language as well as thought:

So what makes it correct to say that x is green? The realist says: the fact that x *is* green, and so goes round in a circle. The nominalist says something quite different. We regard the use of the word "green" to describe x as a correct use. This is a fact, but it is a fact about *us*. According to the rules of our language, x is correctly classified as green but we could have classified x in a quite different way. Classifications merely gather individuals under a common label, and at some level, all classifications arise from our *decisions*.

[The realist] will argue that our use of language is not arbitrary, but is *constrained* by reality. If we use words as we do, it is because the world constrains our communications. The world contains universals, like redness, which we try to capture in our use of general terms. Moreover, the realist will argue, the nominalist has embarked on a dangerous journey. He seems to tell us that the world depends on language: that we *make* the world

by speaking. Indeed that is what the more radical nominalists
. . . explicitly *say*.[158]

By relying on will rather than reason (namely, *deciding* on a term rather than seeing it as part of reality), nominalism effectively robs us of any confidence that our mental images correspond to realities that exist elsewhere, that is, outside of our mind. A famous exchange between Abraham Lincoln and his Cabinet during the American Civil War illustrates how nominalism works. Ever the scholar of human behavior and language, Lincoln wanted to make the point that terms such as *union* or *emancipation* used by his administration had specific meanings referring to actual events and things, and were not simply abstractions. Lincoln saw the skepticism of members of his Cabinet and asked, "Gentlemen, if we call a horse's tail a hoof, how many hooves would the horse have?" His Cabinet members took the bait, answering, "Five." Lincoln retorted that the correct answer was not five but four hooves because, regardless of what we choose to call it, a horse's tail is still a tail. Lincoln was decidedly not a nominalist. He was, like Thomas Aquinas, a *realist*, holding that a real connection exists between the mind and the thing (*res-realis*) outside of the mind.

Not only do words have meaning but that meaning establishes a correspondence between the mind and the world. To identify the appendage at the rear end of a horse as a tail is not simply indulging a common habit of using a particular term, *tail*, it is an affirmation that this equine appendage truly exists and it rightly identifies an anatomical part not to be confused with a hoof. Words have meaning and meaning is found in the world, disclosing intelligible patterns to rational inquiry. These intelligible patterns are part of creation and essential to the attainment of meaningful freedom. Contemporary philosophers who opt for subjectivism, relativism, nihilism, or deconstructionism choose a path other than realism and are apt to confuse a freedom *for* excellence with a freedom of indifference.

One contemporary philosopher who has brought enormous lucidity to the issues of philosophical nomenclature and the need to anchor terms in empirically verifiable reality is Mortimer J. Adler. Over more than half a century of astute philosophical analysis, serving for many years as Chairman of the Board of Editors of Encyclopaedia Britannica, Adler had a gift for communicating foundational truths in accessible language. His link between needs and goods demonstrates the realist perspective of Aristotle and Aquinas at its contemporary best:

> Our common understanding of needs provides us at once with
> the insight that there are no wrong or misguided needs. That is
> just another way of saying that we never need anything that is
> really bad for us—something we ought to avoid. We recognize
> that we can have wrong or misguided wants. That which we
> want may appear to be good to us at the time, but it may not be
> really good for us. Our needs are never excessive, as our wants
> often are. We can want too much of a good thing, but we can
> never need too much of whatever it is we need. We can certainly
> want more than we need. . . . We cannot ever say that we ought
> or ought not to need something. The words "ought" and "ought
> not" apply only to wants, never to needs. This means that the
> natural desires that are our inborn needs enter into the sphere of
> our voluntary conduct only through the operation of our acquired
> desires or wants.[159]

Clearly no one can deny the existence of natural desires or "inborn
needs," so the frame of reference for the language of real goods rests within
the constitution of the subject. There is no appeal to an extrinsic authority
to document, let alone prop up, the realities described by the terms.

Adler builds upon his distinction of wants and needs to show how
another critical distinction can be grasped: "The distinction between needs
and wants enables us to draw the line between real goods and apparent
goods. Those things that satisfy or fulfill our needs or natural desires are
things that are really good for us. Those that satisfy our wants or acquired
desires are things that appear good to us when we consciously desire them.
If we need them as well as want them, they are also really good for us."[160]

The pellucid realism of Adler illustrates splendidly the need for
liberation from the shackles of medieval nominalism. As Pinckaers shows,
nominalism exalted a content-free notion of freedom that ignored human
inclinations to the truth. This fourteenth-century aberration from realism
set the stage for the freedom of indifference indistinguishable from Enlightenment autonomy. With a push from the doctrinaire skepticism of
David Hume, it anticipated the confusion of the contemporary relativism
that hampers moral discourse and nullifies the import of human freedom
today.

Is this affirmation that words have real meaning and correspond
with the reality of the world around us just a desperate attempt to impose
some kind of coherence on an otherwise meaningless world? To accept
such a cynical view buys into a minimalist view of human intelligence: we
are just poor creatures trying to cobble together some sense of things in a

big universe filled with gaps, voids, and puzzles. The conclusion that words truly matter on the human and natural level inspires a comparable confidence that words matter insofar as they pertain to the divine.

A Christian perspective sees profound and pivotal meaning embedded in creation with Christ as the Keystone of that creation, the *Logos*, the Lord whose life and divine wisdom provide unfathomable meaning. We can be confident that words mean things, that thoughts correspond to reality, and that we can debate with one another about such meanings and thereby grow through refinement of reflection as reasoning individuals and a reasonable community. One could hardly expect a community that worships Christ as *Logos* to lack confidence in the capacity of human reason (created reason) or in the capacity of words to communicate a range of truths extending from the minutely human to the cosmically divine.

It is dismaying that one must go to these lengths to demonstrate what should be self-evident. Still, we cannot ignore the baneful and widespread stances of nihilism and relativism—the views, respectively, that nothing is really true or that nothing is independently true apart from the accident of being someone's opinion—which most people are too sensible to adopt explicitly but, as with an occasional puddle, can stumble into from time to time.

Why did the nominalists put such a priority on law and obligation? The answer is two-pronged—theological and anthropological. The nominalists stressed the liberty and omnipotence of God. William of Ockham (1285–1349) vitiated the Incarnation by teaching that God could have redeemed the human race by coming to earth as a donkey.[161] This theological stance may have maximized God's freedom, but it also rendered creation indecipherable since God could act in any way possible. The only way to provide coherence and predictability in this situation would be to legislate what seemed to be God's will. This "solution" increased the likelihood that God's will might be construed erroneously and also that laws would proliferate willy-nilly to announce whatever was deemed to be God's will.

Since words in the nominalist framework were merely human constructs, not symbols and expressions of underlying reality, one could not rely on terms to correspond to reality in such a way that meaning might be verified and universally shared. This inadvertently inflated the importance of law since society must somehow adopt or impose yardsticks of meaning. Truth is imposed rather than discovered. In nominalism, it is law that informs us about reality. It will necessarily be arbitrary in that it depends on the perspective of a fallible lawgiver. For the realist, it is reason and reality that inform us about what constitutes law, an ordinance of reason for the common good, promulgated by one who has responsibility within the community (to repeat, profitably, Saint Thomas's definition of law).

What Pinckaers is accomplishing here is truly significant. He is doing three things. First, he is retrieving the unalloyed wisdom of Saint Thomas Aquinas, rescuing the "Angelic Doctor" from uninformed followers as well as vehement critics. Second, he is meticulously freeing this Thomistic wisdom from the deformities and caricatures of the nominalist legacy that turned the wisdom of Saint Thomas on its head, replacing happiness and the virtues with law and obligation. Third, Pinckaers is articulating for those not immediately engaged in the historical development of Catholic moral theology a vision of anthropology, morality, and happiness which may be quite novel, inherently Catholic, and yet congenial to many schools of thought open to the importance of rational discourse and not allergic to convictions of faith as elements or even partners within that discourse.

Pinckaers is waging a brilliant two-front war. His first battle is to challenge the obsolete neo-scholastic distortions of a Thomistic template that at its best sees freedom, the good, and human happiness as interdependent yet dynamic realities. On the second front, responding to contemporary secularism, the heir of nominalism, Pinckaers engages the many divisions of nihilism, relativism, and deconstructionism that have led intellectual elites to lose confidence in the power of reason and truth.

ANTHROPOLOGY: HUMANITY AS THE HEART OF MORALITY

As we look formally at the five natural inclinations found in Saint Thomas and their application to issues of sexual morality, it is good to recognize exactly where we are starting. We are looking at the structure and meaning of humankind. We are examining the very core of human desire and how the constitution of persons orients choices and acts in the light of perceived and real goods understood as goals.

How different this is from a morality that starts with commands, laws, or obligations. Yes, there are, in the Catholic view of things, commands, laws, and obligations, but they are derived from love and circumscribed by the reality of human personhood. When authentic obligations arise, they are seen to flow from the nature of the person. The scope or extent of an obligation only goes as far as the orientation of the subject toward the good. We can say in summary a number of things that ought to dispel prevalent stereotypes about Catholic moral teaching.

First, it is clear that any obligation of morality is interior at its origin, that is, an obligation flows from the needs and goods of the person; no command is merely imposed upon the subject from an external force. When natural inclinations within freedom are recovered, the dualism of autonomy and heteronomy dies. The moral teaching of the Decalogue shows that freedom and morality flow from within human need and meaning. When the moral and civil law prohibit theft, the reason is not that a hypothetical lawgiver has arbitrarily opted for private property over stealing—a reasonable preference but originating in an external authority—but that the legitimate goal of using earthly goods in a manner consistent with basic human needs requires that those earthly goods be available for human needs. (If someone steals your car, it cannot transport you to the doctor.)

Second, this interior origin of commands means that everything derives from a horizon of human goods and human needs. This is the banquet of life or cornucopia of creation whereby human reason can look at a vast array of possibilities and choose those means and ends most conducive to the good. Who determines what is authentically good? Is this not the point where obligations are smuggled into the picture, ushering in the dreaded loss of freedom, the heteronomy loathed by the Enlightenment? No, if we stay with our proposition that anthropology is our starting point of analysis—what *is* occurs prior to what *ought* to be—then we can answer the question of who defines the good by looking again at the anthropological tableau: it is people themselves who recognize and pursue authentic goods. It is the natural order of things that determines whether their recognition and pursuit is in accord with reason.

We have seen how people can confuse a real with a merely apparent good. Our choices are contingent upon the accuracy of our perception which in turn rests on our own degree of moral awareness. But there is no code or secret formula that smuggles an a priori notion of the good into human calculation. It is true that the definitive notion of the good is found in God and God has revealed to humankind a Decalogue, ten "words" of wise conversation that orient us definitively toward the truth.

God always forgives those who are contrite in the wake of their disobedience of the Decalogue. It is, in the words of the adage, nature that does not forgive. The consequences of breaking any instruction of the Decalogue are harmful to the sinner. It is not the intent of God that sinners suffer; suffering is the consequence of their deeds that the Lord, the Creator of human freedom, permits in order to allow for the exercise of human freedom. With that creation is of course redemption and the call to communion with God and each other. No failure is permanent, no confessed sin unforgiven.

Third, since moral obligations originate from within the nature or being of humankind and hence are derivative, we can logically conclude that obligations are limited to what genuinely promotes the good. Obligations are circumscribed by human identity, which includes a capacity for making distinctions of reasonable versus unreasonable, and by the very logic of creation. We are partners in the divine plan, not puppets. A puppet is subject to the strings being pulled perpetually in the absence of freedom, whereas a partner enjoys freedom and trust in a cooperative venture: "I call you no longer servants, I call you friends" (John 15:13).

1. *The Trajectory of Teleology*

Many dividends of analysis and reflection result from a goal-oriented or teleological approach. In looking at the human species and its ongoing effort to fulfill basic human needs, both the subject and the entire species peer beyond their own immediate circumstances to larger goals, goods, and purposes. This larger view generates a trajectory that orients choices toward the real goods perceived and sought. This trajectory, when fully realized, precludes narcissism because the subject, in looking beyond himself toward real goods, sees the connection between basic human goods and goals. The subject recognizes that it is necessary to aim at and work toward goods in concert with other subjects. In short, the trajectory of teleology makes clear the existence and priority of a community. One cannot procure food, shelter, and clothing or any basic necessity, without the cooperation of spouse, family, neighborhood, society, and community. All have a stake in real goods.

The intentions of the subject are part of the meaning of creation: "The teleology of ancient philosophy is interesting, because we have forgotten what teleology implies. It means the science of *telos*, of the intention or purpose of a thing, or person, or institution. The intention is another word for *meaning*: there is a meaning behind creation, a meaning that can be discovered. This also means that there is an *ordo*, a connection between the parts, in life itself."[162]

Recall also that this trajectory originates from the interior identity of subjects. There is no template or grid imposed on individuals from without. There are no deterministic forces that compel individuals to search and work for real goods. The incentive and necessity come from within ourselves. We are self-actualizing, thanks to the prodigal generosity of our Creator. We have seen the deterministic outcome of Kant's adoption of Newtonian mechanism. Every *thing*, including the subject, is part of a closed system having a predetermined outcome. The quest for unfettered freedom via autonomy leaves the subject—the person—subordinated to a cold, instrumental system likely to instill anomie. It is the very antithesis of the reality of creation.

2. *Natural Law: Ends and Purposes*

A distinguished philosopher whose approach tends to be phenomenological, Robert Sokolowski, has written about the distinction between ends and purposes. His analysis occurs within a context of human goods and the natural law: "An end, a *telos*, belongs to a thing in itself, while a purpose arises only when there are human beings. Purposes are intentions, something we wish for and are deliberating about or acting to achieve. Ends, in contrast, are there apart from any human wishes and deliberations. They are what the thing is when it has reached its best state, its perfection and completion in and for itself. Ends and purposes are both goods, but goods of different ontological orders."[163]

An example given by Sokolowski is the case of medicine and a doctor. The end of the medical profession is the "restoration and preservation of health" but a doctor may have various purposes for practicing medicine such as becoming wealthy or famous, serving the poor, advancing a related career, or even becoming an adept torturer.[164] I believe it is consistent with this view to see ends as the objective dimension of human goods and purposes as the subjective dimension of these human goods.

Natural law can be understood as the intersection of ends and purposes where the subjective purposes are clearly subordinated to the objective ends. Sokolowski puts it this way: "To the question, 'What is natural law?' one can answer very simply: 'Natural law is the ontological priority of ends over purposes.' Natural law is shown to us when we recognize that there are ends in things and that our purposes and choices must respect their priority."[165]

Sokolowski gives as examples of the operation of the natural law the gradual abolition of polygamy in Western countries and the Hindu practice of suttee in India. Whatever subjective purposes may have existed to continue or preserve polygamy or suttee, these purposes yielded to the objective ends of the natural law which disclosed the radical inconsistency of both polygamy and suttee with the institution of marriage.

This brilliant and helpful articulation of the distinction between objective ends and subjective purposes (that may or may not be consistent with the ends of nature) gives us a complementary elucidation of Pinckaers's natural inclinations, corresponding with objective ends, as distinct from the various subjective purposes that human beings, considered as moral agents, may have in realizing, appropriating, or in some instances, opposing those ends. Clearly, there is a direct link between natural inclinations, ends (that is, objective goods in the sense described by Sokolowski), and meaning, both subjective and objective. These are all connected ways of describing natural law.

It should be clear that this vision of all human beings as naturally inclined to fulfilling goods is directly at variance with the Enlightenment notion of autonomy that is indifferent to ends and meaning. Originating ultimately in Ockham's freedom of indifference, Enlightenment autonomy prides itself on being "free" of any inclination to truth, good, or beatitude. This independence is touted as great freedom, but in fact it is a tragic blindness to those ends, purposes, and meaning that allow for the completion of eros in authentic human communion.

Pinckaers works hard on every page of *Sources* to show that natural inclinations are not embodied in a theory of natural law but are literally embodied in human beings. The existence of these inclinations demonstrates the fragility, complexity, and relationality of every subject. Their existence does not in any way limit authentic human freedom. These inclinations, when acted upon through virtuous choices, contrast a freedom of excellence (liberty ordered toward real goods) with a freedom of indifference that neglects the natural inclination to goods and ends perfective of the person.

This thumbnail summary cannot possibly capture the full treatment and brilliance of Pinckaers; it is hoped that its brevity manages both to describe and appeal. We can now proceed to consider specific virtues in this context of natural inclinations and genuine freedom. As we walk through natural, individual inclinations, we do well to remember that they are nothing more, nothing less, and nothing else than distinct aspects of a philosophical and theological anthropology essential for understanding the morality of human choices.

3. *Practical Wisdom and the Natural Inclination to the Good*

The two natural inclinations that Pinckaers puts first and last—the natural inclination to the good, a premise foundational for everything else, and the natural inclination to sexual union—are the inclinations most pertinent to our inquiry on autonomy, freedom, happiness, and communion. Every important component of the moral life rests on the natural inclination to the good, which Pinckaers describes as the "source of all moral action."[166] Since our specific concern is autonomy, communion, marriage, and the family, we will focus greatly on the natural inclination to sexual union in its implication for hot-button issues of sexual ethics.

Nevertheless, one of the most powerful arguments for this Thomistic template of natural inclinations is the fact that *all* of the natural inclinations inhere and cohere so closely. None can be inflated, isolated, or neglected. It is impossible logically to speak of the foundational inclination to the good without considering at the same time how some particular instances, such as family, society, and sexual union might flow from the foundational or primordial good in the very constitution and consciousness of human life.

Another distinguished Catholic theologian who pursues a parallel, Thomistic path is Benedict M. Ashley, OP. His *Living the Truth in Love*[167] describes the close link between the theological virtue of faith and the moral virtue of practical wisdom (the Greek *phronesis* or prudence): "This practical wisdom as a gift of God is closely related to divine faith, but differs from it: the problem of faith, even its practical aspect, is how to listen to God's self-revelation, while the problem of practical wisdom is how to discern what the Christian should or should not do to live in God's Kingdom. Thus practical wisdom applies what God has revealed about our journey toward him to actual life decisions in their particular circumstances."[168]

We can see from Pinckaers and Ashley that human beings are endowed with the capacity to know as well as to believe; these two aspects of understanding are eminently compatible and interactive. To be naturally inclined toward the good means that there is a capacity for practical wisdom to distinguish means and ends, choosing wise means to advance worthy ends. This human capacity orients us directly toward the good in an almost unfathomable way. Saint Thomas was not content with narrowly qualified or esoteric nuances. In the first part of the *Summa Theologica*, he boldly links our nature with goodness and perfection: "Since every nature desires its own being and its own perfection, it must be said also that the being and the perfection of any nature is good."[169]

It is no accident that this section of the *Summa* is Thomas's reflection on the meaning of creation and how its effects enable us to distinguish between good and evil. It is not only the impact but the intent of creation that all human beings desire the fullness and excellence of their very being since the perfection of that being is truly good, a real and surpassing good. In one powerful sentence, Saint Thomas aligns the following propositions: (1) All of us have a human nature that is dynamic, free, rational, and open to desire. (2) The desire that wells up from our interior nature directs us toward being, *esse*, as living, breathing, and striving creatures. (3) What "must be said" as a matter of necessity emerges not as an edict from a cosmic Zeus or angry Lear-like monarch but as an intrinsic dimension of what we know we are, beings endowed with a nature desirous of perfection, that is, being at its fullness. (4) Being and perfection are recognizable as realities truly good. They are good not because anyone so classifies them but by the very dynamic of their existence and relationship to us, the person and subject. We are naturally inclined toward them.

Such a brilliant conceptual beginning for our exploration of human nature gives us confidence that we can indeed distinguish good from evil. We need not resort to any a priori schema or consult with any code to figure out what is good and what is not. Since it is a good thing that we are as we are, we have a heads-up, so to speak, on how to account events, phenomena, or choices. Those that promote being and perfection can be accounted good.

If we cannot confidently identify some realities as good, with substantial agreement on the existence and meaning of the good, then nothing else matters. Pinckaers explicitly states that "the break between metaphysics and ethics was a direct effect of nominalism."[170] We saw how the rejection of metaphysics by Kant led to an ethical conclusion, an arid autonomy, essentially a caricature of eros, that did not serve human needs.

Pinckaers returns to the metaphysical heritage of both Aristotle and Saint Thomas, pointing out that these two giants began their ethical accounts with the meaning of the good but left it undefined. Saint Thomas followed Aristotle in simply stating that "the good is that which all desire."

We can also complement Pinckaers's contribution by turning to a twentieth-century scholar whose long and productive life led him to (almost single-handedly) restore Aristotle to a place of intellectual prominence in the public square, Mortimer J. Adler. Adler succinctly provides an Aristotelian-Thomistic sense of goodness and basic goods: "All the goods that fulfill our needs or satisfy our wants belong in the category of human goods, real or apparent. These are things that are good *for* man. When we use the word "good" substantively to call them "goods," we are using the word in its primary connotation to signify objects of desire. The goods thus named are diverse embodiments of goodness, the idea of which identifies the good with the desirable."[171]

Moralists have imaginatively used the metaphor of a mountain chain to describe the range of goods that can be recognized and pursued by human striving. If anything, the mountain range metaphor limps insofar as a mountain eventually leads to a plain or valley whereas the possible array of human goods, originating in infinite goodness and stretching through human choices, returns to infinite goodness without any limit whatever.

In looking at human nature as part of a philosophical and theological anthropology, we actually discover a reason why atheism is irrational. If one were to argue that all of us can come to a point where there could absolutely be no more good, no chance or choice of good whatsoever, then it would follow that at this point of no return—no possibility of goodness in thought, deed, or desire—we would have reached a void or vacuum where no being, let alone a divine being, could be said to exist. But the evidence points overwhelmingly toward an unlimited range of possibilities of goodness. For every human need or want, another human being, upon discovering this need or want, is likely to use great powers of will and imagination to find a solution. On and on it goes. If we are truly prepared to put boundaries around goodness, we do far more than exclude the possible existence of divine goodness. We actually argue against the existence of humanity, understood as sensitive, intelligent, responsive life itself. To be human is to be radically more than human: *homo non proprie humanus sed superhumanus est.*[172]

Why should such a foundational concept not be defined? Pinckaers explains that, for Aquinas, "the perception of the good was a primordial experience; no other could explain it. The good, therefore, could be described only in terms of its effects."[173] In describing the good as the lovable and the desirable, that which every human being seeks, Pinckaers describes the moral content of the good as follows: "The good is what all men desire, or again, it is what causes love and desire in every human being, or finally, it is what we desire in all our willing."[174]

Clearly we have in the good something far greater than morality and much more expansive than any laundry list of duties, rules, or obligations. Pinckaers makes it plain that the good is an anthropological reality since we are not just talking of a concept in the abstract but studying the way in which people of every era and culture begin to fashion their lives and priorities. It is an awareness of and desire for the good—that which attracts as lovable and desirable—that can truly be described as universal. There is no known human being who lacks a desire for what is good. It is true that individuals suffering from a cognitive disability may lack the capacity to know what is good, but the desire for the good is coterminous with their humanity, a universal attribute of every human being.

Pinckaers illuminates the paradox that while *all* human beings desire what is good as something lovable and desirable, no one is able to experience the universal good directly.[175] While we can speak of the good as universal in the abstract, it will only be in specific, limited encounters—particular desires—that we are able to experience goodness. Goodness in its universal and transcendent magnitude is not an enemy of limited goods but rather the whole of which they are a part.

Nor is goodness a foe of truth but, as we have seen in the classic Aristotelian sense, the good is in some underlying way linked with truth and beauty as aspects of being. This means that there is not only a universality in the good, present for all human beings, but there is a unity of the good, the true and the beautiful under the auspices of being. The fullness of being is of course God.

Pinckaers quotes Saint Thomas at the beginning of the *Summa Theologica* to the effect that "to be is to desire perfection."[176] We see here an application, or perhaps corollary, of the teleological—goal-oriented—approach of Catholic moral theology. Being, both the origin and result of creation, is something good and oriented inexorably toward perfection, that is, the perfection of being, ultimately, God. Being is not content with mediocrity or minimalism. There is nothing static about being: its inherent trajectory is toward perfection and plenitude. That is why even a human being who suffers from a hideous deformity or paralyzing handicap cannot be dismissed as a static or meaningless nonentity. That person too desires perfection, even if the fulfillment of that desire appears impossible for now.

Pinckaers notes that the excellence of goodness has an attractive force, summoning the desire by the person for perfection toward ever greater heights. This orientation or trajectory toward perfection provides Pinckaers with a working definition of a person: "The perfection proper to the human person comes from the intellect and will, from the power to love and will the good as such, to know it and be open to it in its universality. We could therefore define the person as a being aspiring to perfection and the plenitude of goodness."[177]

He goes on to say that "the perfection of the good coincides with the fullness of freedom."[178] The portrait of the person, as sketched by

Catholic moral theology with Saint Thomas as master artist, is slowly taking shape: a human being endowed with reason and the ability to choose, constantly aspiring to perfection and the fullness of both goodness and freedom whereby the essence and completion of that freedom coincides with the fullness of the good. This is precisely the portrait presented by the natural law tradition at its best. The person is neither cog in a machine nor puppet, but a vibrant, reflecting, choosing subject whose *telos* inclines toward the good in all of its perfection.

Lest this surpassing portrait become inaccurate, however, Pinckaers reminds us that there will always be relativity and contingency in regard to the subject's desire and striving for perfection. Just as we cannot encounter the perfection of good as a universal principle, but only draw closer to it by limited experiences, so we cannot as creatures cross the boundary separating the finite from the infinite in this earthly arena.

The unity and universality of the Thomistic portrait means that there is no separation between goodness and happiness. Rather, Pinckaers describes their relationship as a "reciprocal implication": "For Saint Thomas . . . the good was the cause of happiness, and happiness was the plenitude of the good. Yet they could be distinguished by a certain nuance: the good resided in the objective reality, while happiness subsisted in the subject who experienced the good. . . . Perfection and happiness were two aspects of the one object of morality, *bonum*, the good."[179]

This means that there is no radical or fundamental clash, at least in principle, between objective, transcendent good and subjective desire. There is a triad of perfection, happiness, and the good in which the subject experiences happiness as the subjective appreciation of objective good.

The above vision of the good, linking perfection and happiness, subject and object, is a consistent, empirically verifiable account of human activity. It is a rich treasure of divine revelation and saintly wisdom combined. This portrait of virtues as choices revolving around authentic goods stands in contrast to the ephemeral quality of values. Values are essentially vessels into which one can pour lemonade, deadly poison, or Merlot. A virtue is itself the vessel of perfection.

Since our approach, mining the veins of historical Catholic theology, is teleological or goal-centered, it is necessary to look at the meaning of the good as an end. Pinckaers states that "after the good, finality is the first essential element of human or moral action—these two are one for Saint Thomas."[180] For those unfamiliar with scholastic terminology, it is necessary to point out that the term *finality* traces to the Latin *finis* or "end" as goal. *Finality* probably suggests to most people today an approaching hearse; the importance of the end is actually the beginning, as T. S. Eliot and Thomas would both insist.

This finality acquires a universal dimension. (It would be impossible otherwise since end and good are two sides of the same phenomenon and we have seen how personal, private, limited goods are directed inexorably toward perfection and plenitude, the realm of the universal.) Since there is a universality to human goods and ends, it means, Pinckaers notes, that a hierarchy exists. In looking at the list of natural perfections, we can see a hierarchy where, for example, the natural inclination to self-preservation takes precedence over the natural inclination to live in society. There is no opposition between the two but unless I exist, the point about living in society is entirely moot.

How does a personal end or good relate to the common good? While the particular elements of a situation must be known to answer this in the concrete, we can at least preclude any clash in principle between an individual and communal end. We can stipulate that since the end is also a good, it has, insofar as it is part of goodness in general, a universal character that transcends any particular end, so the universal and the particular cannot in principle ever be pitted against each other as radically antagonistic opponents. Individual goods and the common good always need to be discerned correctly and balanced, but theirs is an underlying and inherent harmony.

For example, does a society have the right of conscription, forcing citizens to enlist in an army whereby they risk their lives? Other things being equal (for example, a just government fighting a just war), it may well be the case that a society is within its rights to establish a draft. Does this not pit a universal good or end (the needs of the society) against a particular good or end (the life of a soldier), contradicting the claim made above of harmony between the universal and the particular, the social and the personal? No, when you look at it, the soldier who risks his life does benefit from living in the community and may be called upon to make the ultimate sacrifice for the survival of a just society in repayment for the benefits of citizenship.

Another point of fundamental unity is that between personal and social ethics. Too often, partisans of left or right split whereby there can be broad agreement on social issues but sharp clashes on issues of personal or sexual morality. Many political liberals agreed wholeheartedly with the stance against the death penalty of Pope John Paul II but strongly opposed his views on contraception and abortion. But if the vision of goods and ends is correct, there is a radical consistency between supporting the natural inclination of a human being to self-existence by opposing contraception and abortion, on the one hand, and supporting the same natural inclination to self-existence of a criminal whose misdeeds do not nullify the reality and rightness of that same natural inclination to self-existence shared with an innocent fetus.

Pinckaers brings together his summary of Saint Thomas on goods, ends, happiness, freedom, and morality: "Saint Thomas's morality may thus be called a morality of finality and of the last end, as well as a morality of the good. In this, it is profoundly human as well as divine, for finality thus conceived relates us directly to God. It makes us sharers in divine goodness and freedom, in a work wholly finalized by the good."[181]

Anyone familiar with the basics of Catholic theology will recognize in the phrase "sharers in divine goodness," the language of grace. While we have been talking thus far of natural inclinations, these attributes of the nature or character of human beings are inclined by both nature and grace toward divine goodness. After all, our lives are the result of divine goodness, the pre-eminence of grace.

4. *Love of Friendship and Love of Concupiscence*

At this point in his summary of many attributes of the good, Pinckaers expands on a crucial distinction made by Saint Thomas, namely, the radical difference between a love of friendship versus a love of concupiscence. It is in the *Prima Secundae*, the beginning of the second section of the *Summa*, where Saint Thomas—in tackling the questions of how we make our pilgrimage to God, the path of morality—makes a sharp distinction, breathtaking in both its simplicity and effect.[182] While Aristotle distinguishes three kinds of friendship, corresponding to three kinds of moral good—authentic or honest, pleasurable, and useful—Saint Thomas restricts friendship to the first kind of good, an honest or authentic good, which is itself the object of human love. The other two kinds of Aristotelian friendship—pleasurable and useful—are different in kind from a love of friendship which is focused on the honest or inherent good of the friend and not any other good. We have seen this distinction earlier but have not yet explored the alternative to friendship, concupiscence.

Pinckaers describes the implications of the distinction:

> There is the love of concupiscence or desire, which consists in loving a good for some other reason than itself alone. For example, I may love some good for my own sake. That is the way I love wine. Then there is the love of friendship, which consists in loving a good, a person in fact, in himself and for his own sake. *The love of friendship is love in the proper sense.* . . . This is why the intention of the one who loves cannot and will not go further and consider this good as a means to some other end. This is true particularly of our last end, which is our last end because it is the object of our absolute love. The end is therefore the object of love and desire, and of the love of friendship, but of the latter primarily because it is the good, properly so-called.[183]

It is then a love of friendship—desiring what is good for the friend for his or her own sake—that constitutes love in the authentic sense. To love someone for another reason (such as for what that person may do for us) is not, strictly speaking, love. We shall see in a minute that a love of concupiscence or disordered desire is not, in the Catholic view, sinful. But this kind of desire is not really love since it aims at an end or a good which does not allow the interest or good of the other person, the friend, to be the uppermost consideration.

St. Thomas is using the distinction of love of friendship versus love of concupiscence found in Aristotle's *Nicomachean Ethics*. A keen student of Aristotle, Martha Nussbaum, demonstrates the importance of friendship to the perception of reality. This contribution of friendship to perceptual acuity is another indication that the customary Aristotelian standard of self-sufficiency is inadequate for the purposes of perceiving one's truth and the full picture of reality: "The Aristotelian view stresses that bonds of close friendship or love (such as those that connect members of a family, or close personal friends) are extremely important in the whole business of becoming a good perceiver. Trusting the guidance of a friend and allowing one's feelings to be engaged with that other person's life and choices, one learns to see aspects of the world that one had previously missed. One's desire to share a form of life with the friend motivates this process."[184]

To summarize Aristotle's elements of friendship, we have (1) a mutual attraction by two subjects to a good, (2) a desire for good to the friend, (3) an awareness of the other's benevolence and reciprocity of this goodwill, (4) some regular communication of this goodwill in light of the overarching good that began and continues to ground their friendship, and (5) the value of friendship in the subject's ability to perceive the truth.

Aquinas in his *Commentary on the Nicomachean Ethics* begins the creative enterprise of transforming the natural genius of Aristotle into the language and wisdom of graced love. First, he moves the entire discussion into the realm of love understood as the premier theological virtue. If we may borrow the language of computers, this shift from a focus on the subject to an inquiry on the meaning of love in light of the divine, caritas, means that a menu bar of revealed propositions (for example, Paul's hymn to love in 1 Corinthians 13) is now available for the fleshing out of both eros and agape by incorporating the elements of friendship into a definition of caritas.

How much richer is this Thomistic elevation of the meaning of love to the orbit of grace. It differs radically from both Aristotle and Kant. In his second of three formulations of his categorical imperative, Immanuel Kant made the point that a person must never be reduced to a means to an end. The Catholic perspective certainly agrees with that, but the context of creation, redemption, and communion is so much more evocative of personal engagement than the sterile and rationalistic dryness that Kant was forced to accept by his rejection of metaphysics.

Kant devises a rule; Pinckaers looks at a person. The difference is an anthropology as opposed to an abstraction. Thomists look at the person as a being of desires, capable of ordering them toward a hierarchy of ends and goods, even while dealing with the proneness toward disordered desires, a weakness resulting from the impact of Original Sin on human life. This is not simply a philosophical principle but a theological appraisal—realistic, sensitive, and sympathetic—of the human journey to God.

A constant theme that runs through Pinckaers is the modern deformation and devaluation of scholastic terminology. This devaluation is particularly acute in regard to the term *honest*. Pinckaers notes that he feels compelled to put quotation marks around it because in current parlance *honesty* simply means giving a customer the correct change. In the world and imagination of Saint Thomas, *"honest* meant authenticity and inherent value, something corresponding to highly prized and morally praiseworthy goods and ends. It is not surprising that a culture which will dumb down intellectual content will similarly devalue integrity so that honesty becomes a somewhat mechanical aspect of goodness, 'a simple respect for law.'"[185]

Allow Pinckaers to speak for himself:

> The discussion [of goods in Saint Thomas] reaches its climax with the establishment of the primacy of the "honest" good over the "useful": only the "honest" good is truly useful. The "honest" good is the good that deserves to be loved for its own sake, beyond all interested or utilitarian considerations. It is identified with virtue. For St. Thomas, too, the "honest" good means moral excellence at its highest, in conformity with man's rational nature. The notion of good finds its proper and principal realization in the "honest" good, and only secondarily in the "useful" or "delightful" good. . . . The "honest" good is the culmination of goodness.[186]

Catholic moral teaching on sexuality takes the popular adage "honesty is the best policy" and applies it to sexual issues with the result that honesty, in the rich Thomistic sense described above, is the *only* policy for sex because our sexuality is at the core of our identity.

A final aspect of the natural inclination to the good as a goal-oriented linkage of happiness and perfection, as described by Pinckaers, is the generosity or fruitfulness of the good. The neo-Platonic tradition of Christian thought underscored this reality with the adage *bonum diffusivum sui* or "the good is diffusive of itself," rich and radiant beyond any confinement. Pinckaers identifies this generosity and fruitfulness of love with freedom for excellence, the capacity to strive for and realize those goods which are most in conformity with human excellence, reason, and revelation.[187]

A critical weakness of Kantian autonomy is that the notion of freedom being indifferent to truth, goodness, and beatitude has no room for *kenosis*, the self-emptying love of a subject for the beloved. It is the fruitfulness of virtue that allows love to grow by being given. This theological template is marvelously open to the communion of lover and beloved in the transforming *kenosis* of eros gradually yielding to agape. The Enlightenment has no such conceptual references to describe what every lover who wills to sacrifice for the beloved already knows.

This aspect of goodness—its richness, radiance, outgoing, and outpouring dimension—figures greatly in the Catholic view of desire and fulfillment in a communion discerned and pursued by virtue.

5. Concupiscence

What exactly is concupiscence? The *Oxford Dictionary of the Christian Church,* a classic reference work, summarizes it as follows:

> In moral theology [it is] the inordinate desire for temporal ends which has its seat in the senses. The notion of concupiscence has its biblical foundations especially in the teaching of St. Paul (Ephesians 2:3, Romans 7:7ff., etc.) and was developed by St. Augustine in his struggle against Pelagianism. According to Augustine the cause of concupiscence is the fall of Adam, who, having lost original righteousness, transmitted to us a nature in which the desires of the flesh are no longer subordinated to reason. St. Thomas Aquinas, elaborating the Augustinian teaching, regards it as the material (i.e. passive, because residing in the senses) element of Original Sin, the formal (active, residing in the will) element being loss of Original Righteousness. . . . Orthodox Protestant theology . . . both in its Lutheran and its Calvinist forms, regards concupiscence itself as sin and its very existence as an offence against God; and the Jansenists held a similar view. The Council of Trent (session 5) followed St. Thomas's teaching against the Reformers, and in post-Tridentine theology it is usually regarded as a consequence of Original Sin rather than as part of it.[188]

This means that for Saint Thomas and the Catholic moral tradition we can speak of inordinate desires, rooted in the senses, which fall short of and are distinct from sin. Concupiscence is the arena of temptation, to be sure, but also the environment where weakness or the proclivity to inordinate desire can be tempered and transformed into a possibility of virtue. When the Catholic tradition sees the failings of frail human flesh to be something other than sin, it is not a "tolerance" for weakness but a view of life through a much larger lens that takes into its scope the full measure of creation, sin, redemption and, yes, natural inclinations toward the goodness of creation notwithstanding the many obstacles, weaknesses, and barriers that complicate the realization of the truly good.

We have stressed creation and communion in our Catholic "trifecta," but a word should be said about redemption. The judgment that all have sinned is not a verdict against humanity but a truth of realism and compassion. Redemption is not an exception, a gift granted to the scoundrel, but a path of conversion and growth that must be taken by all.

In short, there cannot be the fruitfulness of creation that fulfils the call to communion apart from the path of redemption.

CONFIDENCE IN KNOWING THE TRUTH

The Enlightenment popularized atheism, or at least agnosticism. Inevitably, it also popularized agnosticism about the good. If one does not know about the ultimate, plenary good, the divine, there is virtually no chance that one will be aware of incomplete or imperfect instances of the good in human experience. In standing with the Catholic tradition against Enlightenment agnosticism, Pinckaers affirms that human beings have the capacity to know the good: "The good of a being lies in the perfection proper to its nature. Human good will be a good conformed to the human intellect, as grasped by our distinctive faculty. This is 'the known good' (*bonum apprehensum*). . . . The known good includes . . . all the knowledge of goodness that we can gain through study, education, reflection, perception, and, above all, personal experience."[189]

It is fascinating that a culture so often addicted to the notion of self-esteem cannot even be sure about its capacity to distinguish good from evil or right from wrong. Granted that no human perspective will ever be unerring in grasping the meaning of a real good, nevertheless we can with asymptotic confidence come closer and closer to the meaning of real goods. We can and must debate with each other concerning the scope or significance of a good. In that kind of give-and-take, we learn all the more about the parameters of goodness, truth, and beauty.

By contrast, the Catholic tradition has a robust assurance, strengthened by divine revelation, that we can apprehend the good. The starting point for all that is good is God, a mystery whom we can never claim to know except as he makes it possible. But the Psalmist proclaims that only the fool denies the existence of God. Sadly, our recent century has endured much foolishness not only from claims denying the existence of God but from the relativism and nihilism that deny the reality of objective good. Scripture recognized the link between God and the good centuries before the birth of Christ: "The fool has said in his heart, 'There is no God.' They are corrupt, they have committed abominable deeds; There is no one who does good."[190]

When we look at moral choices, the overall arena of our discussion of human ethics, we are not talking of speculation or abstraction but practical reason working in tandem with our appetites and desires, whether those rightly ordered or those disordered by concupiscence—the hangover from Original Sin, as it were. In speaking of "study, education, reflection, perception, and, above all, personal experience," Pinckaers emphasizes that our capacity to know the good is an active engagement on the part of the subject, not the object of a command. Once again he confronts the distorted view of the natural law which twists it into an impersonal system of command and conformity. It is anything but that.

In discovering known goods, human beings become aware of the distinction between a real and an apparent good. Sometimes these can coincide, as when a desire to exercise is consistent with the overall good of one's health. But at other times, what appears to be good can in fact *not* be a real good. Pinckaers gives the example of someone who is so bent on amassing a fortune as to act unjustly. He notes that "repeated acts of injustice deform the judgment even as they corrupt the will."[191] The fact that people can make serious mistakes in choosing an apparent over a real good reminds us that philosophical distinctions do not present the complete picture. We cannot merely speak of the possibility of choosing apparent goods but must also look at the reality of sin. Sometimes our choice of an apparent good—for example, Raskolnikov (in *Crime and Punishment*) killing the pawnbroker—is a deliberate action that merits the warranted description of sin, whether mortal or venial.

Having argued for the existence and knowability of the good, aligned toward happiness, perfection, and ultimately God, Pinckaers concludes his section on the natural inclination to the good by citing the primary precept of the natural law: "Good is to be done and evil to be avoided."

The conventional description of this axiom as a "primary precept" to describe a universally realized truth which becomes, through its inherent meaning, a self-willed mandate, is accurate and well-established. Nevertheless, we must be careful in designating a guiding principle at the very start of all human reasoning as a precept. Some moralists, such as Germain Grisez, state this axiom as "good is to be done; evil is to be avoided" to demonstrate that we are not operating in a legalistic framework. The imperative nature of doing good and avoiding evil is not an edict directed at individuals from an exterior authority; it is a truth that arises from the initial awareness of the good and consequent human goods. It is *not* heteronomous (to use Kant's bugaboo), something imposed by an outside force on a subject. This axiom properly describes a *component* of authentic autonomy, one measured by and in relation to a transcendent good. Aristotle pointed out five centuries before Christ that the good is that for which all human beings aim. To do any less or to choose any end violative of a real good is to aim for something incompatible with authentic humanity and divine love.

Pinckaers makes the point that the impact of the primary precept of the natural law is felt on two different levels. At the foundational level, Pinckaers considers the natural desire for the good to be the "source of all moral action," as noted above. But this foundational insight and desire is given form and flesh by the person in a variety of concrete choices, the second or implementing level of the basic desire for the good. We have seen Mortimer Adler's insight that "we cannot ever be mistaken about our wants"[192] even though we can be very mistaken about our genuine needs. Nevertheless, even in one's error, the desire and inclination toward what one considers at the time to be a real good is invariant, universal and, even if flawed, fully human. As is often the case, G. K. Chesterton said it best when he observed that the young man knocking on the door of the bordello is actually seeking the love of God. The lothario's means are gravely mistaken, but his desire for the good is real and perhaps so real that it will propel him eventually to abandon counterfeits and discover the genuine good of sacrificial love.

1. *Solidarity and the Natural Inclination to Self-Preservation*

As with all of the natural inclinations found in the constitution of human life and consciousness there is empirical documentation to show that people are constantly oriented to preserve their lives by working tirelessly to achieve the basics of survival—food, shelter, and clothing. Pinckaers makes the astute point that, as powerful as it may be on the natural level, the inclination to preserve one's life is even more radically operative on the spiritual level. One could cite the popularity of the self-help genre of popular books, groaning endlessly on shelves at Wal-Mart or Borders, which people read so that they can not only fix plumbing problems but also get in touch with their inner plumber. P. T. Barnum must be laughing somewhere about the profits realized from the craze of pop psychology texts. Yet the urge is real enough, not only to live, *esse*, but to live well, *ad bene esse*. Books on religion, mysticism, contemplation, mysteries of the universe, and astrology provide a dizzying array of windows into the meaning of life. If some of the texts are silly, the urge to live and live well is quite serious, quite universal.

The civil and the criminal law have universally recognized the right of self-defense even to the point of using lethal force against an assailant. The U.S. Constitution includes in the Bill of Rights a number of safeguards which serve the interests of self-preservation such as the right against unreasonable search and seizure (the Fourth Amendment) and the right against self-incrimination (the Fifth Amendment). The Declaration of Independence put the right to life at the outset of its concerns.

Is the desire to preserve one's life a matter of vanity and egoism? Not at all. The mother may well want to live as long as she can so that she can help her handicapped child. The great double commandment of Christ—first, love God with your whole strength, soul, mind, and heart, and second, love your neighbor as yourself—rests on the proposition of self-love. Because of our human origin and shared destiny, no life is isolated from a larger communion. Pinckaers quotes Aristotle to the effect that the martyr who chooses to die for a truth does not forfeit his natural inclination to self-preservation but chooses to love his life in a more noble way.[193]

If the desire to live and live well is not egoistic, neither is it simply "conservative." At an early age, every individual realizes the dynamism of life. To survive is to adapt. Cardinal Newman rightly said that to live is to change and to live well is to change often. This changing dynamism and development occurs in tandem with the virtues, the interior dispositions that further activate the natural inclinations already present in human consciousness. To live life to the fullest is hardly a sentence of boredom; it is the greatest adventure to orient life toward maximum integrity and communion with others. As the Lord so powerfully put it, only by losing our life (that is, losing the self-absorption of egoism and narcissism) will we succeed in keeping or saving it.

The great philosopher Josef Pieper describes the virtue of temperance as "selfless self-preservation." This apt, paradoxical, and pithy description of moderation connects sexual desire with the love of friendship by rightly suggesting that one's desire to preserve one's life is precisely so that the love for another (his or her real interest and genuine good) can continue to be lived out. There's nothing selfish about wanting to live when your motivation is to give your life to another. Our solidarity with each other includes a witness to ultimate truths about our personal identity. No one is alone in the arduous struggle to resist the forces of greed, cruelty, and eroticism: each is a temptation to love on the cheap not worthy of the name.

The propensity of some Catholic moralists to see solidarity only as a virtue of social justice is disappointing. It is a corollary of creation that all creatures have a commitment to each other in every aspect of the wide range of basic human goods.[194] Catholic social teaching has since Pope Pius XII spoken of it from different vantage points—as principle, law, and virtue—and used equivalent terms of *friendship* and *social charity* to describe its contours.[195] Solidarity understood as both principle and virtue has application to like-minded peers who are struggling with a common burden, such as disordered or addictive sexual desire, and who are in daily need of support from others to keep them on the right path. This is another instance where *autonomy* or *privacy* fall short. A self-definition based on freedom, independent of truth, goodness, and beatitude, will not be compatible with the *kenosis* or self-emptying, self-sacrificial love essential to supporting the beloved in dealing with personal struggle.

Considered as a virtue, solidarity is invaluable for avoiding pharisaism and polarization. As a commitment to the common good, the virtue of solidarity makes it easier for all parties in a dialogue to come to terms with a radical honesty that replaces grandstanding or rhetoric. When biblical morality and the Judeo-Christian tradition teach that contraception is intrinsically wrong, or that a homosexual orientation is not sinful but disordered, or that cohabitation is a distortion of God's plan of covenantal love for couples, it is much easier to examine humbly the implications of that teaching when there is a solidarity of shared commitment to chastity at the outset of any discussion or debate. All are caught up in the fallout of original sin, concupiscence. Creation calls for redemption and makes it possible through Christ, the New Creation.

Sometimes, an individual is afraid to speak to a friend when there is convincing evidence that a moral issue is present and harmful. There may be compelling reasons to avoid an intervention (lack of opportunity, inadequate resources, a desire to wait for professional assistance at the right time), but the basis of a decision to intervene or not cannot be "what will my friend think of me?" as opposed to what is truly in the best interest of my friend.

The individualism of our culture has fostered a "don't get involved" and "live and let live" passivity that invariably results in harming countless individuals. Mere tolerance is clearly insufficient. There must be respect and solidarity, flowing from the practical wisdom or prudence that is unafraid to challenge our egos with the humbling reality that we are all sinners and in need of critical corrections from one another. Solidarity is a remedy for alienation, a correction of autonomy and a deterrent to anomie.

2. *Humility and the Natural Inclination to Knowledge of the Truth*

Pinckaers describes the love of truth as "the most human of all desires."[196]Clearly there is not a dual track here of a desire for the truth of science versus a desire for the truth of the humanities. The radical capacity for truth and the accompanying natural inclination to know the truth provides reason to believe that truth is indivisible. Children are well-known for asking endless questions, often socially awkward: "Why does Aunt Florence have such a red nose?" This desire to know the truth grows alongside our capacity to know the truth.

Saint Augustine said the right to know the truth is a splendid illustration of the common good. We owe one another the truth. At times it may be circumscribed by prudence, rights, and responsibilities, but clearly we are not free to dissemble in a community where the truth is an essential component of human well-being. When George Orwell said that our first duty to each other is to tell the truth, he was applying a moral truth to a political context. It is not by accident that Satan is known as the Father of Lies. Lies about the reputation of others are not only defamatory but damaging to the entire community. No one can afford the luxury of being indifferent to the truth or cavalier about the consequences of violating it.

The desire to know the truth advances to the contemplative domain, Pinckaers observes. We are not content with the mundane, technical, or functional aspects of life. The awareness of wonder and mystery gradually leads our desire for the truth to the source of all truth, the Logos who is the way, the truth, and the life (John 14:6).

Individuals are likely to disagree sharply and substantively about what constitutes the truth. That is not cause for alarm or dismay but confirmation that truth is universally accessible. If there were not the prospect that our dialogue and debate could refine our reflections and move us toward some shared grasp of basic truths, Augustine's common good, then we should be dismayed indeed. It is especially heartening to those who inquire about the truth of sexuality to be able to communicate, listening and learning from one another. Our desire for truth in general, elevating us to the contemplative plane as we survey the mystery of the person, propels us to see sexuality as part of that mystery. We cannot be content with a reductionist, purely functional view of human sexuality as simply a commodity or incidental experience that increases pleasure.

Once again, Pinckaers shows how science, supposedly the great legacy of the truth of the Enlightenment, has been caught up in a dreadful inversion of reality:

> Paradoxically, the development of modern sciences, which has extended human knowledge beyond all imagination, has boomeranged in a general relativism in all areas of learning and even in the perception of truth. The temptation to determinism in regard to scientific truth has been followed by the temptation to relativity in all branches of science and truth. Truth has become dependent on the thinker. It is bound up with his history, milieu, culture, interests, and social or political pressures. We say, therefore, "To each his truth," which amounts to a frank admission that there is no truth anymore.[197]

Pinckaers has again put his finger on what is depressing in this context. It is not the fact of disagreement about ethical models or sexual issues but the suffocating prejudice that no definitive or objective truths can be known. Relativism is not only at war with reality, it is utterly harmful to the needs of human beings whose lives depend on knowing and living the truth in communion with one another.

Notice how democratic is the Thomistic notion of a universal, natural inclination to know the truth. We are not dependent on elites, on ukases from church or state, or on solemn pronouncements by anointed or self-appointed guardians and keepers. Each one of us has the capacity and the desire to know the truth. This universal desire extends to children and the cognitively disabled. *All* have a desire to know the truth. If a patient who is comatose is unable to express or attain the truth in a coherent fashion, that defect does not vitiate the inherent desire for truth that is part of all human consciousness. This conviction that the natural desire for truth inheres in all human beings, presupposing as it does the capacity of each to understand the truth at some level, is the most anti-authoritarian proposition one could suppose.

As recorded in the Gospel of John, it is shortly after Jesus saves the life of an adulterous woman about to be stoned by the Pharisees for her misconduct that he utters the definitive truth about the truth: "You shall know the truth, and the truth shall make you free" (John 8:32). We shall not be free as moral agents until we have ascertained and begun to live the truth of our personhood, which includes the fragile links between eros, human identity, love, friendship, and communion.

3. *Justice and the Natural Inclination to Live in Society*

A Rand Corporation study released in August 2006 disclosed the finding that teenagers who downloaded sexually-charged music onto their iPods were more likely to have sex much earlier than other teenagers whose iPods did not contain sexually suggestive lyrics. An AP report carried by CNN.com summarized the findings as follows: "Teens who said they listened to lots of music with degrading sexual messages were almost twice as likely to start having intercourse or other sexual activities within the following two years as were teens who listened to little or no sexually degrading music. . . . Exposure to lots of sexually degrading music 'gives them a specific message about sex,' said lead author Steven Martino, a researcher for Rand Corp. in Pittsburgh. 'Boys learn they should be relentless in pursuit of women and girls learn to view themselves as sex objects,' he said."[198]

Pinckaers begins his consideration of justice by quoting Aristotle's *Politics* to the effect that only human beings have the power of speech. The above news account shows how the power of speech can have a dramatic impact on human behavior. The explosion of texting through digital devices so popular among young people highlights the importance of a virtue closely associated with justice and chastity, namely, modesty, the virtue of moderation in speech as well as attire. It is the young and impressionable of societies who have the most to lose by making poor decisions in matters of sex and love. Surely this kind of autonomy is not envisioned as ideal or helpful for adolescents by advocates of sexual liberation who continue to view the 1960s as a liberating epoch.

But is the above account from the Associated Press, reported by CNN, really news? Does it require two news services to inform us that extended, sexually explicit conversation with youngsters who are dealing with a riptide of hormonal confusion are likely to be influenced to act on the music and lyrics that they hear? Once again, common sense trumps ideology, leading all civic-minded individuals to recognize that the sexual arena is not exempt from principles of cause and effect.

Is this a call for censorship? Perhaps. At the very least it is a wake-up call for a society that cannot consistently choose unlimited sexual expression in every possible medium except for those accessible to teenagers. There is an almost schizophrenic conflict between uninhibited sexual expression in the culture and strict restrictions on any kind of sexual communication in the workplace. The split in models of acceptable behavior —culture versus workplace—is hard either to comprehend or observe. A worker is inevitably left confused about what constitutes "autonomy" in the workplace. Does it mean the absence of any affective dimension at all? How much is too much or the wrong type?

The natural inclination to live in society presupposes our capacity to communicate with each other. The desire for communion (*koinonia*) displays the universal need for friendship. The virtue of friendship can be seen here in sharper relief as one of the linked desires and inclinations—the good, knowledge of the truth, self-preservation, and sexual integrity.

It is certainly no surprise that a Thomistic template is largely consistent with the work of Aristotle. Accordingly, in the *Nicomachean Ethics*, Aristotle remarks that where friendship exists in a society there is no formal need for the virtue of justice since the object of friendship, whereby the subject treats a friend as his other self, accomplishes all of the goals of the virtue of justice. Saint Thomas totally agrees that friendship covers the waterfront more effectively than justice but with the one important amendment that friendship includes not only interaction between human peers but also encompasses divine grace since Thomas considers grace to be friendship with God.

What a different template this is than that found in much popular speech. Raunchy lyrics on iPods hardly inspire friendship, love, or communion. But, speaking of justice, it is not fair to criticize teenagers for responding with technical imagination to their own natural desires of curiosity and sexual energy. This disturbing news account of the link between suggestive speech and irresponsible behavior places a premium on communications between generations. Where are the parents to inform, counsel, direct and lead these youngsters away from the temptations of the streets? Aristotle also wisely states in the *Nicomachean Ethics* that parents cannot be the friends of their children since friendship requires a relationship of equals and children do not yet have a background sufficient to render them as peers of their parents.

A possible corollary of the Rand Corporation study is to take it one step further and hypothesize that those youngsters who do not have healthy or regular conversations with their parents are more likely to download objectionable and obscene music onto their iPods. It seems that a contemporary news account, disturbing in its implications, confirms the wisdom of Saint Thomas that there is indeed a natural inclination to societal interaction of which speech is an essential part. The quality of that speech will to a great degree dictate the quality of the community. It will determine whether individuals struggling with the burst of sexual energy will find themselves part of a genuine communion, a *koinonia*, or be left to experiment for themselves about the mysteries of human intimacy with ear buds in their ears and a huge void in their souls.

4. *Chastity and the Natural Inclination to Sexual Integrity*

One can understand how a reader today might well be skeptical about any discussion of sexuality coming from a Catholic priest. The torrent of clergy sex abuse cases is not only scandalous but sickening. There is terrible pain and justifiable outrage as reports of sexual abuse of minors have emerged and there can be no doubt that youthful victims of horrendous crimes have been wounded by actions that have hurt them at a most vulnerable time in their life. At the same time it is necessary to resist the temptation to search for simplistic explanations for reprehensible behavior. The church must constantly reaffirm her efforts to maintain a mandatory safe environment to protect children.

There is reason to believe that the Charter for the Protection of Children and Young People adopted by the U.S. Conference of Catholic Bishops has provided substantive guidance and direction toward accountability and transparency. I believe that instances of sexual abuse do not in any way negate the dominant thesis of this essay that the standard of autonomy is very limited in its capacity to provide the basis for friendship, love and truly virtuous relationships. The effects of a value-free autonomy generate a most dangerous environment where abuse can overpower accountability.

In the Old Testament, Moses led the Chosen People through the desert to the very brink of the Promised Land. Similarly, the late Servais Pinckaers has provided us with a creative recovery of the thought of Saint Thomas sufficient to set foot in the arena of sexual integrity. Pinckaers's monumental contribution can be thematically summarized as follows: sexual desires and deeds which are consistent with the natural inclinations to real goods and corresponding truths such as self-preservation, friendship (society), and the marital covenant (an exclusive, lifetime union of one man and one woman, open to children) constitute sexual integrity. The converse holds as well: any desire or deed at variance with real goods, authentic truths, self-preservation, friendship, and the marital covenant is morally deficient and cannot count as sexual integrity. As with the format of the Ten Commandments, the use of negative prohibitions (no stealing, no lying) can be misleading. The content could not be more expansive or positive: there is no limit on created goods to be enjoyed or truths to be told. Similarly, there is no limit on the ways in which all human virtue—and sexual integrity, in particular—can be lived.

The *Catechism of the Catholic Church* identifies chastity as a vocation as well as a virtue: "Chastity means the successful integration of sexuality within the person and thus the inner unity of man in his bodily and spiritual being. Sexuality, in which man's belonging to the bodily and biological world is expressed, becomes personal and truly human when it is integrated into the relationship of one person to another, in the complete and lifelong mutual gift of a man and a woman. The virtue of chastity therefore involves the integrity of the person and the integrity of the gift."[199]

Chastity as a virtue is linked intrinsically with the full array of real goods that characterize human flourishing. This means that chastity is not a label attached by an extrinsic authority but a goal-oriented call or challenge to live out a unity of body and soul. The human body is not incidental or accidental to our personhood.

It is not surprising that there should be a link between human desire and divine grace: "Chastity is a moral virtue. It is also a gift from God, a grace, a fruit of spiritual effort."[200] The link here between human endeavor and divine gift could not be more explicit. The calling to live in a way compatible with all related goods and natural inclinations toward excellence demonstrates that our Creator loves us beyond measure, intending for us to "taste and see the goodness of the Lord" (Psalm 34:8), an invitation that is fulfilled through, and not apart from, our human sexuality.

Grace is always provided where there is a struggle. The virtue of chastity is no exception to this truth of revelation. Chastity is an arduous good and gift, requiring the full cooperation of human endeavor and divine grace. That it is a calling, a vocation, means that it is worth pursuing over the course of one's lifetime, as a struggle for daily growth and an ennobling experience of ongoing conversion. The Enlightenment model of autonomy, dominant for centuries, makes no room for vocation since it is devoid of any teleology. Virtues are by definition the antithesis of isolation in that they dispose the subject to real goods outside of the self. Autonomy is an antagonist of relationships, communion, and marriage because it is blind to the importance of truth, beatitude, and the goodness that exists outside of the self.

This means in specific terms that our sexuality is inclined toward union, a uniting or communion not merely of two bodies but of two persons—unities of body and soul—of the opposite sex who are committed to each other in a sacramental bond forever, open to the possibility of children and oriented toward a family that images in a human yet very real way the life of the Trinity.

Once again, it is the core constitution of human beings that verifies the nature of this sexual union to which individuals are inclined. First, it is a union, which is by definition a bond between *two* different parties. Since our bodies are not interchangeable, this means that the bond is between male and female. Only in the bond of two sexes can there be a genuine union of differences, of a subject loving *another*. The vision of Genesis (2:24–26) that the union of husband and wife is a two-in-one-flesh union receives the explicit affirmation of Jesus in the Gospels (Matthew 19:4–8; Mark 10.6–9). The path to divine love and human life passes through human flesh, including its inclination to perfect good. Reason and revelation are fully in accord. Eros is the subject of a call to communion. Communion is made possible by the gift of creation and redeemed by the atoning love of Christ.

FIVE

TRANSCENDENCE AND TRANSFORMATION

Only the thinker who starts from the integral existent being and
uses as his lever the radical integrity and transcendent power of
Being (*esse*) discoverable in that integral existent, can hope to
reach the Absolute Esse, the Infinite Act of Being who is God.
Any thinker who takes the mind as his starting point is bound to
be caught in the wash of the intrinsic finitude of the human dimension and sucked down into the ontological void.

— Cornelio Fabro

We have looked at the concept of autonomy associated with Immanuel Kant
and examined its impact upon the sexual revolution, a result that occurred
through landmark rulings of the Supreme Court. In the previous chapter,
we explored an alternative vision of human identity and moral choice in
the teleological perspective of Servais Pinckaers. This vision underscores
the importance of one's orientation, by natural inclination and virtue, to the
good—understood most fully and expansively as God, the source and goal
of all human goodness. This inclination to the good is, for Pinckaers and
the Judeo-Christian tradition, not merely an incidental aspect of human
identity but a constitutive element of human action in the moral sphere.
Good is to be done and evil is to be avoided, as the primary precept of the
natural law affirms, but if good is amorphous and limited, devoid of a transcendent focus, it is only partially a good.

In our critique of autonomy and our argument that it leaves the
supposedly liberated subject terribly vulnerable to alienation and anomie,
we have essentially been looking at a world view where transcendence and
transformation—realities at the core of the Pinckaers sense of inclination
toward the truth, goodness, and beatitude—play little or no role. Transcendence and transformation only make sense if there is a God. There is a vast

and growing body of literature on theism, antitheism, and atheism; there is no effort here to duplicate these efforts. But having looked at the role of reason and revelation, we can ask a final question. Is it reasonable to believe in God today? We ask this because, if there is no God, there is no point to transcendence, transformation or, for that matter, Pinckaers's theological anthropology. This is our quest in this concluding chapter, an argument that transcendence, transformation, and the divine are not only reasonable but indispensable to human well-being.

For the good to be open-ended and beyond boundaries such as irrationality, narrow self-interest, or disorienting sentiment (the Humean alternative to Kant's fixation on duty, omnipresent today as ethical emotivism), there is required, simply, God. Nietzsche may get his due in killing the clockmaker deity who is nothing but pure human abstraction, rather than pure spirit or absolute good—the understanding of God mediated by the Old and New Testaments. One does not have to be a disciple of the political philosopher Leo Strauss to take his point that Athens and Jerusalem, eponyms for the competing claims of human reason and divine revelation, continue as an ongoing polarity of fruitful tension in which both reason and revelation have a contribution to make: "Strauss denied that modern philosophy had put an end to this conflict by refuting revelation; indeed, its unsuccessful efforts to do so through transforming philosophy into systematic certainty had only blurred or destroyed that awareness of ignorance that is the philosopher's primary evidence of the need for philosophy."[201]

But is the pursuit of good the same thing as the pursuit of God? If there is at least a connection, as the West has historically argued, then we are presented with a problem in the eclipse of God in an increasingly secularized world. Without an ultimate, unconditional, and transcendent *telos*, the good without God loses perspective and content.

To complete our assessment of Enlightenment autonomy and its contemporary consequences, in determining whether a Thomistic recovery typified by Pinckaers can lead us out of some serious problems, we must address to some degree the "God Question." Otherwise we will not have an intelligible or even defensible view of the good. Our central contention is that the autonomy of the Enlightenment has not equipped contemporary people with the spiritual, moral, and religious tools needed to make moral decisions in a way that supports sexual integrity, marriage, the family, and the common good of society. What is needed is an alternative vision of an authentic, measured autonomy—participated theonomy, in the language of

Pope John Paul II—not absolute but personalist, relational, and communitarian, whereby each self (each person) enjoys a vital relation to a transcendent absolute and thereby has the essential capacity to be in communion with others.

The Finality and Fragility of the Good

The eradication of any serious theology of creation by the Enlightenment reduced the creative power of God to mere efficient causality: the divine is simply the prime mover that brings about something new. Final causality—the rationale of purposive activity—disappears in this ideological attack on the role of creation. Yet the human reality of acting for a purpose cannot disappear because people are ontologically wired to act for reasons in behalf of perceived goods. The "to-do" list arrives in the mind as soon as the subject emerges from sleep. We can report then that reports of the death of teleology (as with that of Nietzsche's God) are greatly exaggerated. But teleology, final causality, remains as fragile as the goods with which it is connected. They must be considered together.

One can readily admire the insight underpinning the very title of Martha C. Nussbaum's widely read and well-received *The Fragility of the Good*. As a distinguished philosopher and student of ancient Greek philosophy, Nussbaum is tireless in charting the views of Plato and Aristotle on major issues such as love, friendship, power, and society. Although questions arise on the exact nature of eros in her scholarship (Charles Taylor, for one, sees it differently), Nussbaum is invaluable in her sketches and comparisons of the Greek philosophers.

We have already noted her insight that Aristotle stresses the importance of friendship in empowering a subject to perceive reality accurately through the experience and wisdom of friends. The insight and counsel of friends is invaluable for discovering the truth. This is one of the few areas where Aristotle departs from his standard of self-sufficiency as the norm for the magnanimous person. The problem today is that the autonomy left us by the Enlightenment is simply an updated version of self-sufficiency not well-equipped to discover truth apart from the experience and insight afforded by friendships. It is no surprise that Aristotle, given his empirical approach, would see clearly a point missed by the legacy of a rationalism inclined to deal with abstractions rather than experience. Neither friendship nor love can qualify as an abstraction.

Nussbaum makes a further point supportive of our critique of autonomy or self-sufficiency when she shows how Aristotle departs again from his favored and almost invariable standard of self-sufficiency when the subject is love: "There are, however, other important human values that lie at the opposite end of the self-sufficiency spectrum: above all, the good activities connected with citizenship and political attachment, and those involved in personal love and friendship. For these require, and are in their nature relations with, a particular human context that is highly vulnerable and can easily fail to be present. Love requires another loving person. . . . Furthermore, love and friendship . . . are in their nature *relations*, rather than virtuous states (*hexeis*)-plus-activities."[202]

Nussbaum's observation that the Aristotelian notion of love and friendship is a relation rather than a state brilliantly summarizes the limits of autonomy understood as a self-sufficient power or status. Not only does this attempt at self-sufficiency fail to qualify as a relation, needed for love, but it actually opposes love and friendship by so emphasizing the self-sufficient state as to render otiose the very vulnerability and mutuality needed for love to be fulfilled.

Nussbaum amplifies the implications of this point: "Love and friendship . . . are in their very nature contingent relationships between separate elements in the world. Each rests upon and is in complex ways connected with other traits of the person, such as generosity, justice, and kindliness; but there is no trait of being loving or being friendly, that stands to love exactly as being courageous stands to courageous action, viz. as its mainspring and, impediments absent, its sufficient condition. . . . Love is not simply a loving state of character plus a suitable context for its activation."[203]

This means that being autonomous is a state of desired self-sufficiency that might be compared to courage: one can be courageous independent of the traits of another. But love and friendship—eros, agape, and *philia*—are fragile, vulnerable relationships with another, dependent to a great degree on the kind of mutuality that characterizes the relationship. One will have a genuine love and friendship if the mutual relation is virtuous; if the mutuality is merely one of usefulness or manipulation, the eros of desire and the *philia* of a quest for friendship will not be reciprocated. Desire will remain unfulfilled, possibly in a painful way.

Nussbaum emphasizes that for Aristotle the other person, the beloved, plays a central role as subject: "The other person enters in not just as an object who receives the good activity, but as an intrinsic part of love itself. But if this is so, . . . then these components of the good life are going to be minimally self-sufficient. And they will be vulnerable in an especially deep and dangerous way. . . . [Aristotle] announces quite clearly, towards the beginning of the *Nicomachean Ethics*, that the sort of self-sufficiency that characterizes the best human life is a communal and not a solitary self-sufficiency."[204]

I believe that Nussbaum has accurately and powerfully identified the contradictions of a view that claims autonomous self-sufficiency to be the best stance or state for experiencing desire. This notion of autonomy does not recognize that desire and love are part of a mutual relation, laden with fragility and vulnerability, as opposed to a status of power indifferent to truth, beatitude, and goodness and in tension with the autonomy of another. The claim of self-sufficiency is antithetical to any expression of eros, let alone its fulfillment, because self-sufficiency rebuffs mutuality, reciprocity, or vulnerability.

If Aristotle, seen through the lens of Nussbaum, is right that the good of love (including desire and friendship) is quite fragile, then it is imperative to provide it with a firm and lasting foundation. I submit that the contingencies of this good, this relation of love and friendship, are so fragile that they require the support of unconditional love for any human, frail, utterly contingent good of love to survive.

If the human or complete good (*teleion*) is dependent upon the plenitude of divine goodness, we must necessarily explore the role of the divine. This is not at all an onerous task because our whole thesis proposes that authentic autonomy, participated theonomy, and human integrity are an integral part of a theological anthropology, an understanding of persons as bearers of the very image and likeness of the divine. To pursue the implications of the divine good is not an extra task but an inquiry essential to our view of the human.

The intellectual horizon of this inquiry today is secularization, the fact that the West has moved decidedly, if not decisively, away from a reliance on divine causality to explain human phenomena. The medieval synthesis of virtues directing human actions toward God and ultimate goods cannot simply be transferred to the contemporary scene as though secularization and atheism did not exist. They are, after all, forces flowing in turbulent currents of contemporary unbelief, both causing that unbelief and changing the conditions under which people can still claim to believe in God. We have to consider the theoretical possibility that the secular and atheistic critiques of the Judeo-Christian moral tradition have rendered pointless anything proposed about a Pinckaers-inspired *ressourcement*[205] toward a classic synthesis of virtue, sex, and the good oriented toward God. If atheism has triumphed, eliminating the notion of unconditional good as a plausible hypothesis, then our efforts have sadly failed. Clearly we need to consider whether secularity, secularism, secularization, and atheism have made the recovery of a virtue-based ethic impossible.

THE CONTRIBUTION OF CHARLES TAYLOR

We are quite fortunate in the timing of this inquiry to have the definitive study of contemporary secularization now available in the work of the Canadian philosopher Charles Taylor. His *A Secular Age*[206] is a massive tour de force of philosophy, theology, culture, and sociology, published in 2007, that asks what has led to the decline of religious belief (and a religiously based view of human sexuality) from 1500 to the present. He spends considerable time examining the "nova effect" of the second half of the twentieth century that has opened up new expressions of both belief and unbelief.

Taylor is a Catholic critical of what he calls the "cramped, desire-obsessed mode of spirituality"[207] of contemporary Catholicism in regard to sexual ethics. His unhappiness with Vatican pronouncements on sex is modified by his conviction that secularization has not destroyed the foundation of religious belief but has instead changed the circumstances of believers. I shall try to summarize some of his major points that link secularization, belief, morality, the Enlightenment, autonomy, the sexual revolution, transcendence, and transformation. Using Taylor's framework as a guide, I will then propose a *ressourcement* or recovery of classical philosophical and theological themes to energize a practical anthropology and jurisprudence that moves us beyond the quagmire of an absolutized privacy that has become sexual anarchy.

As a meticulous and masterful scholar who carefully traces patterns of belief and unbelief in the mindsets of believers and unbelievers from ancient times to the present, Taylor describes "exclusive humanism" as a stance that combines two polarities: (1) the negative polarity of a Weberian "disenchantment" from earlier myths of fairies, spirits, and magical powers that held the pre-scientific world captive with an attachment to myth, a world view of sacred symbols that dominated and controlled popular consciousness; and (2) a universal commitment to benevolence as a positive equivalent to agape formerly understood as the unconditional love of God for humanity. This would amount to a totally immanent expression of unconditional love exclusive of God. The problem is that, in the absence of God—unconditional love—there is no other foundation for a universal, unconditional love. Expressions of benevolence would inevitably be contingent on human preferences, prejudices, and limits.

This narrative of exclusive humanism "closes the transcendent window, as though there were nothing beyond."[208] Taylor is pleased with the achievements of the Enlightenment but opposed to the hostile attitude of exclusive humanism toward transcendence. He describes his incredibly detailed effort to comprehend secularization as a story largely about transcendence and transformation. It is the link of these polarities limned by Taylor that I borrow to entitle this chapter and conclude our inquiry on eros, autonomy, and the quest for communion.

Taylor sees the eighteenth-century era of "Providential Deism" as critical in ushering in the now formidable worldview of exclusive humanism, that is, atheism. As the Deists focused more and more on God as a distant force, a clockmaker unconcerned with the mechanics of this world's operation, the Enlightenment forces succeeded in bringing about an anthropological turn with four key components that would reinforce one another in the diminution of transcendence as a dominant influence.

Initially an entirely immanent, this-worldly horizon began to dominate European consciousness, as Taylor notes: "Now the first anthropocentric shift comes with the eclipse of this sense of further purpose; and hence of the idea that we owe God anything further than the realization of his plan. Which means fundamentally that we owe him essentially the achievement of our own good."[209]

This stance would make sense in light of the religious upheavals of the Reformation and religious wars that divided Europe. If no universal consensus on the identity and role of God could be found, individuals of different faiths could still strike an agreement at least on what kind of flourishing should be pursued in this world.

The second result of Providential Deism, following upon the eclipse of the transcendent, was the turn against grace and toward reason, powered by scientific inquiry and human experience, the laboratory of progress: "The second anthropocentric shift was the eclipse of grace. The order God designed was there for reason to see. By reason and discipline, humans could rise to the challenge and realize it."[210]

What Taylor's anthropological tableau does is enflesh and elaborate the consequences of the demand by the Enlightenment standard of autonomy that there not be any extrinsic—heteronomous—force to restrict the self-defining, self-sufficient individual. By moving away from tran-scendence, there is no larger-than-human presence required for human well-being, and by moving away from a theology of grace, there is no longer a concession that divine support might be required to achieve the well-being of humanity in the context of creation.

A third consequence, following immediately as yet another anthro-pological turn, is the loss of the sense of mystery associated with provi-dence, transcendence, and grace:

> The third shift follows from the first two. The sense of mystery fades. . . . If God's purposes for us encompass only our own good, and this can be read from the design of our nature, then no further mystery can hide here. If we set aside one of the cen-tral mysteries of traditional Christian faith, that of evil, of our estrangement from God, and inability to return to him unaided, but we see all the motivation we need already there, either in our self-interest well understood, or in our feelings of benevo-lence, then there is no further mystery in the human heart.[211]

I believe that this loss of the sense of mystery plays an enormous role in the unfolding of the jurisprudence of American courts in looking at issues and affected institutions (such as marriage and the family) of sexual ethics as matters of privacy rather than mystery. The courts are using a functional framework to evaluate ontological realities such as love, friendship, and, yes, mystery.

It is not the role of a court to be a referee or arbiter of mystery but to recognize its limitations in doing so. The courts are using a functional construct of instrumental reason derived from the self-sufficient persona of a contemporary, autonomous agent in an area where self-sufficiency or autonomy simply doesn't work, as Nussbaum shows above in her interpre-tation of Aristotle on the limits of autonomy or self-sufficiency when the subject is love. Eros and communion lose their synergy in the absence of mystery; any reduction to a purely functional status impoverishes human subjectivity and the prospects of communion with other individuals.

The fourth and final anthropological turn identified by Taylor as part of the Providential Deism of the eighteenth century was the loss of any urgent sense of transformation:

> The fourth shift came with the eclipse of the idea that God was planning a transformation of human beings, which would take

them beyond the limitations which inhere in their present condition. In the Christian tradition, this has usually been expressed in terms of humans becoming partakers in the life of God. The Greek fathers, followed by the Cambridge Platonists, spoke of "theiosis," a "becoming divine," which was part of human destiny. This prospect is, in a sense, a counterpart to the demand to go beyond merely human flourishing. The call to love God, and love Creatures in the fulsome way that God does, is matched by the promise of a change which will make these heights attainable for us.[212]

The loss of transcendence effectively diminishes any need for transformation. An entirely immanent, this-world-only humanism, exclusive of God, grace, and mystery, has become not only an attractive but generally preferred stance of secularization in most of the West. It cannot be construed, Taylor insists, as merely a succession of "subtractions" (that is, removals of myths, fantasies, and religious rituals) or negative trends within Latin Christendom, (such as the loss of faith, the loss of reverence) but is a positive affirmation of human flourishing as an end in itself, and a move toward universal benevolence as the exclusive, humanist alternative to notions of agape tainted by conflicting theories of God, virtue, sin, and grace.

We can begin to appreciate how profound are the consequences of this four-pronged anthropological shift by contrasting it with the classic, premodern view of Thomas Aquinas on the importance of grace: "Now the gift of grace surpasses every capability of created nature, since it is nothing short of a partaking of the Divine Nature, which exceeds every other nature. And thus it is impossible that any creature should cause grace. For it is as necessary that God alone should deify, bestowing a partaking of the Divine Nature by a participated likeness, as it is impossible that anything save fire should enkindle."[213]

In this thirteenth-century treatise on the importance of grace, Saint Thomas clearly identifies the overarching realities rejected by the Enlightenment (transcendence, grace, mystery, and transformation) and contrasts them with each of the four shifts identified by Taylor as consequences of the Enlightenment and eighteenth-century Providential Deism: there is, first, transcendence ("Divine Nature"), now lost; second, grace ("partaking of the Divine Nature"), now dismissed; third, mystery ("participated likeness"), now abandoned; and, fourth, transformation ("every *capability* of created nature"), no longer needed.

I believe that any inquiry about ethics, religion, and history is deeply indebted to Charles Taylor for providing this imposing account of a theological and anthropological sea change. I have only made scant—but I hope, pointed—reference to the assessment of Taylor. It buttresses my conviction that the issues of sexual integrity and jurisprudence are ultimately a matter of theological anthropology. I will propose now a return to the rich fountain of theological insight, the *Summa Theologica* of Saint Thomas, as appraised and recovered in the contemporary setting by Pinckaers, among others, and discover there a roadmap away from the jejune, flattened landscape of Enlightenment-generated autonomy and self-sufficiency that militate against love, friendship, and communion.

Taylor summarizes his belief that, while the meaning of *transcendence* may not be easy to pin down, "I hold that religious longing, the longing for and response to a more-than-immanent transformation perspective, . . . remains a strong independent source of motivation in modernity."[214]

Taylor affirms his conviction that a "transformation perspective" continues as a strong option for our contemporary society even though there are competing visions of transformation. The range would include traditional Christian perspectives on service in this world as a path toward salvation (including the Social Gospel movement), at one end, and a Marxist emphasis on class conflict and praxis to achieve a purely immanent but just society, on the other end of the spectrum of quasi-salvific agendas.

Taylor argues persuasively that we live in an intellectual setting radically different from the predominant Latin Christendom of the early eighteenth century, an axial point in changing anthropological perceptions. This intellectual setting is more than just a collective mindset or social theory but a "social imaginary," that is, "the way that we collectively imagine, even pre-theoretically, our social life in the contemporary Western world."[215] A new anthropology of markedly different theological premises has come into existence. One cannot simply claim the triumph of atheism because atheism itself is a theological stance, an assertion of chance, randomness, or denial as opposed to an affirmation of being.

It is to these theological dimensions of the contemporary milieu, as sketched by Taylor's four components of the post-Enlightenment anthropological view—the losses, respectively, of transcendence, grace, mystery, and transformation—that we shall now turn. The contrary vision, found in the work of Pinckaers and succinctly stated in the quotation above from the *Summa Theologica* of Saint Thomas in his treatise on grace, serves as a classic parameter by which we can assess the enormous difference between a theistic, pre-Reformation understanding of God and grace and today's social imaginary or daily, prethematic sense of an immanent world—humanist, yet exclusive of and separate from transcendent being and its accompanying dimensions of grace, mystery, and transformation.

A RETURN TO THE ROOTS: *RESSOURCEMENT*

Each of these "turns" also prompts the proposal here for a "return," in my view, to allow Pinckaers to serve as the salient for a recovery from the wintry blast of an environment quite cold to the influence of transcendence, grace, mystery, and transformation. I believe that scholars of contemporary patterns of belief and morality are hugely indebted to Charles Taylor for identifying precisely and imaginatively these four eclipses caused by Providential Deism. At the same time, I now propose to use Taylor's terms but move beyond them, quite possibly in a direction he would not favor. Frankly, I do not see "the Vatican" as a coterie of rule-makers but as a singular voice speaking authoritatively about the very transcendence, grace, mystery, and transformation whose departure Taylor laments. It may be that transcendence has no better earthly friend than the Vatican; at this point, transcendence needs every friend possible.

The work of the *Ressourcement* school of Catholic scholars led them to probe the tradition of faith beyond its immediate Tridentine contours. Reaching back to scriptural and patristic sources, theologians such as Yves Congar (1904–95), Jean Daniélou (1905–74) and Hans Urs von Balthasar (1905–88) demonstrated that neo-scholasticism did not capture the full breadth of the tradition. Their scholarship is at the heart of varied theological achievements of the Second Vatican Council (1962–65). I believe that a similar recovery of the larger Western tradition of transcendence, grace, mystery, and transformation can prompt an enriched appreciation of Western humanism beyond its present contours dictated by the Enlightenment.

After we see how there can and should be a recovery of these dimensions at the theological and philosophical levels, we shall conclude by calling for a jurisprudence that is at least respectful of these historical currents.

1. *The Recovery of Transcendence*

A tradition of theism marks the story of human civilization.

Whether Western or Eastern, ancient or modern, the sense of a divine being is never far from appraisals of human life and moral choices. It is possible to believe in transcendent goods or values such as love, loyalty, and friendship, but unless that belief includes a horizon beyond boundaries, these ideals shall run up against limits such as self-interest or tribal identity which will severely restrict the scope and influence of love, loyalty, or friendship. Not only is the transcendent dimension of human searching a shorthand for the divine, it also touches upon two topics of premium importance to our inquiry about autonomy and eros, namely, the role of a *telos* or moral purpose and the proper scope of natural law. I believe that the recovery of a teleological perspective allied with an understanding of natural law as the identifier, exponent, and servant of human goods, is not only possible but eminently desirable.

Is it ethically wise or morally astute to posit a human existence that is irretrievably limited? Does not the capacity for growth in learning and human endeavor defy any placement of boundaries upon human achievement? How ironic that at a time when science takes ever more seriously the possibility of life on other planets, actively moving to explore those planets, that an ideological cloud should cover the possibility of transcendent life beyond known human confines.

Charles Taylor examines the thought of Martha Nussbaum in some of her recent works (*Love's Knowledge*; *The Fragility of Goodness*) on the topic of transcendence.[216] Taylor sees Nussbaum as an ally of Nietzsche on the claim that Christianity has attempted to destroy eros in the name of transcendence: "Here Nussbaum takes up one of the central themes, one of the constitutive polemics of our secular age, as I am trying to describe it. Hatred at Christianity for having defamed, polluted, rendered impure ordinary human sensual desire is one of the most powerful motivations which impelled people to take the option for an exclusive humanism, once this became thinkable."[217]

Taylor is at great pains to avoid a polemical battle between the Nietzsche-inspired, Nussbaum-supported battle against transcendence; he does not want to provide any encouragement for "cramped, obsessed"[218] proponents of a transcendence that does not value sufficiently the body or the demands of erotic desire. My effort here is probably close to the polemic that Taylor seeks to avoid but I believe his own scholarship impels him to defend the concept of transcendence, which he does in superlative fashion, in a way that requires an ordering of sexual priorities. The whole point of transcendence is that human desires are ordered to a horizon that surpasses human finitude. How could we exempt or exclude sexual desire from this kind of ordering? Taylor seems to suggest that any sort of argumentation in favor of sexual restraint is mere polemic. Much more is at stake. The issue is not the style of argumentation but the foundational meaning of the transcendent good.

To recover an awareness of God, a transcendent, entirely good reality, consistent with sacred texts of the Judeo-Christian tradition, is very much in the interests of humanism today. To those who argue that the forces of religion have unleashed violence born of religious belief upon those stigmatized as unbelievers, one must, with Pope John Paul II, acknowledge that sins have indeed been committed in the name of serving God. Nevertheless, the ongoing debates within Christianity and those larger clashes of religious belief involving Islam and atheism are all attuned to the urgency of defining and pursuing what is truly good. All adherents of belief or unbelief are compelled by reason and experience to acknowledge that harming innocent parties violates the humanity of both aggressors and victims, even if disagreement exists as to which party is innocent.

I believe it is fair to say that a commitment to a transcendent notion of the good is required by any version or variant of humanism. To "exclude" (using Taylor's sense of "exclusive humanism") the transcendent from the experience of humanism is actually to maim and deform such a species of humanism, rendering it a caricature of real instances of human flourishing arising from divine communion. One thinks readily of ancient Greece, the Stoics of Rome, Augustine, Aquinas, Baroque art, the Renaissance, and religious-friendly literature from the nineteenth century into the present (Dostoyevsky, Tolstoy, T. S. Eliot, Evelyn Waugh, Dorothy Sayers, Walker Percy, Allen Tate, W. H. Auden, Shusaku Endo, and Flannery O'-Connor). Belief in the God of Jerusalem is not at all to abbreviate the reason of Athens.

Two aspects of transcendence desperately in need of recovery are the sense of *telos* (purposiveness, goal-oriented striving that transcends immediate self-interest) and a sense of natural law that permits and encourages such teleological striving. Taylor is typically insightful in describing how Natural Law is seen much differently in the "modern moral order." After speaking of a change in the nature of science, Taylor turns toward the rejection of a teleological perspective and the resulting atomism of what emerges essentially as a utilitarian calculus:

> A lot in this scientific revolution turns on the rejection of a mode
> of normative thinking in terms of *tele*. Now this rejection was

also a central part of much of the moral thinking which emerges
from the modern idea of order. This found expression in the anti-
Aristotelian animus of Locke and those he influenced. Of course,
the rejection of teleology was famously motivated by a stance
supporting the new, mechanistic science. But it was also animated by the emerging moral theory. What distinguished the
new, atomist, Natural Law theory from its predecessor as formulated by Aquinas, for instance, was its thoroughgoing detachment from the Aristotelian matrix which had been central for
Thomas. The correct political forms were not deducible from a
telos at work in human society. What justified the law was either
its being commanded by God (Locke), or its making logical
sense, given the rational and social nature of humans (Grotius),
or (later) its providing a way of securing the harmony of interests.[219]

The rejection of teleology is also the rejection of relationality because the transcendent, to which every human *telos* is connected, happens
to be, in the experience of the Judeo-Christian narrative, a *personal* transcendent. This was precisely the reality lost in the aftermath of Providential
Deism, namely, the rejection of a personal *Deus* (whether understood as
Yahweh, Adonai, El Shaddai, or the Father of Jesus Christ). To speak of
"the transcendent" is in fact erroneous because it is merely adjectival, a
modifier in search of a substantive. The God of Abraham, Isaac, Jacob, and
Jesus Christ is a Supreme Being, not only a *personal* deity but the very
model of all human personhood, in whose image and likeness believers
sense themselves to be fashioned.

Taylor's reference above to Hugo Grotius (1583–1645), the Dutch
jurist, is noteworthy because the suggestion by Grotius in his 1625 work
On the Law of War and Peace, that the natural law (*jus naturale*) would
apply whether or not there is a God, and whether or not God takes any interest in human affairs, lays the groundwork for Thomas Hobbes's total rejection of Aristotelian-Thomistic natural law. The first major work of
Hobbes (1588–1679) was entitled *De Cive* (*On the Citizen*, 1642) and was
published just seventeen years after Grotius's *On the Law of War and
Peace*, 1625. "Grotius' derivation of Natural Law doesn't follow the path
of an Aristotelian–Thomist definition of the ends of human nature. . . .
Grotius, who was a follower of Lipsius, thinks that this law is binding in
reason alone (hence his famous assertion, that the Law would hold, "*etsi
Deus non daretur*" [even if God did not exist])."[220]

When Grotius speaks of law apart from God, he opens the door to a view of natural law not only devoid of God but devoid of a notion of transcendent good intrinsically linked with God: "This statement—which Grotius, it should be noted, instantly acknowledges as blasphemous—constitutes an indication that a desacralization of natural law is conceivable to Grotius without thereby necessarily destroying its essential validity as a rule of reason to reasonable creatures. But even this cautious statement, because it suggests the possibility of the independence of natural law from both revealed and natural theology, was interpreted by a number of Grotius' contemporaries as marking a decided break with medieval and classical doctrines."[221]

Not only will Hobbes continue this foray into a nontheistic understanding of law but he will also move the entire concept of law away from reason toward the arbitrary exercise of the will in search of self-interest and power. The loss of deity is also the loss of transcendence and even the loss of any transcendent reason or good:

> Hobbes defines law in terms of will, not reason. Counsel, on the other hand, bases itself on reasons, reasons deduced from the benefit to be gained by the one counseled. Counsel aims, or pretends to aim, at the good of another. But law is command, not counsel, and a command is expected to be obeyed only because it expresses the will of the one commanding. Since the object of every man's will is some good to himself, every command aims at the good of the one commanding. Law is a command addressed to one who has been obliged formerly to obey, a command from one who has already acquired a right to be obeyed.[222]

We can clearly trace, in the incremental influence of Grotius, Hobbes, and Locke, a dramatic change from the Thomistic view of how natural law operates—the ordering of desires, goods, and loves toward a human flourishing willed and graced by a benign, utterly beneficent and transcendent God through the subject's reasonable discernment of authentic human ends—to a desacralized anticipation of contemporary "exclusive humanism" in Grotius, then to the Hobbesian notion of law as the power-seeking exercise of human will designed to keep *the Leviathan* at bay and, finally, the Lockean view that "in man's natural condition there is no law, or at least there is no known and settled law."[223] This condition, which cannot be traced to God (since God has disappeared from the scene), is the dominant philosophical paradigm found in much of the jurisprudence of the United States Supreme Court from the 1960s to the present.

What is at stake in the use by courts of John Locke's "law of nature," the residual American view embedded in jurisprudence, is its rejection of the existence, claims, or centrality of transcendent good found in classic (Cicero; the Stoics), medieval (Saint Thomas Aquinas) and modern (Jacques Maritain, Yves Simon) perspectives on natural law. It is not a malicious conspiracy but an unwitting consensus that uses a functionalist model to sort out ontological questions.

This loss of a personal identity of the divine in the post-Enlightenment phase of Providential Deism, serving as a halfway house for today's atheism ("exclusive humanism"), is enormously damaging because it deprives humans of the most apt model for the communion that they are created to experience and enjoy, the communion of God as Trinity and the related communion of God with humankind in creation.

The reality of God as triune—Father, Son, and Holy Spirit—can neither be overlooked nor underestimated as the *fons et origo* of the existential human community. Christianity has since the time of the Gospels seen God as both subsistent and relational. God is in no way dependent upon any other being, thus transcending any sort of contingency or accident, but also, in the expressed missions of the three persons of the Trinity by Jesus, accessible and even interior to all human life, a sort of *in*clusive immanence. In short, without the Trinity, it is impossible to keep the fragile continuum of transcendence and immanence in balance.

Revelation is needed for reason; divine love is needed for human communion, whether eros, agape, or *philia*. If we abandon the transcendent, we lose the sense not only of divine but also of human purpose in its authentic and unfettered expression. Part of that loss is the corruption of natural law—a compass useful for the attainment of real goods—into a law of nature, a mere barometer of human crudity and conflict.

2. The Recovery of the Reality of Grace

Admittedly, it sounds quite foolish to speak of a human venture to recover grace when grace is identified with divine power and purpose. Is it not beyond human power to realize what is divine? There is no futile attempt to define the indefinable but to point to the contradiction within exclusive humanism of simultaneously stressing the unbounded scope of human agency while dictating that no appeal to a higher power is intellectually justifiable. This is a matter of epistemology, pursuing meaning and truth. If we accept a rigid rejection of grace and the divine, the hard-edged legacy of the Enlightenment thought, we deprive ourselves of what Taylor calls "the aspiration to wholeness."[224] It is this aspiration to move beyond sin, selfishness, and baser impulses that identifies the human quest at its richest and most fruitful.

By grace is traditionally understood a divine gift to human beings, something free (*gratia-gratis*) and unearned that has the power to elevate (*gratia elevans*) and heal (*gratia sanans*) otherwise unwieldy and tragically flawed human efforts. If we rule out the possibility of this divine power being made available to human striving, we effectively rule out the possibility of forgiveness, reconciliation, and transformation—all qualities desperately sought and needed by humankind but not justifiable simply by a yardstick of self-interest or a this-world-only horizon.

The rejection of the reality of grace removes the necessary horizon for considering issues of sexual integrity, human bonding, friendship, love, marriage, and any pursuit of the common good. These are all areas where human weakness is glaringly apparent. Simply to accept this weakness as inescapable and definitive, which would be the result of expelling grace from our narrative, is to ignore human growth and progress not fully explicable by human means alone.

3. *The Recovery of Mystery*

Any good which is fully good (or potentially capable of further good, as is any virtuous attitude or action) is transcendent and open to unconditional love. This means a love that is not contingent on human willfulness, power, or self-interest. This unconditional love is coterminous with grace understood as inherently a gift and, by extension, a given, a possibility for human existence. An example comes to mind: countless people work and pray, one day at a time, for recovery from addictions. It is their conviction that a Higher Power assists them in this arduous task. In light of the abundant evidence that such programs of recovery provide genuine growth and liberation from the consequences of addictions, otherwise unaddressed, do we dare to claim that their achievements are delusional or chimerical?

Love is the realm of mystery. It is impossible to say anything worthwhile about love and ignore mystery—Taylor's insight that the "disenchanted" society identified by the sociologist Max Weber has emptied our world not only of myth but of mystery.[225] Our communal narrative has become cold, functional, impersonal, and instrumental. Mystery is the very language of love. It must be recovered if there is to be any personalism worthy of a new millennium since the human person is inherently an icon of divine mystery.

4. *The Recovery of Transformation*

Perhaps the one constant of the sexual revolution, its meaning, and consequences is that no one is content with the status quo. Those who have fought for sexual liberation, judicially recognizing autonomy and the largest spectrum of options in regard to sex, marriage, and family, have succeeded in changing what they perceived to be a status quo of moralism, repression, patriarchy, and religious intolerance. Today there are also a significant number of people who believe that the sexual revolution has weakened the bond between sex, marriage, and children, distorted sexual truths built into our bodies by a loving Creator, and seriously damaged the moral compass of responsible behavior. Those caught up on opposite sides of the Culture War would agree that the need to transform society toward desired goals remains a priority. There is not agreement on the content or direction of the goals, but there is consensus on the need for transformation.

Charles Taylor's linkage of transformation with transcendence, grace, and mystery provides a brilliant connection of influences lost by Providential Deism. Some may seek a Marxist transformation of society into an equitable environment free of class differences. Others seek a recovery of traditional virtues that will, it is devoutly believed, transform individuals and society into a communion respectful of traditional virtues and inclined to struggle to achieve the promise and potential of those virtues. The first view is ideology triumphant, the second is faith recovered.

It is clear beyond debate, as are few other issues, that the potential for transformation toward growth, maturity, respect, love, family, and communion must remain viable. The fact that we live in a pluralistic society does not negate this priority: all camps, tribes, and perspectives must be free to work for the transformation of whatever is perceived to be injurious to the common good. The various components of a pluralist society cannot ignore the various messages delivered by cultural activists. All can debate and dialogue in the conviction that transformation is needed. There will never be a society-wide consensus on what needs to be transformed, but the whole point of debate and dialogue is that transformation is not only *desirable* but *possible*. Otherwise all parties would be condemned to the prison of an unbending status quo.

For a Christian, the path of transformation is the call to holiness. It is the recognition that we are part of a good creation but must work strenuously in response to divine grace to allow the fruitfulness of that creation to open hearts, enlighten minds, and transform love.

A JURISPRUDENCE OF MODERATION

The term *jurisprudence* literally means "wisdom in regard to the law." Built into this very term, used to describe wise actions by courts, is the name of a virtue essential to the attainment of justice—prudence or practical wisdom in the alignment of means and ends. Built into the very meaning of prudence is moderation, a balancing between undesirable extremes.

Traditionally, jurisprudence has included various schools of thought. Each of these, however, shared a commitment to the idea that a virtue, prudence, has a central role to play in the making of laws. It is precisely the virtues of prudence and moderation that American courts, starting with the Supreme Court, have most jeopardized and are now in greatest need of recovering.

The Enlightenment teaches that worthy ends, goals, or goods are purely a matter of individual interest and preference. They are not transcendent and inclusive of God, we are told, and they do not benefit from grace nor call for transformation. With this wholesale rejection of any *telos* or goal as transcendent, it is impossible to choose wisely because the ends or goals to which means must be aligned are arbitrarily dismissed as unknown. When society becomes agnostic on the subject of God, it logically becomes agnostic also on the subject of transcendent goods.

What is it that a good can transcend? In short, a good is transcendent because its scope and compass are larger than individual or private goods. If we reduce all goods to the strict boundaries of a private sphere, we are left with the vulnerability, critiqued above, that the standard of autonomy does not suffice to evaluate justice, friendship, or love. To speak in this context of a "common good" becomes self-refuting; there is no good or *telos* that commands common adherence. What is left is an abstraction, an empty vessel into which we pour whatever we think might be advisable as a common good. This is the legacy of Locke, Hume, Hobbes, and Kant. We must do better.

American courts can and must remain faithful to the Constitution, not adopting a world view of religious belief but allowing such a world view to continue to exist within an inevitable and beneficial spectrum of pluralistic options. The concept of pluralism that commands intellectual assent from all quarters has to an alarming degree become a facade for the exercise of raw, arbitrary power. Differences are permitted, but they are increasingly subject to political whim and power. The naked public square of the late Richard Neuhaus remains unclothed. This is especially true where religious beliefs and practices can be removed from the public square because they are inconsistent with a secular orthodoxy that rejects *any* display of or deference toward the transcendent. At the very least, the concept of pluralism requires that courts remain neutral in regard to the religious ways of people for whom the transcendent continues to make sense and make a difference in their lives.

This is not an appeal for substantive due process. It is not a claim that religious beliefs should enjoy a privileged or normative status in American jurisprudence. Pluralism includes authentic toleration of religion, a toleration forever enshrined in the First Amendment to the Constitution. The Founders laid the foundation for a democracy that is authentically respectful of and responsive to the religious practices of the *demos*, the people of religious belief who happen to pay taxes, fight and die for the country in armed conflicts, and labor generously for a common good that includes the interests of believers and nonbelievers alike.

All jurisprudence seeks fairness, but fairness, to be informed, must be conscious of history. I believe that the United States Supreme Court has in several dangerous instances (*Dred Scott, Lochner, Buck v. Bell, Korematsu, Roe v. Wade*) stumbled into uninformed conclusions precisely because ideology trumped historical awareness. The historical claims of African-Americans, workers, and the unborn were lost to the superior force of a species of autonomy—either race, profit, or choice—that caused great harm to a great many people.

Moderation in judicial decisions means that *stare decisis* is not simply a mechanical repetition of an earlier holding but a historically astute awareness that history plays a considerable role in the definition of rights and responsibilities. These rights are forged in the crucible of historical conflict; they cannot be at the mercy of ideological abstractions. Edmund Burke recognized prior to the French Revolution that political force based upon abstract claims of liberty, fraternity, and equality would lead to a Reign of Terror. It is our task to recognize that abstract claims of autonomy, strong on ideology but weak on civil bonds, have inflicted suffering after the sexual revolution.

A jurisprudence that recognizes and respects legislative prerogatives is much more likely to realize the best of an informed tradition respectful of both belief and unbelief. To allow debate, disagreement, and diversity to unfold in the chambers and councils of state legislatures is to fulfill the general scope of federalism envisioned by the Founders. Democracy may not be tidy, but it cannot be short-circuited by an approach to law and social policy that has no time for transcendence, grace, mystery, or transformation. Judicial fiat will not correct social ills in a lasting way; *Roe v. Wade* has demonstrated that.

It is true that some problems such as racial prejudice had to be addressed by U.S. courts in a definitive way, as the landmark case of *Brown v. Board of Education* did in 1954. (Note, however, that *Brown* permitted the different states to achieve desegregation, each in their own way while *Roe v. Wade* peremptorily struck down the enactments of state legislatures and mandated, across the board, a trimester framework for competing interests in regard to abortion.)

But the actual achievement of racial progress and reconciliation owes much more to the faith-based efforts of Dr. Martin Luther King Jr. and his use of natural law reasoning (human law—a segregated lunch counter—does not trump God's law) over a period of decades. This message that racism was inconsistent with human decency, proclaimed in churches with heroism and often at great cost, eventually changed the culture, whose expanded values of freedom courts have come to reflect.

The decisions of courts are critical, but changing the culture is even more fundamental. The excesses and distortions of the sexual revolution of the 1960s are increasingly evident. There is a desire across the political spectrum to reduce the number of abortions, for example, even as people opt for pro-life or pro-choice stances. It is time for a recovery of foundational virtues that are consistent with what Russell Kirk called "the permanent things." If we change the culture, we shall, over time, change the courts. Such has to be the hope of generations who will not otherwise enjoy the experience of life.

I would like to conclude this plea for moderation and even-handedness in striking a balance between legislative laboratories and judicial decisions by quoting an eminent theologian invited to address the United Nations in April 2008. The setting was the sixtieth anniversary of the Universal Declaration of Human Rights (1948) a United Nations document praised by Eleanor Roosevelt and greatly indebted to the political thought of Jacques Maritain (1882–1973), a French Thomist prominent in drafting the first global effort to set forth universal rights. The theologian delivered this reflection:

> Human rights are increasingly being presented as the common language and the ethical substratum of international relations. At the same time, the universality, indivisibility and interdependence of human rights all serve as guarantees safeguarding human dignity. It is evident, though, that the rights recognized and expounded in the Declaration apply to everyone by virtue of the common origin of the person, who remains the high-point of God's creative design for the world and for history. They are based on the natural law inscribed on human hearts and present in different cultures and civilizations. Removing human rights from this context would mean restricting their range and yielding to a relativistic conception, according to which the meaning and interpretation of rights could vary and their universality would be denied in the name of different cultural, political, social, and even religious outlooks. This great variety of viewpoints must not be allowed to obscure the fact that not only rights are universal, but so too is the human person, the subject of those rights.[226]

The theologian, Pope Benedict XVI, affirmed that not only are human rights universal but so too are the persons who are the subjects of those rights. He points toward a universality that includes transcendence, grace, and mystery and requires the daily challenge of transformation toward the good life in a communion of love, blessed by a Creator and sustained by courts, classrooms, and homes attuned to the abiding presence of divine love.

CONCLUSION

Faith is open to the effort of understanding on the part of reason; reason, in turn, recognizes that faith does not mortify it, rather it drives it toward wider and loftier horizons. . . . Faith and reason, in reciprocal dialogue, vibrate with joy when both are animated by the search for profound union with God. When love vivifies the prayerful dimension of theology, knowledge, acquired by reason, is broadened. Truth is sought with humility, received with wonder and gratitude: In a word, knowledge grows only if it loves truth.

— Pope Benedict XVI

All of us desire to live a good life, one characterized by meaning and value. The good life is to be lived in communion with beloved friends. But we cannot live the good life without the good, a transcendent reality, supported by grace, open to mystery, and calling for transformation. The critical question that faces our culture in the unfolding aftermath of the sexual revolution of the 1960s is to locate what exactly provides meaning and value, their source and inspiration. I believe it is the foundational reality of goodness and the various qualities or virtues affiliated with goodness that give meaning to life. Since it abridges the potential of the human being to put any limits on that goodness, the door must be kept open to an ultimate goodness—God. I believe the most engaging, satisfying, and redemptive revelation of that goodness is found in the life and Gospel of Jesus of Nazareth. Just as meaning is found in the orientation toward the good and its realization in countless virtues or desires ordered toward further goods, so it is virtue that provides values which last and unify.

Simply to speak of values fails to address the question of their meaning, their validity, their intensity, and their staying power. Those who rail at the ambiguity of the term *family values* have it right. But the struggle to live out a life of virtue is an arduous task. We often find ourselves in a setting where it is good versus good that perplexes and perhaps divides us. It may be a case of need versus want and there are no bumper-sticker slogans to resolve our quandary.

At the same time, we have in our very being a natural orientation to the good life and real goods which provide a feast of rich choices. We are able through reason and faith to identify choices that are at war with an intrinsic inclination to truth, beatitude, and goodness. We are wired for happiness by a Creator who redeems us when we fail and calls us to everlasting communion, a communion that includes both eros and agape in our journey of redeemed, transforming love.

We cannot opt for attitudes or actions that contradict the goodness of an all-loving God and still remain consistent with our own humanity. Plainly, some choices are wrong. For too long we have made choice the purpose and object of our love. Love must be the purpose and object of our choice.

The Enlightenment provided countless valuable ideas for our modern world. The idea of autonomy may well count as one. But its direction has left us disengaged from the good life. We have paid the price of its atomizing shape by living fractured lives. We have contracepted our future to the point where we have insufficient workers for the many tasks of a multi-tasking world. What happens in the bedroom affects the marketplace and vice versa. Privacy is not a sufficient standard to assess the links between marriage, family, community, and society.

Ours must be a path of redemption. We have aborted so many of our peers as to bring shame on our own lives, diminishing our own humanity even as we exterminate it when inconvenient. We have allowed the termites of pornography to eat away at the foundations of character and family, destroying subtly and over time. Households without fathers have left a generation unsure of how the tenuous bond between a man and a woman is to unfold. Infidelity and divorce compound the uncertainty of a moral system that focuses exclusively on actions rather than souls. The casualties of the sexual revolution are all around us. Perhaps we are in that number. But we are not without choices.

Profound thinkers such as Servais Pinckaers, Alasdair MacIntyre, Charles Taylor, and Josef Ratzinger have shown us a way out of the morass brought about by an absolute autonomy that becomes a secular god of choice at odds with the wisdom of the God of Abraham, Isaac, Jacob, and Jesus Christ. We have about us the recovery of virtue. We are beginning to awake from a groggy acceptance of cold, instrumental, and content-free autonomy as the uncontested meaning of meaningless lives. Our freedom must be oriented toward truth, goodness, and beatitude for it to serve human purposes.

Yes, we are sexual beings. Yes, it is a good thing to be autonomous beings. To link these paramount features of our existence, we can point to specific virtues and identify them as the path to a sexual autonomy truly compatible with the good life, an autonomy that participates in divine love through the elevation and healing of grace.

Authentic sexual autonomy consists of the virtue of practical wisdom that recognizes and acts on our orientation to the good life with its inclusion of countless enriching human goods. This sexual autonomy includes a solidarity with each other in the compassionate awareness that none of us is perfect and all of us need each other. Our solidarity must be rooted in virtue and the shared search for the good life. True solidarity does not wink at evil or tolerate the intolerable but supports fellow sinners with a judgment-free love and works toward the kind of recovery that brings us into the presence of an ineffable Higher Power without whom we will remain addicted to our own demons. Our sexual autonomy requires a humility that respects the truth of each Ash Wednesday's marking with the *humus* (dust) of our origins. From these modest beginnings come the gifts of life and love that carry us into the farther shores of eternal life and divine love.

These are truths that we dare not neglect and cannot afford to forget. Sexual autonomy requires that we render to one another that which is due; there cannot be love without justice. We begin with chastity, modesty, reverence, and respect, knowing that each is to be seen and valued as an image of the divine, an icon of God, not merely as an object or means to an end. The ultimate gratification is not in receiving pleasure from someone else's body but in communicating a language of gift with every inch of our own body. True autonomy includes the option to give, sacrifice, and love, taking risks and accepting vulnerability as building blocks of communion.

Finally, sexual autonomy is marvelously and mysteriously a life of authentic freedom. It is a life beautifully teleological or end-oriented. Unless we make choices that aim toward the communion of self-giving love, we choose against humanity and bet against goodness. Such a wager never wins.

A choice for the good life requires God and goodness at every level of our being. It alone is a life worth living. It is the life that takes us from unworthy choices and hurtful deeds. It is the life toward which we are inclined from the moment of our conception. We cannot live it fully without the love of one another. It is the pursuit and sharing of that love that makes sex something truly beautiful.

NOTES

INTRODUCTION

EPIGRAPH. From an address given May 22, 2005, before praying the Angelus with the crowds gathered in Saint Peter's Square.

1. *The Pastoral Constitution on the Church in the Modern World* (*Gaudium et Spes*), 1965, n. 22.
2. See Henri de Lubac, *The Drama of Atheistic Humanism* (New York: World Publishing, A Meridian Book, 1950), ix.
3. See Iris Murdoch, *The Sovereignty of Good* (London: Routledge & Kegan Paul, 1970).
4. See Servais Pinckaers, *The Sources of Christian Ethics*. Translated from the third edition by Sr. Mary Thomas Noble, OP (Washington, DC: Catholic University of America Press, 1995).
5. John Rziha, *Perfecting Human Actions: Saint Thomas Aquinas on Human Participation in Eternal Law* (Washington, DC: Catholic University of America Press, 2009), 262–63.

ONE: AN IDEAL AND A REVOLUTION

EPIGRAPH. Theodore Dalrymple [Anthony (A.M.) Daniels], *Our Culture, What's Left of It: The Mandarins and the Masses* (Chicago, IL: Ivan R. Dee, 2005), 234.

6. See J. B. Schneewind, *The Invention of Autonomy: A History of Modern Moral Philosophy* (Cambridge: Cambridge University Press, 1988).
7. See Martin Rhonheimer, *Natural Law and Practical Reason: A Thomist View of Moral Autonomy* (New York: Fordham University Press, 2000).
8. E. F. Schumacher, *A Guide for the Perplexed* (New York: Harper Perennial, 1977), 1–2.
9. Ibid. 1–14.
10. Lewis White Beck, ed., *18th-Century Philosophy* (New York: Free Press; London: Collier-MacMillan, 1966), 1.
11. See Edmund Burke, *Reflections on the Revolution in France* (1790; reprint Oxford: Oxford University Press, 2009).

12. Jay Winik, *The Great Upheaval: America and the Birth of the Modern World, 1788–1800* (New York: HarperCollins, 2007), 274.

13. Roger Scruton, *Modern Culture* (London: Continuum, 1998), 24–25.

14. Vernon J. Bourke, *Will in Western Thought: An Historico-Critical Survey* (New York: Sheed & Ward, 1964), 159–60.

15. Robert Nisbet, *Prejudices: A Philosophical Dictionary*, s.v. *authoritarianism* (Cambridge, MA: Harvard University Press, 1982), 20.

16. Louis Dupré, *The Enlightenment and the Intellectual Foundations of Modern Culture* (New Haven, CT: Yale University Press, 2004), 25.

17. Schumacher, *A Guide for the Perplexed*, 38. A reference for Schumacher's quotation can be found in Saint Thomas Aquinas, *Summa Theologica*, I–II, q. 61, a. 2, which discusses how the theological virtues elevate human subjects into a divine context.

18. Pope John Paul II, Encyclical, *Veritatis Splendor* (1993), n. 41.

19. James Collins, *God in Modern Philosophy* (Chicago: Henry Regnery, 1959), 173.

20. Benjamin Wiker and Jonathan Witt, *A Meaningful World: How the Arts and Sciences Reveal the Genius of Nature* (Downers Grove, IL: InterVarsity, 2006), 106.

21. Robert P. Kraynak, *Christian Faith and Modern Democracy: God and Politics in the Fallen World* (Notre Dame, IN: University of Notre Dame Press, 2001), 33.

22. Sally Sedgwick, *Kant's Groundwork of the Metaphysics of Morals* (Cambridge: Cambridge University Press, 2008), 22.

23. Immanuel Kant, *The Doctrine of Virtue: Part II of The Metaphysics of Morals*. Translated with an Introduction and Notes by Mary G. Gregor. Foreword by H. J. Paton (Philadelphia, PA: University of Pennsylvania Press, 1964), 54.

24. Ibid., 62.

25. Alasdair MacIntyre, *After Virtue* (Notre Dame, IN: University of Notre Dame Press, 1981). It is a fascinating factoid, suitable for starting cults, that at the very end of his critique, MacIntyre says that the world is not waiting for a Godot but for another Benedict. On April 19, 2005, Cardinal Joseph Ratzinger was elected the 264th successor to Saint Peter and chose the name of Pope Benedict XVI.

26. Ibid., pp. 190–91.

27. Charles Taylor, *A Secular Age* (Cambridge, MA: The Belknap Press of Harvard University Press, 2007), 610.

28. Pinckaers, *The Sources of Christian Ethics*, 428.

29. Louis Dupré, *Passage to Modernity: An Essay in the Hermeneutics of Nature and Culture* (New Haven: Yale University Press, 1993), 40–41.

30. Taylor, *A Secular Age*, 20.

31. Thomas Hobbes, *Leviathan* (1651), pt. I, ch. 13.

32. Alasdair MacIntyre, *A Short History of Ethics: A History of Moral Philosophy from the Homeric Age to the Twentieth Century*. Second Edition. (Notre Dame, IN: University of Notre Dame Press, 1998), 138.

33. Ibid., p. 187.

34. Jean-Jacques Rousseau, *Emile*, in R. L. Archer, ed., *Jean Jacques Rousseau: His Educational Theories selected from Émile, Julie and Other Writings*, (Woodbury, NY: Barron's Educational, 1964), 55.

35. Jeremy Bentham, *A Fragment on Government,* preface to the first edition, in Mary Peter Mack, *A Bentham Reader* (New York: Pegasus, 1969), 45.

36. John Stuart Mill, *Utilitarianism* (1863), ch. 2.

37. John Stuart Mill, *On Liberty; Representative Government; The Subjection of Women: Three Essays*. Introduction by Millicent Garrett Fawcett (London: Oxford University Press, Humphrey Milford, 1940), 115, 118.

38. John Locke, *Some Thoughts Concerning Education* (1693), section 54.

39. MacIntyre, *A Short History of Ethics*, 157.

40. Pope John Paul II, *Crossing the Threshold of Hope* (New York: Alfred A. Knopf, 1994), 51–52.

41. Dupré, *Passage to Modernity*, 159.

TWO: AUTONOMY AND MARRIAGE, STRANGE BEDFELLOWS

42. Will and Ariel Durant, *The Story of Civilization IX: The Age of Voltaire* (New York: Simon and Schuster, 1965), 784.

43. Janne Haaland Matláry, *When Might Becomes Human Right: Essays on Democracy and the Crisis of Rationality* (Leominster, Herefordshire: Gracewing, 2007), 31.

44. See Richard A. Davis, *Principles of Oceanography*, 2nd rev. ed. (Boston, MA: Addison-Wesley, 1977).

45. Karen Armstrong, *The Case for God* (New York: Alfred A. Knopf), 166–67.

46. Philip Larkin, "*Annus Mirabilis*," 1974, first stanza.

47. Gay Talese, *Thy Neighbor's Wife* (New York: HarperCollins, 1980, 2009), 188, 25–51.

48. Ibid., 188.

49. Ibid., 191–92.

50. Ibid., 193.

51. Ibid., 198.

52. Ibid., 551, 560, 563.

53. Camille Paglia, *Sex, Art, and American Culture* (New York: Vintage, 1992), 212.

54. Ibid., 216.

55. Taylor, *A Secular Age*, 485.

56. Several powerful cultural assessments of the longstanding consequences of 1960s radical feminism have come from right-leaning critics: Christina Hoff Sommers, *Who Stole Feminism? How Women Have Betrayed Women* (New York: Simon & Schuster, 1995) and Kate O'Beirne, *Women Who Make the World Worse*

(New York: Penguin Books, 2006). The *New York Times* columnist Maureen Dowd combines social analysis with political satire in her *Are Men Necessary? When Sexes Collide* (New York: G. P. Putnam, 2005).

57. Scruton, *Modern Culture*, 9.

58. Roger Kimball, *The Long March: How the Cultural Revolution of the 1960s Changed America* (San Francisco: Encounter Books, 2000), 14.

59. Allan Bloom, *Love and Friendship* (New York: Simon & Schuster, 1993), 13.

60. Ibid., 13–14.

61. Ibid., 15, 17.

62. See T. Brian Mooney, "Plato and the Love of Individuals," *Heythrop Journal* 43 (2002): 311–27.

THREE: AUTONOMY BECOMES PRIVACY IN THE COURTS

63. *Planned Parenthood of SE Pennsylvania v. Casey*, 505 U.S. 833 (1992), at 851.

64. *Lawrence v. Texas*, 539 U.S. 558 (2003), at 571.

65. Ibid.

66. Justice Scalia in dissent, *Lawrence v. Texas*, 539 U.S. 558 (2003).

67. *Roe v. Wade*, 410 U.S. 113 (1973).

68. *Dred Scott v. Sandford*, 60 U.S. (19 How.) 393 (1857).

69. 60 U.S. (19 How.) 393, 407 (1857). The entire opinion of Chief Justice Taney can be accessed at http://supreme.justia.com/us/60/393/case.html (last accessed March 29, 2010).

70. Cass R. Sunstein, "*Dred Scott v. Sandford* and Its Legacy," in *Great Cases in Constitutional Law* ed. Robert P. George (Princeton, NJ: Princeton University Press: 2000), 65.

71. Ibid., 74. Professor Sunstein is of the view that Taney was an "originalist" in the Scalia and Bork mode, but his emphatic point that Taney misread the Constitution, the original text, on slavery makes the "originalist" thesis much harder, in my opinion, to sustain.

72. U.S. (19 How.) 393, 404, 405 (1857).

73. *Roe v. Wade*, 410 U.S. 113, 158 (1973).

74. McLean in *Dred Scott v. Sandford,* 19 Howard 393, at 550 (1857).

75. Abraham Lincoln's Speech on *Dred Scott*, June 26, 1857. Available at www.teachingamericanhistory.org.

76. Michael McConnell, "Symposium on Interpreting the Ninth Amendment: A Moral Realist Defense of Constitutional Democracy," 64 Chi.-Kent. L. Rev. 89, 101 (1988), citing 60 U.S. 621 (Curtis, J., dissenting). This article is cited in Mark R. Levin, *Men in Black: How the Supreme Court is Destroying America* (Washington, DC: Regnery, 2005), 15. Levin provides a brilliant review of judicial excesses and much of the analysis of this chapter is indebted to his work.

77. McConnell, "A Moral Realist Defense," 101.

78. Robert H. Bork, *The Tempting of America: The Political Seduction of the Law* (New York: Free Press 1990), 31.

79. Lawrence H. Tribe, *The Invisible Constitution* (Oxford: Oxford University Press, 2008), 111.

80. Ibid., 111–12.

81. Ibid., 113.

82. *Korematsu v. United States*, 323 U.S. 214 (1944), at 233 (dissenting).

83. Lucas A. Powe, Jr., *The Supreme Court and the American Elite, 1789–2008* (Cambridge, MA: Harvard University Press, 2009), 219.

84. Ibid., 220.

85. *Korematsu v. United States*, 323 U.S. 214, 243 (1944) (dissenting).

86. Tribe, *The Invisible Constitution*, 112.

87. *The Federalist Papers*, n. 78.

88. Joseph R. Biden, Jr., "Law and Natural Law: Questions for Judge Thomas," *Washington Post*, 8 September 1991, C1, C4.

89. Lawrence H. Tribe, "'Natural Law' and the Nominee," *New York Times*, 15 July 1991, A15.

90. Michael W. McConnell, "Trashing the Natural Law," *New York Times*, 16 August 1991, A23.

91. Saint Thomas Aquinas, *Summa Theologica*, I–II, q. 91, a. 2.

92. Pinckaers, *The Sources of Christian Ethics*, 327–78.

93. Edwin Black, *War against the Weak: Eugenics and America's Campaign to Create a Master Race* (New York: Thunder's Mouth Press, an imprint of Avalon, 2003), 105–17.

94. *Buck* v. *Bell*, 274 U.S. 200, 205 (1927).

95. Ibid.

96. *Lochner v. New York*, 198 U.S. 45 (1905).

97. See Liva Baker, *The Justice from Beacon Hill: The Life and Times of Oliver Wendell Holmes* (New York: HarperCollins, 1991), 408–29.

98. *Lochner v. New York*, 198 U.S. 45 (1905), at 74.

99. Christine Rosen, *Preaching Eugenics: Religious Leaders and the American Eugenics Movement* (Oxford University Press, 2004), 6.

100. *Lochner v. New York*, 198 U.S. 45 (1905), at 74.

101. *Buck* v. *Bell*, 274 U.S. 200, 207 (1927).

102. See Albert W. Alschuler, *Law without Values: The Life, Work, and Legacy of Justice Holmes* (Chicago, IL: University of Chicago Press, 2000).

103. Ibid., 65.

104. Baker, *The Justice from Beacon Hill*, 603.

105. Ibid., p. 67, citing Holmes to Laski, May 12, 1927, in Mark DeWolfe Howe, *Holmes–Laski Letters: The Correspondence of Mr. Justice Holmes and Harold J. Laski, 1916–1935* (Cambridge, MA: Harvard University Press, 1953), 942.

106. Holmes to Einstein, May 19, 1927, in *Holmes–Einstein Letters* at 267, cited in Alschuler, *Law without Values*, 67, 234.

107. Powe, *The Supreme Court and the American Elite,* 196.

108. Rosen, *Preaching Eugenics*, 139–64.

109. John 6:66 ("Because of this, many of his disciples turned back and no longer went about with him").

110. Catherine Drinker Bowen, *Yankee from Olympus* (Boston: Little, Brown, 1944). This is a fictionalized and idealized account of the life of Holmes.

111. Liva Baker, *The Justice from Beacon Hill*, 601–2.

112. Rosen, *Preaching Eugenics*, 150.

113. See David Kennedy, *Birth Control in America: The Career of Margaret Sanger* (New Haven, CT: Yale University Press, 1970).

114. Richard A. Posner, ed., *Introduction to the Essential Holmes: Selections from the Letters, Speeches, Judicial Opinions, and Other Writings of Oliver Wendell Holmes, Jr.* (Chicago, IL: University of Chicago Press, 1992), xxix, cited in Alschuler, *Law without Values*, 28.

115. *Roe* v. *Wade*, 410 U.S. 113 (1973), at 154.

116. Thomas Hobbes, *Leviathan* (1651), pt. I, ch. 13.

117. *Griswold v. Connecticut*, 381 U.S. 479 (1965).

118. Ibid., at 527.

119. Ibid., at 484.

120. Levin, *Men in Black*, 57.

121. Robert H. Bork, *The Tempting of America: The Political Seduction of the Law* (New York: Free Press, 1990), 185.

122. Ferguson v. Skrupa, 372 U.S. 726, 732 (1963). The reference to Spencer was of course an endorsement of Holmes's famous dissent against substantive due process in *Lochner*.

123. Stanley Morrison, "Does the Fourteenth Amendment Incorporate the Bill of Rights? The Judicial Interpretation," *Stanford Law Review* 140, 166 (1949).

124. *Eisenstadt v. Baird*, 405 U.S. 438 (1972), at 453.

125. See Linda Greenhouse, *Becoming Justice Blackmun: Harry Blackmun's Supreme Court Journey* (New York: Time Books, Henry Holt, 2006).

126. *Eisenstadt v. Baird*, 405 U.S. 438 (1972), at 453.

127. Mark 10:7–9; see Genesis 2:24; Matthew 19:1–12; Mark 10:1–12.

128. *Eisenstadt v. Baird*, 405 U.S. 438 (1972), at 453.

129. Max Boot, *Out of Order: Arrogance, Corruption, and Incompetence on the Bench*. Foreword by Robert H. Bork (New York: Basic Books, 1998), 115–16.

130. Ibid., p. 116.

131. John Hart Ely, "The Wages of Crying Wolf: A Comment on *Roe v. Wade*," *Yale Law Review* 82 (1973): 920–49.

132. Levin, *Men in Black*, 65.

133. *Roe v. Wade*, 410 U.S. 113 (1973), at 159.

134. See *Stenberg v. Carhart*, 530 U.S. 914 (2000).

135. Black, *War against the Weak*, 401–2.

136. Ibid., 427.

137. Phillip Longman, "The Global Baby Bust," *Foreign Affairs* 83:3 (May/June 2004): 64–79.

FOUR: THE RECOVERY OF VIRTUE: FROM AUTONOMY TO THEONOMY

138. In addition to the works of Charles Taylor, see Dinesh D'Souza, *What's So Great About Christianity* (Washington, DC: Regnery, 2007); Francis Collins, *The Language of God: A Scientist Presents Evidence for Belief* (New York: Free Press, 2006); John Polkingthorne, *One World: The Interaction of Science and Theology* (London: SPCK Publishing, 1986); John Micklethwait and Adrian Wooldridge, *God Is Back: How the Global Revival of Faith is Changing the World* (New York: Penguin, 2009).

139. Christoph Cardinal Schönborn, "The Designs of Science," *First Things* 159 (January 2006): 34–38, at 38.

140. Armstrong, *The Case for God*, 284.

141. Pope John Paul II, Apostolic Exhortation, *Christifideles laici* (1988), n. 37.

142. Ibid.

143. J. Brian Benestad, "Doctrinal Perspectives on the Church in the Modern World," in *Vatican II: Renewal within Tradition*, ed. Matthew L. Lamb and Matthew Levering (Oxford: Oxford University Press, 2008), 151.

144. Pinckaers, *The Sources of Christian Ethics*, 296.

145. Saint Thomas Aquinas, *Summa Theologica*. Literally translated by the Fathers of the English Dominican Province. 3 Vols. (New York: Benziger Brothers, 1947).

146. *Gaudium et Spes* (paragraph 22) in Austin Flannery, *Vatican II: The Conciliar and Post-Conciliar Documents* (Northport, NY: Costello, 1975).

147. Ibid.

148. Wiker and Witt, *A Meaningful World*, 16. The included quotation comes from Friedrich Nietzsche, *Beyond Good and Evil*, trans. Walter Kaufmann (New York: Vintage, 1966), sec. 4

149. Pinckaers, *The Sources of Christian Ethics*, 407.

150. Leo Strauss, *Natural Right and History* (Chicago, IL: University of Chicago Press, 1953), 74.

151. Ibid., 75.

152. My goal in this section is to apply Pinckaers's elaboration of the five natural inclinations—found in the *Summa Theologica* of Saint Thomas Aquinas (I–II, q. 94.2) and presented in chapter 17 of Pinckaers, *The Sources of Christian Ethics*—to issues of sexual morality.

153. Saint Thomas Aquinas, *Summa Theologica*, I–II, q. 90, a. 2.

154. Simon Tugwell, OP, *The Beatitudes: Soundings in Christian Traditions* (Springfield, IL: Templegate, 1980), 4–5.

155. Saint Thomas Aquinas, *Summa Theologica*, I–II, q. 1, a. 1.

156. Pinckaers, *The Sources of Christian Ethics*, 400.

157. Ibid., 168–69.

158. Roger Scruton, *Modern Philosophy: An Introduction and Survey* (New York: Penguin, 1994), 91–92.

159. Mortimer J. Adler, *Six Great Ideas* (New York: Collier Books, MacMillan, 1981), 77.

160. Ibid., 78.

161. Armstrong, *The Case for God*, 150.

162. Janne Haaland Matláry, *When Might Becomes Human Right*, 39.

163. Robert Sokolowski, "What is Natural Law? Human Purposes and Natural Ends," *The Thomist* 68 (2004): 507–29.

164. Ibid., 512.

165. Ibid., 521.

166. Pinckaers, *The Sources of Christian Ethics*, 421.

167. Benedict M. Ashley, OP, *Living the Truth in Love: A Biblical Introduction to Moral Theology* (New York: Alba House, 1996)

168. Ibid., 91.

169. Saint Thomas Aquinas, *Summa Theologica*, I, q. 48, a. 1.

170. Pinckaers, *The Sources of Christian Ethics*, 409.

171. Adler, *Six Great Ideas*, 82.

172. Saint Thomas Aquinas, *Summa Theologica*, I–II, q. 61, a. 2.

173. Pinckaers, *The Sources of Christian Ethics*, 409.

174. Ibid., 410.

175. Ibid., 411.

176. Saint Thomas Aquinas, *Summa Theologica*, I, q. 5, a. 1.

177. Pinckaers, *The Sources of Christian Ethics*, 412.

178. Ibid.

179. Ibid., 412–13.

180. Ibid., 414.

181. Ibid.

182. Saint Thomas Aquinas, *Summa Theologica*, I–II, q. 26, a. 4. Thomas had earlier spoken of the Aristotelian distinction of goods into "honest," "useful," and "delightful" at the very beginning of the *Summa*, I, q. 5, a.6.

183. Pinckaers, *The Sources of Christian Ethics*, 414–15.

184. Martha C. Nussbaum, *Love's Knowledge: Essays on Philosophy and Literature* (Oxford: Oxford University Press, 1990), 44.

185. Pinckaers, *The Sources of Christian Ethics*, 416.

186. Ibid., 415–16.

187. Ibid., 417.

188. F. L. Cross, ed. *The Oxford Dictionary of the Christian Church*, s.v. concupiscence (London: Oxford University Press, 1963), 324.

189. Pinckaers, *The Sources of Christian Ethics*, 418–19.

190. Psalms 10:4; 53:1.

191. Pinckaers, *The Sources of Christian Ethics*, 419.

192. Adler, *Six Great Ideas*, 78.

193. Pinckaers, *The Sources of Christian Ethics*, 425.

194. *Catechism of the Catholic Church*, Second Edition (Vatican City: Libreria Editrice Vaticana, 2000), 344. Hereafter the *Catechism* will be cited as *CCC*.

195. Ibid., 361, 1939.

196. Ibid., 426.

197. Ibid., 428.

198. August 7, 2006: http://www.cnn.com/2006/HEALTH/parenting/08/07/sexlyrics.teens.ap/index.html.

199. *CCC*, 2337.

200. Ibid., 2345, citing Galatians 5:22.

FIVE: TRANSCENDENCE AND TRANSFORMATION

EPIGRAPH. Cornelio Fabro, *God in Exile: Modern Atheism; A Study of the Internal Dynamics of Modern Atheism, from Its Roots in the Cartesian* Cogito *to the Present Day.* Translated and edited by Arthur Gibson (Westminster, MD: Newman Press, 1968), 1150.

201. Nathan Tarcov and Thomas L. Pangle, "Leo Strauss and the History of Political Philosophy," in *History of Political Philosophy*, 3rd ed. ed. Leo Strauss and Joseph Cropsey (Chicago, IL: University of Chicago Press, 1987), 910.

202. Martha C. Nussbaum, *The Fragility of Goodness: Luck and Ethics in Greek Tragedy and Philosophy*. Revised Edition (Cambridge: Cambridge University Press, 2001), 345.

203. Ibid., 343–44.

204. Ibid., 344.

205. Taylor draws upon French sources extensively but is very sparing in his references to mostly French Catholic theologians who have championed a return to classic sources—*ressourcement*—not unlike the revisionist view of secularization that Taylor proposes. Theologians such as Yves Congar, Henrie Lubac, Jean Daniélou, Hans Urs von Balthasar, Marie-Dominique Chenu, and Louis Bouyer were at the forefront of a recovery of classic fonts of Christian theology insufficiently appreciated in the Tridentine era. See Marcellino D'Ambrosio, "*Ressourcement* theology, aggiornamento, and the hermeneutics of tradition," *Communio* 18 (Winter 1991): 530–55.

206. Taylor, *A Secular Age* (See chapter 1, note 22 above for publishing details).

207. Ibid., 631.

208. Ibid., 638.

209. Ibid., 222.

210. Ibid.

211. Ibid., 223.

212. Ibid., 224.

213. Saint Thomas Aquinas, *Summa Theologica*, I–II, q. 112, a. 1c.

214. Taylor, *A Secular Age*, 530.

215. Ibid., 146.

216. Ibid., 625–31. See Martha C. Nussbaum, *Love's Knowledge: Essays on Philosophy and Literature* (Oxford: Oxford University Press, 1990).

217. Taylor, *A Secular Age*, 626.

218. Ibid., 631.

219. Ibid., 183–84.

220. Ibid.,126.

221. Richard H. Cox, "Hugo Grotius," in *History of Political Philosophy*, 3rd edition. ed. Leo Strauss and Joseph Cropsey (Chicago, IL: University of Chicago Press, 1987), 388–89.

222. Lawrence Berns, "Thomas Hobbes," in *History of Political Philosophy*, 3rd edition. ed. Leo Strauss and Joseph Cropsey (Chicago, IL: University of Chicago Press, 1987), 412.

223. Robert A. Goldwin, "John Locke," in *History of Political Philosophy*, 3rd edition. ed. Leo Strauss and Joseph Cropsey (Chicago, IL: University of Chicago Press, 1987), 509.

224. Taylor, *A Secular Age*, 609.

225. Ibid., 426.

226. Pope Benedict XVI, *Address to the United Nations General Assembly*, April 18, 2008.

CONCLUSION

EPIGRAPH. Pope Benedict XVI, Wednesday Audience, October 28, 2009. Accessed at http://www.zenit.org/article-27371?l=English.

INDEX

A

Abolition of Man, The (Lewis), 88
abortion, 26, 53–55, 89–94, 133, 174
Adams, John, 15
Adler, Mortimer J., 119–120, 128–
    129, 140
After Virtue (MacIntyre), 21, 23
agape, 21, 50, 154
AIDS, 43
Alschuler, Albert, 75, 76
American Revolution (1776), 15
Aristophanes, 34
Aristotle
    happiness, 109–110, 112–113
    human well-being, 23
    love and friendship, 133–135, 146,
        153–155
    self-sacrifice, 141
    speech and human behavior, 145
Armstrong, Karen, 98, 179n45 (39)
Ashley, Benedict M., 127
atheism, 97, 129, 138, 163
Augustine, 40, 137, 143
autonomy
    absolute, 11, 30–31
    and dignity, 17–18, 98–100
    eros, conflict with, 40–42, 111–
        112, 175
    of individual in society, 28–31
    and natural inclination to the good,
        126–127
    and nominalism, 118
    prevalence of, 11–12
    and relationships, 19, 136, 148,
        154

    and relativism, 120
    virtue, in service of, 97

B

Baird, Eisenstadt v., 86–89
Baker, Liva, 79
Balthasar, Hans Urs von, 161
Beck, Lewis White, 13, 15–16, 17
being and perfection, 127–128
Bell, Buck v. See Buck v. Bell
Benedict XVI, 1, 172, 173, 178n25
Benestad, J. Brian, 99
Bentham, Jeremy, 29
Biden, Joseph, 66
birth control. *See* contraception
birth rate decline, 96
Black, Eugene, 94–95
Black, Hugo, 84, 85–86
Blackmun, Harry, 59, 83, 89, 90, 91,
    92
Bloom, Allan, 49–52
Board of Education, Brown v., 82,
    171
Bolling v. Sharpe, 62–63
Bolton, Doe v., 89
Boot, Max, 89
Bork, Robert, 60–61, 85, 92
Brennan, William, 86–89
Brown v. Board of Education, 82, 171
Buck, Carrie, 71, 75–76, 81–82, 95
Buck v. Bell, 56, 70–77, 79–80, 81,
    82–83, 88, 94–96
Bullaro, John and Judy, 42
Burke, Edmund, 13–14, 15, 170
Bush, George H. W., 66
Butler, Pierce, 77, 80